Managing Finance for Quality

Also available from ASQC Quality Press

Process Reengineering: The Key to Achieving Breakthrough Success
Lon Roberts

Reengineering the Organization:
A Step-by-Step Approach to Corporate Revitalization
Jeffrey N. Lowenthal

Excellence Is a Habit: How to Avoid Quality Burnout
Thomas J. Barry

Full-Cycle Corrective Action: Managing Quality for Profits
Thomas M. Cappels

The ASQC Total Quality Management Series

   TQM: Leadership for the Quality Transformation
   Richard S. Johnson

   TQM: Management Processes for Quality Operations
   Richard S. Johnson

   TQM: The Mechanics of Quality Processes
   Richard S. Johnson and Lawrence E. Kazense

   TQM: Quality Training Practices
   Richard S. Johnson

To request a complimentary catalog of publications, call 800-248-1946.

Managing Finance for Quality

Bottom-Line Results from Top-Level Commitment

James A. F. Stoner

Frank M. Werner

ASQC Quality Press
Milwaukee, Wisconsin

Financial Executives Research Foundation
Morristown, New Jersey

Managing Finance for Quality: Bottom-Line Results from Top-Level Commitment
James A. F. Stoner and Frank M. Werner

Library of Congress Cataloging-in-Publication Data

Stoner, James Arthur Finch
    Managing finance for quality: bottom-line results from top-level
commitment / James A. F. Stoner, Frank M. Werner.
        p.   cm.
    Includes bibliographical references and index.
    ISBN 0-87389-267-4
        1. Total quality management—United States—Case studies.
    2. Industrial management—United States—Case studies.
    3. Corporations—United States—Finance—Case studies.   I. Werner,
    Frank M.
    HD62.15.S78   1994
    658.5'62—dc20   94-4312
                                                        CIP

Financial Executives Research Foundation is the research affiliate of Financial Executives Institute. The basic purpose of the Foundation is to conduct research and publish informative material in the field of business management, with particular emphasis on the practices of financial management and its evolving role in the management of business.

The views set forth in this publication are those of the authors and do not necessarily represent those of the FERF Board as a whole, individual trustees, or the members of the Project Advisory Committee.

Frisbee® is a registered trademark of Wham-O.

10 9 8 7 6 5 4 3 2 1

ISBN 0-87389-267-4

Acquisitions Editor: Susan Westergard
Project Editor: Kelley Cardinal
Production Editor: Annette Wall
Marketing Administrator: Mark Olson
Set in Garamond by Montgomery Media, Inc.
Cover design by Montgomery Media, Inc.
Printed and bound by BookCrafters, Inc.

ASQC Mission: To facilitate continuous improvement and increase customer satisfaction by identifying, communicating, and promoting the use of quality principles, concepts, and technologies; and thereby be recognized throughout the world as the leading authority on and champion for, quality.

For a free copy of the ASQC Quality Press Publication Catalog, including ASQC membership information, call 800-248-1946.

Printed in the United States of America.

 Printed on acid-free recycled paper

 ASQC
Quality Press
611 East Wisconsin Avenue
Milwaukee, Wisconsin 53202

 Financial Executives
Research Foundation
10 Madison Avenue, P.O. Box 1938
Morristown, New Jersey 07962

Project Advisory Committee

Ralph Karthein (Chairman)
Controller, IBM Canada

Corning Incorporated
Sandy Helton
VP and Treasurer

Jim Chambers
Assistant Treasurer

Federal Express
Chauncey Burton
Senior Quality Administrator, Finance

Motorola
Ken Johnson
VP and Corporate Controller

Larry Grow
Senior Manager of Internal Audit

Solectron
Susan Wang
Senior VP and CFO

Len Wood
Manager of Internal Audit

Southern Pacific
Larry Yarberry
CFO

Joe Doherty
Assistant VP—Finance

Justin Fox
Director—Quality

Contents

Foreword

Many reviewers, readers and researchers will no doubt recommend this book as must reading for all managers and even all members of finance functions. I will go further. This book should be must reading for all members of any of the professional functions so critical to the survival of modern corporations. Almost everywhere in this book, we can easily change the word finance and insert whatever functional name we wish and the lessons will be the same. This book is a major contribution to understanding the practice of quality management. It deserves several readings.

Late in 1992 I was asked to prepare a closing talk for IMPRO, Juran Institute's annual conference on quality management. The topic suggested was the ten most important trends in quality management I saw emerging.

Somehow these trends struck nerves. Many people have asked me for copies, and I have been asked several times since to give various versions of the same topic. In the American Society for Quality Control's new research publication, *Quality Management Journal*, I highlighted the important research issues I feel still exist in these areas. So little solid research has been done in the emerging key areas of total quality management that they are fertile ground for researchers looking for ways to make major contributions.

Fortunately, there is important research already being done. James Stoner and Frank Werner document some of the best in this book, *Managing Finance for Quality*. Over the past few years at Fordham University, they have taken an innovative approach to teaching total quality management. Rather than the traditional approach of reading a collection of articles and books about tqm and speculating on how it might be applied to whatever area of business under study, in this case finance, they have gone straight to the leading companies and studied how tqm is practiced.

These studies, first through inviting leading practitioners into the classroom to describe their approaches and results and then by in-depth study visits to five leading companies, have led to remarkable new insights, clear documentation of best practices, and lessons learned far beyond what was available from any other source. In so doing, they themselves have established a "best practice" for university research in total quality management.

The results of the research Stoner and Werner so clearly describe in this book adds much to our understanding of the ten trends I have spent innumerable months studying. Before going further, perhaps I should summarize these trends:

1. Expansion of quality management concepts, methods, and tools to all industries and all company functions

2. Quality improvement at a revolutionary pace

3. Partnering—forming partnerships with suppliers, with others in our industries, and even with competitors

4. Education and training for all members of the team—management, professionals, workforce, suppliers, and customers

5. Self-directing workteams

6. Information systems for quality

7. Process management and process engineering

8. Customer focus

9. Benchmarking

10. Strategic quality management

The first trend is, in some ways, the entire focus of this book. Stoner and Werner have focused their research on the expansion of the principles of tqm to one important function of a company, the finance function. This remarkably in-depth study has implications for many other functions. With a little imagination we can take their lessons learned and apply them to almost any function in any company in any type of industry.

As they document the tqm activities of the five companies selected for in-depth study, Corning, Federal Express, Motorola, Solectron, and Southern Pacific, the true meaning of the second trend becomes clear. Quality improvement at a revolutionary pace is becoming a way of life at these companies. They are routinely reporting improvements of a magnitude that, to a company just beginning to change in these ways, seem implausible if not impossible.

The concept of partnering comes through loud and clear without ever being directly addressed. We see in this book many examples. These pioneering finance functions are continually improving their focus on their internal and external customers and building close working relationships. Work previously done by the finance function is being transferred to line functions with resulting savings in time and improvements in accuracy. Audits are becoming "faster, instructional in nature, more accurate, less costly, and more appreciated by the units being audited." Suppliers are being treated as partners by purchasers and long-term, information-sharing relationships are becoming the norm.

One of the refreshing findings in their studies has been that although education and training are important in finance functions—just as they are in other functions—some things come quite easily. Finance people bring special characteristics and skills to the tqm implementation process. Their comfort with numbers, their considerable analytical skills, and their understanding of the "big picture" of company operations give them a head start in many tqm activities. In other areas, education and training may be even more important in the finance function than in other areas. By defining these needs clearly, Stoner and Werner have provided a most useful service.

Although self-directing work teams are not separately discussed, the concept comes through in many parts of this book. Work processes are continuously being analyzed, replanned, improved, and self controls established. In many cases, the finance people are becoming teachers, mentors, coaches as work is transferred closer to the point of initiation. Credit checks are being done before sales, savings in time are great and the empowerment of the sales people is leading to significantly increased revenues. The companies studied are becoming flatter in organizational structure and much less staff oriented as specialization is diffused. Many specialized financial skills are being distributed throughout the organizations.

Two other trends are fundamental to the work described in this book: the emerging need for vastly improved information systems and process redesign and reengineering. These two often are closely linked but perhaps never more so than in the financial areas. Throughout the studies Stoner and Werner describe we see major process redesigns and the concurrent revamping and restructuring of information systems. The building of these information systems makes possible much of the diffusion of specialization described here. The simplification and sometimes refocusing of financial processes make possible the significant gains and bottom-line results so impressively reported.

Throughout the entire book Stoner and Werner emphasize the incredible customer focus these companies have maintained. Defining customers quite broadly, these companies have created information systems that give quick feedback on customer wants, needs, and expectations and how well they are meeting these. They describe intensive measurement systems with clear goals and annual improvements. In Federal Express, for example, the purchasing group has developed its own set of 10 service quality indicators for procurement. These are supplemented by quantitative inputs from buyers, suppliers, and internal customers.

Another trend clearly illustrated is the fascination with external benchmarking displayed by leading U.S. companies. All five of the studied companies have made extensive use of the Malcolm Baldrige National Quality Award criteria as a framework for self assessment and comparisons with the world's best companies. Three of the studied companies are winners of this prestigious award. All are intent on searching out best practices and best processes from any company in any industry and copying, modifying, or using pieces of these proven well-working processes. By doing this benchmarking and quickly adopting lessons learned, they have all accelerated their rates of change and avoided many of the costs and time delays of trial and error improvement strategies.

Quite appropriately for a book about the finance function, Stoner and Werner carefully keep the focus of this book on the bottom line. They integrate all the lessons learned into the basic operations of the company and clearly describe the last trend, strategic quality management. This important focus, far too frequently missed in books on quality management, is clear throughout. Perhaps this focus, more than any of their other many contributions here, makes this book such an important addition to the science and understanding of total quality management.

A. Blanton Godfrey
Chairman and CEO
Juran Institute, Inc.

Preface

Speeding up closing the books from six to four days saves the company $20 million per year, and we anticipate an additional $10 million annual saving now that we've reached two days. But, in addition to the cost savings, the early close frees up several hundred finance people for each day removed from the process. They can devote their attention to more important things than just preparing the numbers—like helping our people run the business.

–Ken Johnson
VP and Corporate Controller, Motorola

In the Finance Department, we first tried to improve our productivity, which translated to doing more and doing it faster. But in those cases where we were just producing junk, we just produced more junk more quickly. So we said, "Wait a minute. The tqm concept tells us that product and task orientation is fine, but we really ought to look at it from a process point of view."

–Susan Wang
Senior VP and CFO, Solectron

Throughout business, financial executives are seeking ways to add more value to their companies. One particularly exciting opportunity to add value derives from the dramatic changes currently occurring in management thought and practice.

There is a "quality revolution" taking place around the world based on a new way of managing organizations. This "global management technology" emphasizes exceeding the expectations of customers, empowering every organizational member, and continuously improving products, services, and the organizational processes that produce them. It has been proven successful in many applications world-wide. We refer to the new management technology as "total quality management," or "tqm."

In this book, we report on the progress of five companies that have made a deep commitment to total quality management: Corning Incorporated, Federal Express, Motorola, Solectron, and Southern Pacific. The first four are well recognized quality leaders—three have won the Malcolm Baldrige National Quality Award, the nation's highest prize for quality excellence. The fifth company, Southern Pacific, is attempting a rapid transformation to quality. Each has demonstrated success in adopting and applying quality management in finance. In addition, financial executives in each company have an interesting story to tell about how quality management has changed their work.

Many other companies are making similar commitments right now or will be doing so in the future. This study is addressed to financial executives in those companies to assist them in adding value to their organizations as their companies adopt and adapt the new quality management practices and systems.

The Opportunity Facing Financial Executives

We believe it is useful to look at all companies as being on a journey from the traditional management systems that have existed since the turn of the twentieth century to tqm. Operating within this transformation adds complexity to finance work, but also creates many opportunities for financial executives and companies in general.

With its focus on customers and processes, concerns which cut across traditional functional lines, tqm requires the participation of all parts of an organization. When major functional groups don't participate, the results are often costly; conversely, full participation in tqm by all organizational units creates important synergies. As companies move toward tqm, the finance function is expected to be a full player.

Quality management has immediate and extensive implications for the day-to-day work and leadership of finance professionals. Finance executives can add greater value to their organizations in two ways: by facilitating and supporting these changes within their company's finance function and by providing leadership for the entire organization's adoption of quality management systems and practices. Finance people will need to acquire new skills and ways of using those skills, but, as demonstrated by the study companies, this has the promise of significantly increasing finance's contribution to the organization.

About this Book

This book is an expanded version of our study *Finance in the Quality Revolution—Adding Value by Integrating Financial and Total Quality*

Management, published in 1993 by the Financial Executives Research Foundation (FERF) as part of its Series on Innovative Management. That book contained the five company case studies, a sixth chapter—"Lessons Learned"—which also appears as Chapter 6 of this book, and a brief Executive Summary and one-page synopsis of each case designed for the book's executive audience.

FERF is the research arm of the Financial Executives Institute, a membership organization of some 11,000 CFOs, treasurers, controllers, and other financial officers of companies throughout North America. In 1991, FERF concluded that members of the Financial Executives Institute would be interested in learning more about the interrelationship of tqm and financial management and funded the case studies upon which *Finance in the Quality Revolution* and this book are based.

The success of *Finance in the Quality Revolution* convinced FERF and us that there was a wider audience for this research, and we approached Quality Press of the American Society for Quality Control, which agreed to the project. The five case studies and "Lessons Learned" chapter were kept as originally published and were supplemented by six additional chapters discussing tqm, how financial management practice is changing in companies committed to systematic quality management, and how finance might continue to evolve as more companies embrace this new management technology.

Methodology of the Study

Our research was conducted using the case study method. We sought companies that were either leaders in tqm or were at particularly interesting points along their tqm journey, whose finance functions were leaders in applying quality management to financial management, and whose finance people believed they had an interesting story to tell. A key tqm concept is "competitive benchmarking," finding examples of best practice to learn what is possible and how it might be accomplished. We feel this is an excellent way to learn about quality management and its implications since many of the advances in tqm are occurring in the field.

We spent from four to six days at each company, interviewing senior corporate executives, finance members, and members of the corporate quality department. At three of the companies, we also attended the formal quality briefing given to suppliers and other interested parties. In addition, we asked for and were given many company documents relating to tqm efforts and progress in both the company as a whole and within the finance function.

In each interview, we asked:

- how the person (and company) became involved in tqm,
- for their best examples of using tqm within corporate finance,
- how the finance function was changing as the company continued to adopt tqm and adapt it to its needs, and
- for evidence of payoffs from tqm.

The interviews proved a rich source of information and insights and became the basis for much of the writing in this study.

Contents of the Book

This book is divided into two parts. Section I addresses finance, tqm, and the issues raised in our research. Section II contains the five case studies.

Section I

Section I of this book is devoted to seven short chapters discussing quality management and its relationship to corporate finance, summarizing themes emerging from the study, and identifying the significance of tqm for financial executives. The seven chapters are:

Chapter 1, "Corporate Finance in Transition," which notes dramatic changes taking place in the practice of financial management in quality-leading companies. We report the six key conclusions of our research, draw similarities and differences between finance's quality experiences and those of other organizational units, and suggest implications and opportunities for corporate finance professionals as their companies move toward quality management.

Chapter 2, "The Global Quality Revolution," which places the changes occurring in corporate finance in the context of changes in the entire organization's management systems. We introduce the Malcolm Baldrige National Quality Award as one model of quality management systems, place the Baldrige model in the context of a global paradigm shift from traditional control and command hierarchical management systems to a new quality based management paradigm, and note implications of this paradigm shift for all managers.

Chapter 3, "Quality Management Comes to the Corporate Finance Function," which places corporate finance in the context of this transition from the traditional management paradigm to the new tqm paradigm by identifying and contrasting characteristics of corporate financial practices consistent with the old paradigm ("conventional corporate finance") and characteristics of corporate finance consistent with the new paradigm ("total quality finance").

Chapter 4, "Integrating tqm into Corporate Finance," which focuses on how the finance functions of the companies in this study contribute to the total organization's tqm effort by integrating "classical" tqm practices, tools, and philosophies into their own operations. We focus on the goals of the finance function, the types of tqm management tools used by finance, and the ways finance does its work and relates to the rest of the organization.

Chapter 5, "Integrating Corporate Finance into the Organization's tqm Efforts," which looks at how finance contributes to the total organization's tqm endeavors from a second angle: how finance aligns its work activities and relationships with the rest of the company's organizational processes and tqm efforts.

Chapter 6, "Lessons Learned," which summarizes conclusions about the adoption of tqm by the finance functions of the companies in the study. Five major themes are the appropriateness of classical tqm approaches for the finance function, the importance of starting, the great yearning for quality, the receptiveness (as opposed to "resistance") of finance members to these approaches, and the opportunities for leadership by finance members.

Chapter 7, "What's Next?—The Continuing Evolution of Corporate Finance," which speculates about the future of tqm in corporate finance. Three questions for the future relate to reinterpreting the "bottom line," rethinking the guidance suggested to financial managers by current finance theory, and inquiring how far "distributed finance" might go toward making all managers financial managers and all financial managers general managers.

Section II

In Section II, we present five case studies, one for each company. In each we first report briefly how the company and its finance function became involved in systematic, company-wide quality management. Then we report examples of finance's quality-driven activities, with one or more major themes for each company. Although one of our most important observations is how similar the quality practices and systems are among the companies in the study, we have selected major examples which differ from company to company to illustrate the breadth of the changes occurring in finance. We conclude each case study with observations on the benefits of finance's and the rest of the company's investments in quality.

Corning: The Corning case illustrates how tqm can play an integrating and linking role permitting a very lean treasury organization to support a large multinational corporation. We look at Treasury's mission statement and "Key Results Indicators" which provide guidance and direction to treasury members. We then discuss quality initiatives taking place in each unit within Corning's treasury.

Federal Express: The Federal Express case profiles new ways for corporate finance to support others in the company. We identify Federal Express' system of Service Quality Indicators, both company-wide and for finance, which count errors and weigh them by their importance to customers. We report on Business Case Analysis, a broad and holistic method of project analysis and evaluation. We also discuss a financial information system which empowers individuals throughout the company to get more involved in financial analysis and which frees up the finance staff to make additional contributions.

Motorola: The Motorola case emphasizes the payoffs from a sustained quality focus. One of the earliest U.S. quality pioneers, Motorola has systematically extended quality management concepts to all parts of the company. Motorola is a leader in understanding the importance of cycle time, and its six sigma defects measurement system is now used widely by many tqm companies, including several others in this study. A particular success at Motorola is extending the six sigma and cycle time concepts to soft finance processes. We illustrate this by profiling Motorola's internal audit process, generally considered to be world class. We also report on payroll accuracy and cycle time reduction in closing the accounting books.

Solectron: The Solectron case presents a company in which quality is a moment-to-moment way of life in every part of the organization. Our primary focus is on ways in which finance has become closely integrated with customers, both Solectron's external customers and finance's internal customers. We also report how Solectron uses quality assessment processes including the Malcolm Baldrige National Quality Award and ISO 9000 as ongoing means of self-improvement.

Southern Pacific: The Southern Pacific case shows that a company does not have to spend many years to get into and start reaping the benefits from a quality management system. We identify how finance joined with the rest of the organization to speed up its rapid quality transformation. We profile progress in improving billing accuracy and in redesigning and integrating the planning process to support quality initiatives. We also report how Southern Pacific was able to use its quality plans and results to gain enhanced access to the financial markets.

How to Use/Read this Book

The seven chapters of Section I are designed to be read in sequence—they build upon one another to tell the story our research uncovered. On the other hand, each of the five case studies of Section II stands on its own. Their order is alphabetical, and readers are invited to enjoy them in whatever order suits their interests. We encourage you to read as much as you find useful in each of the cases, starting with the case(s) emphasizing the issues your own company is facing most immediately. Although all the cases address "getting into quality" and "payoffs from quality," the cases differ in their focus, with each case emphasizing one or more themes about the changes occurring in corporate finance. Finally, you may wish to learn a bit about the research methodology, the authors and other contributors to the study, and suggestions for further reading. These topics appear at the end of the book.

Acknowledgments

Completing a project like this one takes the effort and cooperation of many people. We were fortunate to work with a series of teams that were uniformly supportive, constructive, and a lot of fun. Although it is difficult to acknowledge all those who assisted us, these pages are at least a start.

Our first thank yous go to the good people at the Financial Executives Research Foundation (FERF)—Roland Laing, President; Bill Sinnett, Senior Research Associate; and Kathy Knachel, Publications Manager—who first came to us with the proposal for this study, helped us put together the steering committee and "recruit" the participating companies, advised us, turned the manuscript into a finished work, and consistently supported us over the past year. They have been partners in every respect in this endeavor, and we thank them.

The Financial Executives Research Foundation published the five case studies and the "Lessons Learned" chapter in their Series on Innovative Management under the title *Finance in the Quality Revolution—Adding Value by Integrating Financial and Total Quality Management.* They also worked with us and members of Quality Press in arranging for the publication of this more complete version of our study. For making this volume possible we are again indebted to Roland and Bill of FERF and to the people at Quality Press, in particular Susan Westergard, Kelley Cardinal, and Shannon Eglinton. Three anonymous reviewers also earned our great appreciation—thank you, whoever you are.

We owe a special debt of gratitude to the members of our project steering committee—Ralph Karthein, IBM, Chairman; Sandy Helton and Jim Chambers, Corning; Chauncey Burton, Federal Express; Valerie Lauderdale, IBM; Ken Johnson and Larry Grow, Motorola; Susan Wang and Len Wood, Solectron; and Larry Yarberry, Joe Doherty, and Justin Fox, Southern Pacific. They guided our work along the way, gave us excellent access to their finance and quality organizations, and worked with us on each case and chapter.

Our first task was to select companies for the study. In this effort we started with the help of A. Blanton Godfrey of the Juran Institute, who was also the first person we turned to for assistance in 1989 when we undertook our first study of this type, *Remaking Corporate Finance*. In addition to suggesting companies we might invite to participate in the study, Blan introduced us to many of the people we subsequently contacted for advice and guidance. For this study, we drew once again on individuals who guided us in our first study, and we added a variety of new coaches and "door openers." These include Richard Adams, Jim Anderson, Harry Artinian, David Baldwin, Len Bardsley, Richard Buetow, Charles T. Carey, Carola Crowley, Sharon DesJarlais, Rick Dmytrow, Newt Hardie, David Hickie, Aleta Holub, Ken Leach, David Lindsey, Gabriel Pall, Mary Anne Rasmussen, Kurt Raimann, Bob Simonini, Steve Smith, Terry Smith, Kent Sterett, and Bob Talbot. At this stage, Bill Sinnett and Roland Laing also provided valuable guidance in selecting companies.

In each company, we spoke to excellent, responsive individuals. We thank them all. They are far too numerous to list here, but many made their way into the case studies, and all are listed, along with their titles, at the end of their company's case.

In the Fall 1991 academic term, we conducted a seminar at the Graduate School of Business at Fordham to kick off the project. Students heard presentations from Debra Gray and Phil King of Federal Express, Ken Johnson and Larry Grow of Motorola, and Susan Wang of Solectron. We thank them for the excellent presentations they made to our seminar.

Student teams wrote papers integrating what they heard with their readings, and provided insights into the companies which aided our further interviews and writing. Some teams produced first drafts of the cases that appear in this book. Other teams wrote essays on themes common to the four presentations. One team developed a useful bibliography on finance and tqm. The Fordham student teams that developed company case drafts are acknowledged at the end of the case on which they worked. All of the seminar members are also listed at the end of these acknowledgments.

Several students from the seminar continued working with us after the term ended, researching and assisting on specific cases—Cathy Borzon, Corning; Jeff Deiss and Dave Susswein, Federal Express; Ralph Terracciano, Motorola; Candy Childers, Solectron; and Anne Hardy, Southern Pacific. All of them made valuable contributions as we moved the work forward. Ralph Terracciano deserves particular mention for his drafts of the Motorola case and the internal audit example.

We were fortunate to have Jean-Louis Boulmer as our research assistant during and after his studies at Fordham. Jean-Louis organized our papers, transcribed interviews, and assisted us in our research—giving us far greater access to our materials. Also helping out as required were our Fordham graduate assistants John Diego, Maribeth Holland, Galina Katlikova, Ricky Kintanar, and Eleonora Oropeza.

We also are grateful for the support of our Dean, William J. Small; our former Dean Arthur R. Taylor, now President of Muhlenberg College; former Associate Dean Susan Atherton; and the entire staff at the Schools of Business at Fordham.

Finally, we wish to thank our families—Barbara, Alexandra, and Carolyn; and Marie, Allison, and Eric—who tolerated our travel, long phone calls, and late nights locked up by the word processor. Their support and encouragement were and remain very much appreciated.

Members of the
Finance and Total Quality Management Seminar
Fordham University—Fall 1991

Kimberly Allen
Christopher Amico
Andrea Baker
Brad Barton
Javier Basuri
Lori Beath
Leigh Benowitz
Mirco Bianchi
Thomas Bisighini
Jeffrey Boose
Catharine Borzon
Julie Brennan
Karen Byrne
Fidelma Callery

Scott Caruso
Christopher Connolly
Marianne Craig
Jeffrey Deiss
Gregory DeRosa
David Eastep
Margaret Edwards
Thomas Fitzpatrick
Jeffrey Goddard
Rina Goldman
Andrew Goldner
William Halford, Jr.
Rukshana Haque

Ann Hardy
Melissa Horan
Eleonora Oropeza
Sophia Petsas
Rafael Porras
Donald Quigley
Ellen Radloff
Margaret Riley
Amy Rosenzweig
Marie Sabia
Ann Schroeder
David Susswein
Victor Tan
Ralph Terracciano

Section I

1
Corporate Finance in Transition

I don't see how you can compete in the long run without embracing these [quality approaches]. They are proven; there is no question about it anymore. It is a given fact. You had better get on board on these things or you are going to get left behind, and you are not going to be able to catch up.

–Alan Graf
Senior VP and CFO, Federal Express

A new way of managing organizations, often called total quality management or "tqm," has revolutionized the way many successful companies are operating. Its hallmark is a commitment to exceed customer expectations on an ongoing basis by continuously improving the company's products and services and the processes which make and support them. And, although keeping the customer happy and improving quality seem like obvious things to do, it is only recently that many companies have discovered the power of this new management technology.

As companies adopt and adapt quality management to their own circumstances, they quickly discover that a core concept of tqm is viewing the organization as a system tied together by processes which cross conventional functional boundaries. Every traditional department—including finance—must be involved in the company's tqm efforts to obtain the full benefits of this powerful management technology.

The finance functions of many companies are learning that by being full partners and participants in their company's quality management efforts, they can add even more value to the firm:

- At Solectron, a rapidly growing contract manufacturer of electronic products and components, finance has added greater value by enabling the sales staff "to do finance's credit analysis job" *before* investing time in developing possible customer prospects, saving time for the sales staff and for other Solectron units. The resulting reduction in finance's credit analysis work has added additional value by freeing up time to attack more challenging and satisfying projects.

- Motorola's internal auditors redesigned the audit process to be faster, instructional in nature, more accurate, less costly, and more appreciated by the units being audited. The two-year auditing position is one of the most prized developmental assignments in the company and is highly rated by the auditors at the end of their assignments. Working with Motorola is also seen as a prize assignment for Motorola's external auditor, KPMG Peat Marwick. Their audit staff are jokingly described as "willing to kill" to get assigned to the Motorola audit because it goes so smoothly.

- Federal Express is learning how to measure the key competitive implications of major technological investments and how to make better capital budgeting decisions, by moving away from being trapped into counting only the less important short-term financial impacts. Finance members working on teams evaluating the new investments are enthusiastic about the opportunities to improve the quality of the analyses and about the change in their roles from policing and judging to facilitating, coaching, teaching, and learning.

Solectron, Motorola, and Federal Express are all leaders in managing for total quality, customer satisfaction, and organizational flexibility. In each company, the finance function is a full player in the company's changing approach to management. What these companies and their finance functions are experiencing are the types of changes other companies are also discovering are necessary for competitive survival.

The Quality Revolution and Financial Transformation

This study of changes in the corporate finance function focuses on the adoption of quality management practices in corporate finance. The study assumes that "the jury is no longer out" on quality management practices—that quality management is not just another business fad, but instead represents a fundamental change in how organizations are managed.

Quality management is not a fad because it has worked so well in so many places for so long. Organizations are adopting quality management because the new methods yield higher quality products and services at lower costs, shorter cycle times to complete operational tasks and to introduce new products and services, and growing customer, supplier, and employee loyalty.

The implications of these new management practices for financial executives, and all financial staff, are direct and profound: new attitudes, new skills, new work tasks and methods, and new relationships will supplement and/or replace the successful ones of the past. Tqm brings with it both the proverbial bad news and good news. The bad news is that what used to work may no longer work—personal and professional changes will be required of financial executives and staff. The good news is that the new ways of managing frequently increase finance's ability to add value and are often more rewarding and satisfying for both executives and staff. Finance is becoming more valuable to the firm and more fun for its members.

Purpose of the Study

This study is intended to assist financial executives in adding value to their organizations as those organizations adopt and adapt the new quality management practices and systems of this emerging "global management technology."

Approach of the Study

The study seeks to accomplish its purpose by reporting the experiences of members of the corporate finance functions of five companies: Corning, Federal Express, Motorola, Solectron, and Southern Pacific.

The first four companies are well-recognized quality leaders, members of the "first generation" of quality management companies in the United States. Three—Federal Express, Motorola, and Solectron—have won the Malcolm Baldrige National Quality Award, the nation's highest award for providing quality goods and services, and Corning's Telecommunications Products Division received a site visit when it applied for the Baldrige Award—an event popularly called "being a finalist in the Baldrige competition." The fifth company, Southern Pacific, has not yet established a reputation for leadership in quality, but its experiences may turn out to be particularly valuable for financial and other executives. A relative newcomer to tqm, Southern Pacific is attempting to institute systematic quality management at an accelerated rate by building upon the "lessons learned" by the quality leaders. We see companies like Southern Pacific, which are attempting to "reduce the cycle time" for installing a quality management system and for building a culture of quality, as representing a "second generation" of quality management companies, a generation that—aided by the first generation companies—achieves the benefits of quality faster and at lower costs.

Key Themes and Conclusions

Six major conclusions emerge from this study:

- the payoffs from investments in quality management are high,

- quality works as well in finance as anywhere else,

- members of finance can be full players—even leaders—in their companies' adoption of tqm,

- finance organizations do not always need expensive consultants or an elaborate quality organization to get started with tqm,

- new measurements, information, and reporting are emerging from finance's active involvement in tqm, and

- the decentralization of the analysis and controllership role of finance is accelerating.

The Payoffs from Quality Are High

The financial executives interviewed in these companies are convinced that quality is a good investment, both from a narrow functional view of the "bottom-line" payoff and from a much broader view of the pay-off for customers, employees, and the country as a whole.

As the chapter opening quotation from Alan Graf of Federal Express suggests, these financial executives believe that company-wide quality management systems go well beyond being very profitable; they are necessary for corporate survival.

The financial executives are convinced that the finance organization must be a full and active participant in the company's quality program for it to succeed. Motorola's chief corporate staff officer and former assistant CFO says:

> We've found that it's important for the finance organization to be an integral part of the company's quality processes. If we're not on board 100%, we just make [quality management] more difficult for everyone else.

One of the most striking aspects of the financial executives' comments is the clear message they send about the payoffs for employees—the executives' experience and belief that working and managing within well-functioning quality management systems are more rewarding and satisfying than working and managing in the traditional management systems tqm is replacing.

Quality Works as Well in Finance as Anywhere Else

The financial executives are equally convinced that the quality systems and practices that work elsewhere are fully applicable in finance departments and financial processes. In fact, they believe that quality management is a more natural way to "do" finance than what they had been doing previously. Corning's CFO says:

> The [quality] approach in finance does not look any different from the [quality] approach anywhere else. . . . It's a pretty big shift [from the way finance used to be done], yet now that we do it, it seems pretty straightforward. It's hard to imagine not doing our work this way.

Finance members can use the same types of quality management tools and get the same types of results as the rest of the company. These results include improved internal and external customer satisfaction, reduction of useless work activities and rework, cost savings, reduced cycle time, increased creativity and innovation, and increased professional capabilities.

Members of Finance Can Be Full Players and Even Leaders

In each study company, finance members were strong contributors to quality management, both within finance and by forming new partnerships with other functions. They provided leadership in a number of ways: in aligning financial and quality information systems, in integrating quality planning with financial and strategic planning, in breaking down barriers between the finance function and the rest of the organization, in empowering members of other functions and divisions to become their own financial analysts or their own internal auditors or to do other finance work. In the cases of Corning and Southern Pacific, finance people were involved from the very beginning in the formal planning and executing of company-wide tqm implementation.

There is no indication from the study companies that finance professionals have to wait for others to take leadership before pursuing tqm. Our research identified so many ways finance contributes to the tqm transformation that we know of no reason why someone in finance cannot be the first quality champion for companies that have yet to make the tqm commitment.

Expensive Consultants and Elaborate Quality Organizations Are Not Needed to Get Started

Most of the study companies began integrating quality management and corporate finance by simplifying financial processes and eliminating non-value added work using in-house skills and "a lot of common sense." Many of the benefits from early quality efforts came from simply asking customers whether the work finance was doing for them was useful and eliminating the activities that were not. In their early efforts, finance members were often able to draw upon existing quality training programs and internal quality leaders from other functions. They were also able to get a good start by plucking the "low hanging fruit"—quality and cycle time problems so blatant that both problems and solutions quickly become obvious when first looked at from a quality management perspective.

The greater the internal quality management resources on which finance can draw, the less likely that outside help will be needed. However, for finance to move rapidly or to take advantage of special skills not available internally, outside consultants may have an important role to play. And for companies which have not yet made a deep commitment to systematic quality approaches, outside consultants may be important to help the finance function get started.

New Measurements, Information, and Reporting Are Emerging

Finance people are identifying and incorporating measures of process and quality into corporate reporting systems. By doing so they are changing the way their companies establish goals and measure performance. At Corning, for example, key Treasury processes have been identified and are starting to be rated as being in one of six sequential categories: process mapped, process documented, key control points identified, process benchmarked, continuous improvement in place, or process under tqm management. At Federal Express, a company-wide system called Service Quality Indicators (SQIs) measures the company's and the individual functions' progress in quality improvement. SQIs capture the level of customer satisfaction by counting the number of times the company fails to satisfy a customer. For example, within the Finance Division the purchasing group developed a set of 10 SQIs for procurement. These 10 quantified measures are supplemented by a set of subjective inputs such as comments from buyers about supplier responsiveness and attitude.

The Decentralization of the Analysis and Controllership Role of Finance Is Accelerating

Finance professionals are discovering new ways to "distribute" their expertise throughout the company, moving financial analysis closer to where it is needed and freeing themselves up to do additional value-added work. At the same time, the treasury and service functions of finance are becoming more centralized as tqm permits finance organizations to simplify processes.

Solectron's finance function, for example, is working to change where finance is done in the company structure—distributing financial work so it is performed closer to the customer and sometimes performed by non-financial people. In identifying promising prospects, finance plays an important role in an effective team-based process, supporting sales, marketing, and other personnel in evaluating the potential and suitability of each prospective customer. A step that once came relatively late in the process—the decision on the creditworthiness of the prospect and the amount of credit the prospect would be eligible to receive—is now being performed very early in the process. And rather than being performed by someone in finance, it is now done by people in sales. In distributing this financial task closer to the customer and "giving away" this piece of financial work, finance has improved considerably its contribution to the entire process.

Solectron's attempts to distribute financial skills, tasks, and responsibilities are representative of efforts in the other companies of the study. Solectron's successes with credit analysis, self-audits, and other distributed financial processes are also mirrored by successes at the other companies, such as Federal Express' ELVIS system which permits non-finance members to do their own financial analysis.

Quality Experiences and Opportunities for Financial Executives

Two further themes emerge from the six conclusions discussed above: (1) how finance's quality experiences are similar to and different from those of the rest of the company, and (2) the wealth of opportunities for financial executives and staff members as their companies make the transition toward tqm.

Similarities and Differences

Finance's use of quality approaches and the results achieved have both similarities to and differences from the approaches and results of other parts of the company. The similarities are more numerous and in many respects more important; however, the differences are important to recognize.

Quality methods and results: Finance members use the same types of quality management tools and get the same types of results as the rest of the company. They achieve improved internal and external customer satisfaction, reduce useless work activities and rework, save costs, reduce cycle time, increase creativity and innovation, and increase professional capabilities and work satisfaction.

Need for training in quality and differences in receptiveness: Like all other organizational members, finance members need training in the use of quality management tools, in the philosophy and value of quality approaches, and in understanding the nature and implications of quality management. Also like members of other organizational units, some finance members are quick to embrace quality management while others drag their heels and reject it.

Many finance members do tend to have an advantage in grasping some quality management tools because of their affinity for numbers. Their comfort with quantitative measures and their desire to be precise, concrete, and specific in analysis and prescription make the numerical tools of quality management particularly attractive to them and support them in being quick learners in this aspect of quality management. (On the other hand, many finance people are uncomfortable with the group and team oriented aspects of quality management and the levels of interpersonal skills in listening, acknowledging, sharing, and the like, required for full contribution. For them, the "soft skills" of quality management may come harder.)

Value of a "customer perspective": Like the rest of the organization, finance has customers, a perspective that comes as a bit of a revelation to some finance members. However, once they accept this perspective, they find it valuable and empowering to use the concepts of internal and external customer, customer-supplier relationships, listening to the "voice of the customer," and exceeding customer expectations.

Changes in roles: Like other members of their companies, the roles of finance members change significantly—from defenders of the interests of their particular function, division, or work unit to team players seeking to support the total organization in exceeding customer expectations. In addition, finance has a number of special characteristics: a historical police/judge role, a special responsibility for seeing that corporate resources are used prudently, a special custodial role for the performance measurement system, and work that exposes many members to the total company. These roles, responsibilities, and perspectives give the financial staff special situations to deal with.

Police/judge: Finance is frequently charged with a special responsibility for protecting the interests of shareholders and their agents: the board of directors and the top management of the company. This perspective often leads finance to cast itself and be perceived as the corporate police and as judges of the actions of others—"the only adults in the company." Every business function has its own unique role, and quality creates different role transition issues for each. For finance, the historical police/judge role can be a significant barrier to understanding the nature of quality management and to being willing to embrace the collaborative behaviors and trusting relationships required of all organizational members. Surrendering the role of organizational cop can be seen on the one hand as a significant loss of power and control, yet on the other hand, it may provide an opportunity to escape the stress, isolation, and defensiveness built into any policing role. One of the more striking messages sent by the interviewees in this study is how much finance members value the shift from cop to partner, from judge to team player. They do not miss the police officer's badge and billy club.

Prudent use of resources: Closely related to the cop/judge role is finance's traditional obligation to assure efficient use of corporate resources. As quality management systems become firmly embedded in an organization, that special role of finance virtually disappears, being replaced by company-wide continuous quality improvement processes used by intra-unit, cross-functional, and cross-divisional teams. The efficient use of resources becomes a company-wide responsibility independent of finance.

Custodian of the performance measurement system: Finance has historically played the leading role in defining success for the organization and its members and how success was to be measured. It then played the key role in measuring performance. With the significant changes in management practices that are part of tqm, finance has a special responsibility for re-shaping the performance measurement system and for facilitating the transition from existing systems to new ones. Because this task is a sophisticated and intellectually difficult one and because few companies have achieved clear and dramatic breakthroughs in this area, re-shaping performance measurement systems is one of the greatest challenges facing finance and the rest of the organization at this stage of the quality revolution.

Exposure to the total company: Financial work frequently provides exposure to many other parts of the organization, giving its members a sense of the big picture. However, finance's traditional focus on only "the numbers," and a very limited set of numbers at that, provides a narrow set of lenses through which the big picture is viewed. So, finance people often have the advantage of being accustomed to thinking in terms of the total organization combined with the disadvantage of doing that broad thinking in very narrow terms.

Finance's use of integrative techniques: Financial tools provide devices for integrating and stating very concisely the organization's overall situation and past performance, so finance people are accustomed to thinking in an integrative way. However, the picture they get from traditional financial and managerial accounting reports represents only one view of the organization and its performance.

Special challenges: As organizations progress in inculcating quality management approaches, each function and work unit finds that quality management presents unique challenges. Finance faces both challenges common to other functions and challenges unique to its special roles and responsibilities. And, like the other functions, finance needs to play a lead role in grappling with its own special challenges.

Each business function probably feels that its special quality challenges are more daunting than those faced by the other functions, but finance may have some claim to facing the greatest challenges. Two of these include developing and implementing creative and empowering approaches to defining success for the organization and changing the reward system to support rather than ignore or punish quality improvements. We believe two other special finance challenges will be easily handled by most finance people: allowing other members of the organization to be adults and giving away the power to judge and "make others wrong." From all indications in our interviews, these are "sacrifices" financial staff members are grateful for the opportunity to make.

Implications for Financial Executives and Staff

As companies make the transition from traditional management systems to quality management, members of corporate finance functions will find a variety of new opportunities and challenges for themselves and for their roles within the organization.

The high payoff from quality: The implication for financial executives of the high payoff from investments in quality is clear: as part of their traditional responsibility for assuring sound management practices and the financial viability of their organizations, financial executives must take a leadership role in implementing quality practices in their companies and in their functions.

Achievements and commitment: Finance members can achieve the same types of improvements to their function and contributions to the total organization, and can exhibit the same types of commitment to and enthusiasm for quality approaches as other members of the organization.

Collaboration and teamwork: Using the same quality management tools and approaches, finance members can collaborate fully with the rest of the organization in customer satisfaction and quality improvement projects—they can be expected to be full team players.

Training: Investments in training finance members must be made to get the results. A danger in finance's comfort with numbers is that finance individuals may think they already understand quality's quantitative techniques and do not need to learn them. A danger of failing to value or of being uncomfortable with some of the "people skills" of quality management is that they may attempt to avoid such training. A danger of working in many parts of the organization and seeing the big picture with an integrative view is that they may believe they truly understand a systems perspective and have little to learn about how systems really work and behave. All three mistakes can be serious for the individuals and for the organization. Training in quality perspectives is needed as much for finance members as for anyone else in the organization, even though some parts will come with greater ease and some with greater difficulty.

Customer focus and roles: Finance can be expected to be a full player in building customer-supplier relationships inside and outside the company and in becoming more effective in teaching, coaching, and facilitating the work of others.

Measurement and reward systems: As finance's roles and behaviors change, measurement and reward systems must also change to acknowledge, reward, and support the new behaviors appropriate for their new roles.

Giving up past roles: Finance people need to be supported by their bosses and other organizational members in surrendering outmoded roles and tasks they have learned in the past and whose mastery has frequently contributed to their success. This situation is true for all organization members, but finance has its own special roles and responsibilities to give up or give away. These include cop and judge, feeling like the only adults, and taking more than their share of the responsibility for efficiency and effectiveness.

Special challenges: Every company has a right to expect, and a need for, finance to take a leadership role in grappling with certain quality-related challenges. Some of these challenges will be unique to finance; others will be common throughout the organization. Finance members will need the support and contributions of other individuals and functions if they are to find workable solutions.

Two particular challenges requiring financial leadership are among the most daunting facing management today:

- Dramatically changing reward systems to recognize and support team-based as well as individual-based contributions, quality and process improvements, investments in long-term organizational competencies and capabilities, empowerment of others, and the "invisible leadership" that creates such empowerment. We simply do not know enough about how to encourage, recognize, and reward such contributions. Finance members have a special opportunity to contribute, in collaboration with members of all other functions, by finding ways to do so.

- Renegotiating the relationship between the firm and the capital markets to remove pressure for short-term profit and stock price performance when the actions necessary to produce that performance come at the expense of the company's long-term stability and viability. Just as corporate finance members face challenges in their own understanding and adoption of quality management, capital market professionals also require a period of learning about the need for and benefits of quality. Corporate finance members will play a critical role in "training the markets."

Other challenges which we are unable to see today will arise in the future. Quality management is a changing, evolving phenomenon. As more companies adopt this new management technology and adapt it to their special circumstances, they and others will learn more about its payoffs and implications. We expect this to present new challenges and opportunities to all members of the organization.

2
The Global Quality Revolution

Solectron uses the Malcolm Baldrige National Quality Award criteria as a framework for interpreting the company's quality management system and makes the Baldrige assessment process part of that management system. Ko Nishimura, Solectron's co-CEO, recalls, "We looked at [the Baldrige assessment process] as a key business process that we should use in the company to integrate the pieces. Why should we go out and invent one of these when there were a lot of people who thought this out pretty well? I looked at this and said 'Gee, this is great. It doesn't do everything, but it does a lot of things and it's going to move the company forward if we use it every year.'"

The Baldrige assessment process is one of a growing number of attempts to understand key aspects of the new management processes contributing to and arising from a global quality revolution. The changes associated with this revolution present financial executives, and all other managers and non-managers, with exceptional challenges, opportunities, and risks. One of the most basic challenges is how to interpret what has been happening in the theory and practice of management since the early 1950s when this revolution started to become visible and to bear fruit. These global changes have been called by many names: "a paradigm shift," "a quality revolution," "a new management paradigm," "the Japanese economic miracle," "the end of Taylorism," "the end of Traditional Management." For those who see the global changes as driven by changes in management practices, those practices have also received many labels: "a new management culture," "Japanese Management," "lean manufacturing," "Company-Wide Quality Control," "Total Quality Management (TQM)," "high commitment management," "the Juran management approach," "the Deming Way."

Currently, the most frequently used label is "Total Quality Management (TQM)," the name we have adopted in this book. In adopting that name we have made one change. Very intentionally, we have chosen not to capitalize the three words "total quality management" or their acronym "tqm." We do this because there is considerable concern among quality experts about the efforts of consultants, quality gurus, and academics to determine a single "correct" definition for quality management.

One recent example is the concern that the very desirable commitment of the U.S. Department of Defense to tqm may be leading to an undesirably rigid "official definition" of what tqm *really* is. We share Soren Kierkegaard's concern about rigid categorization expressed in his quotation: "Once you label me, you negate me." Our avoidance of capital letters and these comments signal our belief that many of the different company and consultant names for tqm describe processes that are fundamentally similar. In addition, we believe that the pursuit of quality is creating a new way of managing more rapidly than any official definition will be able to keep up with. We use the generic "tqm" to emphasize that what we see as tqm today will look like something else tomorrow.

As the quotation from Solectron's co-CEO suggests, one of the currently popular frameworks for interpreting what has been happening is provided by the Baldrige criteria. Financial executives in each of the companies participating in this study have used the Baldrige criteria as part of their work and have frequently found them quite valuable.

The purpose of this chapter is to offer readers a framework for interpreting the changes occurring in their organizations. We start by outlining the Baldrige framework—one that many companies and an increasing number of academics have found useful, even if not perfect. Then we place the Baldrige framework in a somewhat larger context, that of a shift of management paradigms. We interpret the paradigm shift as the replacement of a dominant "Traditional Management paradigm" associated with such names as Frederick W. Taylor, Max Weber, and Henri Fayol to a "new quality management paradigm"—a new "management technology"—associated with names like W. Edwards Deming, Kaoru Ishikawa, Joseph M. Juran, and Genichi Taguchi. We close the chapter by speaking to the implications for financial executives, with the understanding that if we are, in fact, in the midst of a management paradigm shift, modesty and humility are necessary—it is always difficult to interpret changes when one is in the midst of them.

The Baldrige Award Framework

The Malcolm Baldrige National Quality Award is the result of concern in the United States about the loss of global competitiveness and market share by many U.S. companies and entire industries. The Award was established by legislation passed in 1987, and the first applications were accepted in 1988. Each year there can be a maximum of six winners—two in each of three categories: manufacturing, service, and small business. Awards to manufacturing and service winners can be for the company as a whole or for a division of the company. In the Award's first six years there were 19 winners: 11 in manufacturing, three in service, and five in small business.

Applying for the Baldrige Award

To apply for the Award, companies submit an application covering seven major areas (Figure 2.1). Applications in the manufacturing and service categories are limited to 75 pages in length and carry an application fee of $4000; the maximum length in the small business category is 50 pages and the fee is $1200. All applications are evaluated by individuals selected from a pool of examiners who provide feedback to the applicants and whose evaluations determine whether the application receives further consideration. Highly rated applications receive a "site visit" from a team of examiners coordinated by a senior examiner, an event frequently referred to as being a "finalist," even though that term is not an official one used by the examiners or judges of the process. Winners, if there are any, are announced in October, National Quality Month.

In the spirit of continuous improvement, the Baldrige Committee has examined its experience each year and has made changes in the items on which applicants are examined. A particularly notable change was the introduction in 1992 of specific attention to the applicant's financial performance, triggered most directly by the much publicized financial difficulties of the Wallace Corporation shortly after it won the Award in 1990.

The Baldrige Framework as a Theory of Excellence

Although the Baldrige Committee does not claim the application represents a theory of managerial or organizational excellence, many managers and academics find it useful to ask the question, "What implicit

FIGURE 2.1 **1994 Baldrige Award Examination Items and Point Values**

1994 EXAMINATION ITEMS AND POINT VALUES		
1994 Examination Categories/Items		Point Values
1.0 Leadership		**95**
1.1 Senior Executive Leadership	45	
1.2 Management for Quality	25	
1.3 Public Responsibility and Corporate Citizenship	25	
2.0 Information and Analysis		**75**
2.1 Scope and Management of Quality and Performance Data and Information	15	
2.2 Competitive Comparisons and Benchmarking	20	
2.3 Analysis and Uses of Company-Level Data	40	
3.0 Strategic Quality Planning		**60**
3.1 Strategic Quality and Company Performance Planning Process	35	
3.2 Quality and Performance Plans	25	
4.0 Human Resource Development and Management		**150**
4.1 Human Resource Planning and Management	20	
4.2 Employee Involvement	40	
4.3 Employee Education and Training	40	
4.4 Employee Performance and Recognition	25	
4.5 Employee Well-Being and Satisfaction	25	
5.0 Management of Process Quality		**140**
5.1 Design and Introduction of Quality Products and Services	40	
5.2 Process Management: Product and Service Production and Delivery Processes	35	
5.3 Process Management: Business and Support Service Processes	30	
5.4 Supplier Quality	20	
5.5 Quality Assessment	15	
6.0 Quality and Operational Results		**180**
6.1 Product and Service Quality Results	70	
6.2 Company Operational Results	50	
6.3 Business and Support Service Results	25	
6.4 Supplier Quality Results	35	
7.0 Customer Focus and Satisfaction		**300**
7.1 Customer Expectations: Current and Future	35	
7.2 Customer Relationship Management	65	
7.3 Commitment to Customers	15	
7.4 Customer Satisfaction Determination	30	
7.5 Customer Satisfaction Results	85	
7.6 Customer Satisfaction Comparison	70	
TOTAL POINTS		1000

theory of management might underlie the application?" Figure 2.2 and the application descriptions of the categories suggest such a theory. The model has four major elements: the goal, driver, system, and measures of progress.

The purpose of the organization—its goal—is customer satisfaction (category 7.0) and from that satisfaction, organizational survival derives, as indicated by competitive success and gains in market share. "The basic aim of the quality process is the delivery of ever-improving value to customers." (Quotations are from page 5 of the 1994 Baldrige application.)

The key driving role is played by senior executives: top management leads and sustains tqm (category 1.0). "Senior executive leadership creates the values, goals, and systems, and guides the sustained pursuit of customer value and company performance improvement."

Four systems are key: systems for gathering and using information on quality (category 2.0), for strategic quality planning (category 3.0), for developing and managing human resources (category 4.0), and for the management and continuous improvement of productive processes (category 5.0). "[Each] system comprises the set of well-defined and well-designed processes for meeting the company's customer, quality, and performance requirements." The quality information system for obtaining, analyzing, and acting upon valid information ("management by fact") is critical in linking the other systems together.

The results of successful leadership of the key organizational systems are measured (category 6.0) by progress in improving inputs, internal processes, and outputs. Progress is measured on the input side by improvements in supplier quality, inside the organization by improvements in internal processes and productivity and reducing or eliminating waste, and on the output side by improvements in product and service quality. "Measures of progress provide a results-oriented basis for channeling actions to delivering ever-improving customer value and company performance."

The Baldrige model presents a clear vision of the key elements of a quality management system, and a detailed set of metrics for measuring progress toward that vision. Although it identifies a number of major dimensions, its usefulness may be increased by adding three supplementary perspectives associated with the conditions that gave rise to the need for a Baldrige process. These additional perspectives are

- the framing of changes in global management practices as a paradigm shift—a shift from Traditional Management practices to a new management technology: total quality management,

FIGURE 2.2 **The Baldrige Award Criteria Framework**

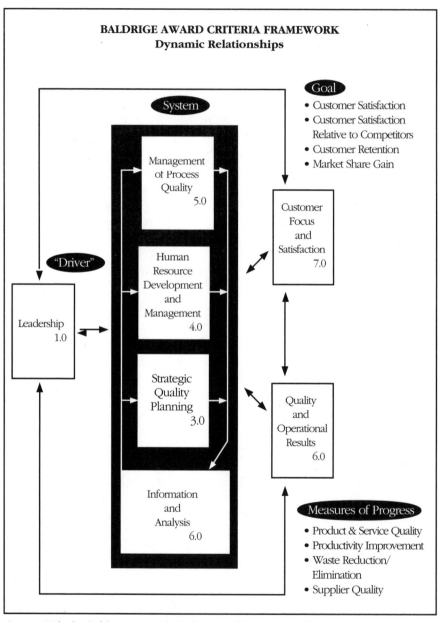

BALDRIGE AWARD CRITERIA FRAMEWORK
Dynamic Relationships

Goal
- Customer Satisfaction
- Customer Satisfaction Relative to Competitors
- Customer Retention
- Market Share Gain

System

Management of Process Quality 5.0

Human Resource Development and Management 4.0

Strategic Quality Planning 3.0

Information and Analysis 6.0

"Driver"

Leadership 1.0

Customer Focus and Satisfaction 7.0

Quality and Operational Results 6.0

Measures of Progress
- Product & Service Quality
- Productivity Improvement
- Waste Reduction/ Elimination
- Supplier Quality

Source: Malcolm Baldrige National Quality Award. *1994 Award Criteria,* 5.

- how the paradigm shift is changing the core elements of management practices and the rest of the organization, and

- the implications of this paradigm shift for financial executives and all other organizational members.

The Paradigm Shift—Contrasting Traditional Management and Tqm

The Traditional Management paradigm is the one associated with the writings of the American industrial consultant Frederick W. Taylor ("Taylorism"), the German sociologist Max Weber, the French executive Henri Fayol, and other influential management writers of the early part of the twentieth century. It is the one within which we have all grown up. Based upon a military command and control model, it seems natural to us and is part of our culture—"in our bones" in many respects. It starts with a well-defined hierarchy, an organizational pyramid, which is frequently quite steep with many layers of management. Jobs are clearly defined, as are authority relationships. Top management provides clear leadership to the rest of the organization. At each level of the organization, managers plan, organize, and control the work of subordinates—providing leadership, motivation, and rewards for high performance; they delegate authority to subordinates below, while remaining ultimately responsible for the action of those subordinates and accountable for the final results. Customers are in some sense important to the organization, although the ultimate goal is to make money for the shareholders—who employ management as their agents for this purpose.

The tqm paradigm sees many aspects of managing and the relationship of the organization to the world very differently. Customers are part of the productive process rather than outsiders; suppliers are also part of the process. The purpose of the organization is to satisfy (surprise and delight) customers and other individuals and groups involved in and impacted by the organization (its "stakeholders"), as well as to improve itself and its products and services. The shape of the organization, if it can really be distinguished enough from the environment with which it becomes increasingly more integrated over time, is less like a steep pyramid resting on its base, than an "inverted frisbee"—a flattened pancake-shaped object. The customers are on top, and what used to be called "top management" is now on the bottom supporting and "empowering" the work of those above, those who do the real work of the organization: delighting customers.

Figure 2.3 suggests the transition from Traditional Management to total quality management. Traditional Management (TM) is represented by a steep pyramid reflecting the shape of the traditional organization chart. By contrast, total quality management (tqm) is shown as an "inverted, flattened frisbee." It is inverted (converging at the bottom rather than the top) to place the customer on top and to identify the most important people in the company as the front-line workers who provide goods and services to the customer; the role of senior management is to serve as a support system, making the jobs of others easier. It is flattened as layers of middle management, no longer necessary now that management is everybody's job, are removed. The path from Traditional Management to tqm involves an upward slope, with tqm representing an improvement over TM. The loop in the line suggests the process of inverting the pyramid, but does not communicate the change in its shape and the many other transformations going on within in the new shape.

Figures 2.4 and 2.5 summarize a few of the many changes involved in the transition, or perhaps "transformation," from the Traditional Management paradigm to the tqm paradigm. Figure 2.4 focuses on changes in three core elements of an organization's management practice: its goals, management methods (or management tools), and the ways in which it is managed (how those management tools are used to pursue the goals). Figure 2.5 looks at seven other dimensions of an organization, identifying one salient transition for each.

Transitions in Management Practices

A firm's goals, management methods, and ways of managing all change as it moves from Traditional Management toward tqm. Among the changes are:

Goals: change from the attractiveness and simplicity of TM's singular goal of "maximizing share price" for management's ultimate "customer," the shareholder, to the complexity and richness of tqm's set of goals encompassing the customers who purchase the company's products and services, long-term survival of the organization, continuous quality improvement, and all the company's stakeholders (including investors).

FIGURE 2.3 **The Transition from Traditional Management (TM) to Total Quality Management (tqm)**

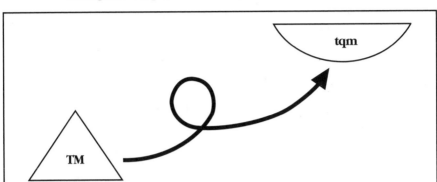

Management methods (or tools): grow deeper as TM's financial and budgeting tools, boss-subordinate command group management practices, and MBO-type planning and control methods are supplemented and in some cases replaced with the quantitative and analytical tools of statistical process control, the behavioral tools associated with quality improvement teams, self-directed work teams and other individual and group work processes, and the process of competitive benchmarking.

Ways of managing (or ways of using the management tools): change from TM's reliance on bosses to plan, organize, lead, and control the work of their subordinates within the functional silos and separated organizational divisions of a hierarchical command and control structure to tqm's team-oriented, participative management environment in which large numbers of quality improvement teams and cross-functional task forces identify and tackle large and small improvement opportunities and in which improving quality is an everyday way of life throughout the organization.

Transitions Throughout the Organization

Many characteristics of the organization change as it makes the journey from TM to tqm. A widely used model to summarize these dimensions is the "7–S" framework developed at McKinsey and Company (Figure 2.5):

Shared Values: from a partially shared value of making as much money as possible for the shareholders to a widely and deeply held commitment to satisfying customers.

FIGURE 2.4 **Changes in Three Core Elements of Management Practices**

	TM	**tqm**
Goals	1) Maximize share price	1) Exceed customer expectations over the long term 2) Achieve high quality through continuous improvement 3) Balance the needs of all stakeholders
Management methods	1) Financial analysis 2) Boss-subordinate command group 3) MBO-type planning and control tools	1) Numerical and analytical quality tools 2) Behavioral tools 3) Competitive benchmarking
Ways of managing	1) Boss-subordinate relationships 2) Functional silos 3) Clear delineation of responsibilities	1) Team-oriented participative management 2) Project-by-project 3) Moment-by-moment

FIGURE 2.5 **Seven Dimensions of the Transition**

	TM	**tqm**
Shared Values	Partially shared commitment to profits	Fully shared commitment to customers
Skills	Persuading, influencing	Listening (generously)
Style	Commander, director	Coach, facilitator
Staff	Expenses to be reduced	Resources to be developed
Structure	Steep, many level pyramid with management on top	Inverted frisbee with customers on top
Systems	Determined by management, changing slowly and irregularly	Determined by users, continuously improved
Strategy	Protection of a safe market niche	Superior learning organization

Skills: from being persuasive and compelling in influencing others to listening well to others—to the "voice of the customer," and to the "voice of the process," and when listening to people, "listening generously."

Style: from a strong commander, directing the troops, to a coach or facilitator, a progressively more invisible leader able to empower others.

Staff: from seeing people in the organization not as expenses to be reduced or eliminated but as resources to be invested in, developed, and used wisely.

Structure: from a steep pyramid with many levels of management to an "inverted frisbee" with the customer on the top and "top management" on the bottom, supporting and empowering the work of those closer to the customer.

Systems: from a set of organizational systems developed and administered by senior management and rarely changed, to team-based systems developed by the users of the systems and continuously improved by them.

Strategy: from finding a safe market niche that can be protected from known competitors to becoming a superior learning organization.

Implications for Financial Executives (and Others)

A management paradigm shift carries a great many action implications for financial executives and all other organizational members. The following chapters discuss many of these in the context of the transition in corporate finance from Traditional Management practices to tqm practices. However, it is important to pause for a minute, before turning our attention to finance, to recognize a danger of using the metaphor of a "paradigm shift" to interpret what has been happening in the world, and, if we accept that metaphor, to note at least three implications of being in the middle of a paradigm shift.

The danger is that the metaphor of paradigm shift may imply that we are moving from one stable state to another, when both states may have considerable elements of dynamism in them, especially the tqm paradigm.

Three implications of being in the middle of a paradigm shift are:

- the likelihood of misunderstanding the true nature of the paradigm shift,

- the likelihood that we will all be living and managing in organizations that are a mix of both paradigms for a considerable period of time, and

- the problems and ambiguities arising from living in both worlds (paradigms) and very likely misunderstanding important parts of each.

The Dynamic Nature of Tqm

Tqm is not a static, unchanging way of managing. Just as the metaphor of "journey" is used to describe the process of adopting the tqm management technology, the technology itself seems "to be on its own journey," progressing and changing in ways that will confound those who believe it to be a specific, rigid, unchanging way of managing.

Although we find the term paradigm, and the concept of paradigm shift, to be worthwhile, their use runs the danger of implying that tqm, the new paradigm, is a concrete, stable, rigid end state. To counteract this impression, it is important to emphasize that descriptions of tqm have consistently had to be changed as the phenomenon itself has continually outgrown the boxes it has been put into. Tqm, or whatever label is put upon the newly emerging and evolving management system, is clearly not a static state—not a stable way of managing that will not change.

On Humility Inside Paradigm Shifts

As valuable as the Baldrige criteria may be as a road map for adopting tqm, and as important as it may be for managers to seek to understand the past, present, and likely future changes organizations and the practice of management are undergoing, it is also important to recognize how little we actually know or can know if we are truly living inside a shift of "management paradigm."

If a paradigm shift actually is occurring, we have to assume that it is easy to misread and misinterpret much of what is happening around us. As tqm has unfolded, we have already experienced many such misreadings, some lasting for decades.

Throughout much of the 1960s and 1970s, many managers and academics insisted that the high quality manufactured products turned out by Japanese companies were either produced by Traditional Management practices using massive amounts of cheap labor to inspect in quality or were the result of a unique culture-based "Japanese management system" that could not be utilized in other countries. Later, when quality successes in manufacturing were demonstrated in country after country, it was argued that the new management methods were applicable only to manufacturing operations—but certainly not services. Still later, with the successes of service companies like Federal Express and the recognition that large segments of manufacturing companies are really deliverers of services—quality services, the denial shifted to organizational functions: maybe the tqm technology works in manufacturing and even services, but only in the operations function, never in finance, or accounting, or the legal function.

Just as many astute observers have sequentially misread the applicability of this new management technology, we are probably making many mistakes in interpreting what is happening right now as the technology continues to evolve. Humility and an openness to reconsidering what we think we have learned will be very appropriate for many, many years to come.

Living in Both Paradigms—Partial Quality Management

For the foreseeable future, all organizational members will be working and living in both paradigms. Their organizations will be a mix of Traditional Management practices and tqm practices. Reward systems, information systems, training programs, even the very words used to talk about managing, will be a mix of the old and the new and may even appear to turn upside down. For example, what do words like "top management," "subordinates," and "superiors" mean in an "inverted frisbee" of an organization with the customer on top and "top management" on the bottom, "supporting" the people above? For years we have described the people now seen at the top of the organization as "subordinates" and have called those whose role is now to support from below "superiors." Changes in business practice have become so great that we truly need to reinvent the language of management. We might start by acknowledging, only half in jest, that we are living in a world of "pqm"—partial quality management.

Consequences of Dynamism, Misunderstandings, and Competing Paradigms

The dynamic nature of today's management environment, as companies move from Traditional Management toward tqm, suggests several consequences and implications.

Questioning and inquiry: Because the final shape of tqm is not known, and because the evidence is that it must be adapted to fit each company, managers will have to develop a degree of comfort taking action with good questions rather than good answers. Much of "management" is likely to become experimentation, active questioning about what works in general, what works in specific cases, and what simply doesn't work. The financial people we interviewed told us they were learning to operate regularly in a mode of "action inquiry."

Paradox, inconsistency, and ambiguity: The transition between paradigms means that leadership from the top must, at times, involve some inconsistencies, ambiguities, and paradoxes—even if senior management is clear about where it wants to go. And many times management may well be unclear where it wants to go even if there is constancy of purpose. Well-meaning individuals may simply be unable to figure out what the next logical step is or may be constrained by customers, shareholders, or suppliers still mired in the practices of the old paradigm.

KISS vs. complexity: The importance of simplifying what managers communicate to the rest of the organization is one of the valid wisdoms of management captured in the immortal acronym KISS (keep it simple, stupid). Simplicity in implementing tqm is no less important. It enables people to do what is expected of them without endless questioning and uncertainty about what is expected. However, much of tqm involves exploration and inquiry, learning new things that cannot be taught in advance, and tqm itself is changing. In our interviews, we encountered situations where organizations successfully communicated a clear simple statement of a quality dimension to virtually everyone in the organization, only to discover that new perspectives and insights made alternative statements more useful. And we observed at least one case where a simple quality statement which later proved of limited use was so attractive and easy to grasp that it was difficult to replace.

Implications

For managers, implications of the dynamism, misunderstandings, and competing paradigms include the importance of:

- using a dynamic definition of tqm, or whatever label is used for the new way of managing, and accepting that what we think is tqm today will soon turn out to be an inadequate description as tqm itself keeps evolving and changing.

- recognizing that a state of questioning and inquiry will often be more appropriate for leaders and other organizational members than a state of certainty.

- accepting that many of us will be living in both paradigms (partial quality management) for many years to come and that an understanding of both paradigms and the skills of each will be important for effective performance.

- accepting in advance that even strongly committed senior management will at times act inconsistently with stated quality commitments and that what is consistent with a quality commitment will not always be clear.

- accepting that attempts to keep things simple for "subordinates" will sometimes backfire, especially as tqm itself keeps evolving.

3

Quality Management Comes to the Corporate Finance Function

By now, doing finance this way is simply the normal thing to do.

—Larry Yarberry
VP, Finance, Southern Pacific

The major difference at Solectron is that, in contrast with some other companies, finance is an ally in the decision-making process.

–Stephen Ng
VP, Corporate Materials, Solectron

Total quality management (tqm) has become an integral part of the way the corporate finance function operates in the companies of this study. In each company, interviewees reported that the finance organization was as deeply involved in tqm, both in its own operations and in working with others, as any other function within their company. From the evidence we have collected, we believe this will be the normal state for companies truly using quality management.

All companies are located at some point on a continuum moving from traditional management to total quality management. Some have barely begun the journey. Others, including the companies of this study, are somewhere along the path, many quite far along. We see this transition to tqm as inevitable, a necessary result of the breakdown of geographic, natural, and technological monopolies that has come with the emergence of the "global marketplace."

A company cannot implement quality management completely without the full participation of all of its organizational functions. Within the firm, tqm focuses on processes, how products and information are transformed as they proceed from raw materials to finished goods. By their very nature, processes are cross-functional. They do not respect the departmental boundaries that delineate the units of a traditional organizational structure. Rather, they acquire inputs and deliver their outputs throughout the organization. Looking outside the firm, tqm focuses on customers and suppliers, creating partnerships to exceed expectations. In its own way, nearly every part of the organization engages in some activities which impact customers and suppliers. Corporate finance, for example, analyzes customer credit and supplier viability, processes accounts receivable and payable, and analyzes capital projects which change products and supplier requirements. Unless all parts of a company participate in its tqm efforts, there will be limits to the firm's ability to improve its processes and service its customers.

Beyond its direct activities in a company's processes and in customer/supplier satisfaction, corporate finance plays a special role in the business organization. It is the owner of the firm's information, defining the data organization members see and how they see it. It calculates the firm's "results," both company-wide and by organizational unit. Through its reporting function it sets much of the tone for what is important. It brings special skills to the business, including its comfort with cash flows and time value of money, which give direction to most of the company's analytical work. By virtue of their training and exposure within the firm, finance members often have the ability to see the "big picture": how choices will affect many parts of the organization. Unless corporate finance participates in the company's tqm efforts, it will be easy for finance and other units to make poor decisions.

Starting to Do Tqm

The five companies profiled in this study began to employ quality management for a variety of reasons, supporting the hypothesis that there is no one critical condition which is the prerequisite for adopting tqm. Interestingly, none were in a state of crisis, on the verge of extinction and looking for some "last-gasp" effort to save the business.

Two of the companies—Corning and Motorola—were highly successful but facing intense competition and aware that their quality could be improved. Both were facing new or increased competition from foreign competitors which were gaining reputations as producing high-quality products and being faster to respond to customers and markets. Both had been founded by strong leaders whose "family style" value systems were consistent with tqm. One company—Southern Pacific—was languishing following an unsuccessful merger attempt and five years in trust that had limited its ability to respond to competition. The other two—Federal Express and Solectron—reflecting their founders' philosophies, had been managed since their inception in a style very close in many ways to quality management. For them, adopting tqm meant systemizing and labeling practices that had begun with their founding.

Corning and Motorola were motivated to look at quality management by a new awareness of future possibilities as company executives observed successes achieved by competitors which were using quality management. In response, senior management made a decision to reorient the company's management system to institute tqm principles. The decisive event for Southern Pacific was the purchase of the company by a new owner who saw the benefits of tqm and chose to "bet the railroad's turnaround on quality." For Federal Express and Solectron, there was no pivotal event that changed the company's management system but rather an evolution and formalization of what was already there.

How Finance Got Involved

Our research suggests there are (at least) five ways that corporate finance becomes involved in the company's tqm efforts: as a source of traditional analytical skills supplying resources to others, as evaluators and judges helping others to understand results, as members of cross-functional teams where finance is one of the functions involved, as team leaders and members working on finance's own internal projects, and as full participants from the beginning as the company starts to do tqm. All of these five are represented by the finance functions of the companies of this study, with some companies doing more than one in their initial tqm efforts. Examples of early participation in tqm by finance include:

A source of skills: Divisional controllers at Solectron contributed their expertise to evaluate improvements to internal operations.

Evaluators and judges: Motorola finance incorporated quality metrics into its regular reporting to raise the importance of quality performance.

Members of cross-functional teams: Early tqm experiences for finance members from all five companies included working on teams which cut across functional lines.

Working on finance projects: Initial team-based tqm projects within finance included improving and/or reducing cycle time in preparing the quarterly information book for the Board Finance Committee at Corning; invoicing, collection of receivables, and mail delivery at Federal Express; book-closing and payroll accuracy at Motorola; and order entry at Solectron.

Full participants from the beginning: Corning included a finance member on its first Quality Council responsible for establishing systematic quality at that company. Finance members at both Federal Express and Solectron joined in the early planning and implementation of systematic quality management practices. At Southern Pacific, the entire company, including each finance area, began to learn about and implement quality together.

Total Quality Finance

In the following section we compare Conventional Corporate Finance (CCF) and "total quality finance" (tqf). By Conventional Corporate Finance, we mean finance within a traditional (pre-tqm) management system: the discipline of corporate finance as it evolved in practice and in academic writings prior to the incorporation of quality management concepts. By total quality finance, we mean the corporate finance function as it is adapting to and adopting the concepts of total quality management. We describe CCF and tqf in their "pure forms"—as polar opposites—to increase the visibility of the differences between them. However, just as virtually all companies practice a mix of Traditional Management and tqm, finance functions also practice a mix of CCF and tqf. It is unlikely that any finance function uses either CCF of tqf in its pure form—all practice some form of "partial quality finance."

How Total Quality Finance Differs from Conventional Corporate Finance

Total quality finance and Conventional Corporate Finance differ along many dimensions having to do with goals and objectives, time horizon, position in the company, relationship to others, and methods of analysis.

The differences largely reflect the new perspectives of focusing energies on customers, processes, and continuous improvement that are the core of tqm.

Purpose of the firm: In Conventional Corporate Finance, the goal of the firm is to maximize shareholder wealth, visible in the capital markets as the price of the firm's common stock. The primary customer of the company is the shareholder, and all actions of the company are to be analyzed from the perspective of their influence on share price. Since financial market prices are present values of future benefits, and since academic studies have suggested a high degree of pricing efficiency, all managerial actions are presumed to translate quickly and accurately into enhanced or reduced share price.

By contrast, total quality finance accepts the tqm goals of exceeding customer expectations, and continuously improving the company's products and services by improving the processes that produce them. All stakeholders, both external and internal, are involved in one or more processes and are valid "customers." High share price is merely one (admittedly favorable and necessary) result of tqm. Exceeding customer expectations and improving product and service quality are seen as the best ways to increase revenues by capturing greater market share at higher sales prices. Improving processes is seen as the way to become the industry's quality leaders and low-cost producers. The combination of higher revenue and lower costs that tqm can produce, along with the realistic prospect of continued improvement, is what drives high shareholder value.

Focus of management: CCF argues for management to pay attention to money and financial results in the belief that they translate directly into shareholder wealth. It places faith in the accounting system since that system is designed to record and report financial transactions. Non-financial costs and benefits are irrelevant, as is, to a large extent, how financial results are achieved.

Tqf points management, and all employees, toward processes in the belief that they are the true drivers of quality and efficiency, hence profits and value for all stakeholders. Processes can be managed directly; results can only be "managed" by managing processes. Tqf finds traditional accounting systems lacking in that they only record and report financial transactions and not customer- or process-related data. In tqf, how a result is achieved is precisely what management must pay attention to, and therefore all costs and benefits are relevant, whether they are financial or not.

Measurement horizon: Traditional financial theory claims a long-run vision. In practice, however, CCF's trust in financial market efficiency, the desire of many managers to show good results in the current year to earn promotions and bonuses, and the predominance in the financial markets of fund managers who are measured by their quarterly performance pressure managers to concentrate on whether their decisions can be quickly evaluated by the financial markets. Actions which will immediately raise share price are prized and those which would push prices down are to be avoided, regardless of their long-run impact.

With its focus no longer solely on share price, tqf is more able to look to the long term. Exceeding customer expectations implies a desire "to have customers return, and to bring a friend." Tqf is therefore much more willing to support actions which appear costly in the short run, but which build customer loyalty or have other long-run payoffs, regardless of whether they are visible today.

Place in the organization: In the traditional management system which spawned CCF, finance is a centralized function. It is a filter through which resources flow out to the rest of the organization. It acts as the eye of the executive, keeping control and track of resource utilization and performance.

In the total quality management system, finance tends to be distributed throughout the organization. It serves as a vascular system for the entire business organism, bringing financial resources and analyses to where they can best be used. It still tracks and reports on resource use, but no longer controls it.

Attitude toward the management system: CCF has little responsibility for, nor interest in, the management system. It takes the existing management system as given and concludes that it must be well functioning, having been designed by and watched over by senior managers. CCF therefore tends to conclude that problems in corporate performance come from externalities or poor employee performance, and it strives to increase output and reduce costs within the existing system.

Tqf is intimately concerned with the system of management since it is the key ingredient of corporate success. It assumes that the management system as a whole and each of its sub-systems must be designed around the processes they support, and that it is easy to have a system which is poorly functioning because it is not congruent with process flows. Tqf is also more optimistic about people, believing they generally try to do their best but are frustrated when the management system does not support them. While accepting externalities as a possible source of difficulty, tqf presumes that the primary reason for poor corporate performance is not poor employee performance but a poor management system. Instead of punishing employees, it asks about improving the system.

Relationship to others inside the firm: Conventional Corporate Finance tends to be insular, independent from the productive parts of the firm. This is thought to increase its impartiality, conducting its analysis and oversight functions at arms length. Information should flow in to finance, be analyzed, and flow back out. As a result, CCF is reactive in style.

Total quality finance tends to be integrated and to work closely with the productive parts of the firm. Its role is problem solving not oversight, and it can better participate in analysis when it is close to the people and processes involved. It forms partnerships to share in problem solving with all parts of the organization. By contrast to CCF, tqf is proactive in style.

Relationship to outsiders: As with insiders, CCF sees it can best carry out its role with outsiders at arms length. It accepts outsiders' performance as a given as long as they meet minimum, often contractual, standards. Should an outsider fail to meet those standards, CCF has few remedies other than adopting a negative approach including withholding payments, using threats, or resorting to litigation.

Also as with insiders, tqf sees it can best work with outsiders in a partnership relationship. It places outsiders in the same role it places itself, a member of a team whose primary goal is continuous improvement of processes, products, and services. Contractual standards are less important than customer requirements. Should an outsider fail to meet those standards, tqf works with them to improve their performance.

Attitude toward variation: In Conventional Corporate Finance theory, variation is synonymous with risk. In traditional finance theory, risk is to be minimized for a given level of return. Therefore, all corporate variation is treated the same way.

Practitioners of total quality finance understand that some variation is natural, a result of the inability of any process to be rock-steady, while other variation is the result of poor management systems which tamper with processes, leaving them out of control. Not all variation should be "managed" in the same way. Man-made variation should be eliminated completely by bringing processes under control; natural variation should be studied to reduce it through process improvements.

Methods of problem solving: CCF takes its decision rules from economic theory. It looks for marginal improvements and decomposes problems into parts for analysis. It places no particular value on cycle time. It has devoted little attention to relationships across organizational boundaries.

Tqf takes its decision rules from systems and process theory as well as from economic theory. It seeks dramatic change by using quality tools to abolish unnecessary work, eliminate waste, and reduce errors. It places a high value on slashing cycle time. It devotes considerable attention to linkages throughout the company, analyzing costs through process connections. Figure 3.1 summarizes the differences between CCF and tqf.

The Deployment of Tqm Technology in Finance

Just as companies as a whole are in the midst of a transition from traditional management (TM) practices to tqm, their corporate finance functions are also making a comparable shift from CCF to tqf. In the TM organization, Conventional Corporate Finance is practiced near the top, as an arm of the senior executives. By contrast, in the tqm firm total quality finance is practiced throughout the organization; it is difficult to locate it at any particular place to the exclusion of others.

The finance function of each study company is located somewhere along this continuum, with CCF at one end and tqf at the other. However, the continuum has many dimensions. It would be difficult to rank-order the finance functions studied from most advanced to least advanced, as some are further along on one dimension while not as far along on others. Taken as a whole, however, these five companies provide excellent illustrations of the progress being made by leaders in total quality finance.

Changing Roles of Finance People

We see three types of changes in what finance people say and do as they move from practicing Conventional Corporate Finance to total quality finance. While still responsible for many of the traditional functions assigned to finance, they perform these old roles in new ways. In addition, they perform new roles as quality management broadens their participation within the business. They also develop new ways of speaking, a new language that plays an important role in changing their self-perceptions.

FIGURE 3.1 **Conventional Corporate Finance (CCF) and Total Quality Finance (tqf) Compared**

	CCF	tqf
Purpose of the firm	Maximize shareholder wealth, the price of the common stock.	Exceed customer expectations and continuously improve products, services, processes.
Identification of the customer	The shareholder.	All stakeholders, both external and internal.
Focus of management	Money and financial results. The accounting system. Irrelevant: non-financial costs and benefits, how results are achieved.	Processes as manageable drivers of quality and efficiency. Important: all costs and benefits, how results are achieved.
Measurement horizon	Decisions which can be quickly evaluated by the financial markets.	Long-term, regardless of whether benefits are immediately visible.
Place in the organization.	Centralized. Filter for resources. Controls resource utilization.	Distributed. Conveyor of resources. Does not control resource utilization.
Attitude toward the management system	Assumes the system is OK—poor employee performance is responsible for problems.	Assumes employees are OK—a poor system is responsible for poor performance.
Relationship to others	Insular, independent overseer. Sees conflict of interest from serving others. Reactive.	Integrated, problem-solving partner. Sees benefits from serving others. Proactive.
Variation	All treated as problematic.	Differentiates types.
Methods of problem solving	Uses only economic theory. Seeks marginal improvements. Decomposes problems for analysis. No value placed on cycle time.	Uses systems, process, and economic theory. Seeks dramatic improvements. Attention to process connections. High value on cutting cycle time.

Among the old roles enacted in new ways are internal analyses such as planning and budgeting, capital project analysis and working capital management, now done more in partnership with the operating units of the organization. Relationships with funding sources are changing as investors are beginning to look for quality initiatives as a basis for estimating future cash flow and franchise value. Perhaps the greatest changes are taking place in finance's traditional internal control responsibility, as tqf practitioners move from checking up on others to coaching others in the art of self-assessment.

New roles include owner and improver of finance processes, partner with other organizational units in improving their own and cross-functional processes, and partner with outside suppliers and customers in exceeding the expectations of all parties.

Finally, practitioners of total quality finance seem to talk differently, to a large extent reflecting their new place in the organization. Some of the new words are from the language of tqm reflecting a new set of skills learned and mastered. Some come from a greater understanding of how the rest of the business works as they work closer with and are trained in the work of other parts of the organization. Yet much of the new talk seems simply to be from the added "joy in work" that comes from being a partner and player rather than a police officer or judge. The finance members we interviewed could not overemphasize the importance of their newfound "freedom."

New Tools Used by Finance People

Quality management has its own set of tools, some similar to and others quite different from those traditionally claimed by corporate finance. The "hard tools," relatively easy for most finance people to grasp and use, include the graphical and numerical techniques which underlie statistical process analysis and control. In addition there are "soft tools" such as team-based problem solving, listening, acknowledging, and coaching—tasks not accorded a particularly high value in a traditional management system—which often require a change of personal style for finance members. We discuss these tools, and their relationship to finance, more fully in the next chapter.

New Goals? . . . or New Routes to Old Goals?

With its emphasis on customers and processes, tqm refocuses management away from stock price maximization and toward customer expectations and process improvement. Tqm asks us to listen to the "voice of the customer," and the "voice of the process," not particularly the "voice of the investor." But is it wrong to maximize shareholder wealth? Are these goals truly new?

The financial executives we interviewed shared a conviction that there was no inconsistency between tqm goals and value maximization. In fact, to a person, they were convinced that the only way to achieve a sustainable high share price is to pursue the goals of quality management: to listen to the customer as the "final arbiter" and to "manage the manageable." They pointed out that pursuit of stock price without attention to customers and processes is dangerous, as likely to destabilize a working system as to make meaningful change for the better. On the other hand, tqm demands the company focus on its key success factors, and if this is done, profits and high share price will follow.

We interpret what we heard as an argument for a sequencing of goals, in which active pursuit of tqm objectives leads naturally to the achievement of the Conventional Corporate Finance end. Federal Express captures this particularly well in their corporate motto: People–Service–Profit. If people are supported, they will improve processes and deliver exceptional and cost-effective service to customers who, in turn, will come back over and over again delivering the company's profits.

4

Integrating Tqm into Corporate Finance

Corning, Incorporated's global treasury function is remarkably lean. The 33,000 person company has a treasury staff of only 54—32 in the U.S. and 22 abroad. Sandy Helton, Corning's Treasurer, and Vice Chairman Van Campbell believe the company's quality processes are the key to the group's ability to run such a lean yet high performing treasury function. Treasury listens carefully to its customers to eliminate non-value added activities, establishes partnerships inside and outside the company to get important tasks accomplished, and develops and continuously adjusts its Key Results Indicators (KRIs) to keep its members focused on the highest priority tasks.

When Motorola's audit department started improving its internal audit process in 1987, it took an average of 20 days to complete a draft report, and 51 days to issue a final report. Within two and one-half years, final reports were being completed in 5 days, and draft reports were so rarely issued that their cycle times were no longer worth tracking. The department's measurements showed that quality improved 25 times, a 33% reduction in management and clerical staff saved $1.1 million a year, and a 26% increase in audit staff productivity saved $1.5 million per year.

Federal Express' finance function uses a technique it calls the Business Case Approach (BCA) to analyze major projects. BCA is part of a trend in the finance organization of working with the rest of the company more as consultants, partners, and facilitators rather than as judges, controllers, and police officers. It also supports a growing ability and willingness to quantify the value of improvements in quality. As Debra Gray, Managing Director, Financial Planning Customer/Systems Support observes, in its attempts to measure the "soft benefits" of quality improvements, the finance staff is moving "from saying 'We will only count it if you can prove it,' to putting much more devotion into quantifying soft benefits. And, today you are much more likely to hear a finance person say: 'I can't prove it, but I think it is the right thing to do.'"

This and the succeeding chapter focus on how the adoption and adaption of quality methods are changing the way finance does its work and makes its contributions to the organization. In this chapter we look at changes in finance's goals, management methods, and ways of managing—the three core management practices identified in Chapter 2—as they come more into alignment with tqm approaches. Chapter 5 discusses other ways in which the finance functions of the study companies are aligning themselves with tqm.

The adoption of tqm elements is clearly apparent in the study companies, either replacing or supplementing the elements characteristic of Conventional Corporate Finance.

Corporate Finance Goals

The tqm adoption process normally pays explicit attention to establishing a shared vision, mission, and goals in each work unit and for the organization as a whole. Therefore, we expected our study companies to have both clearly articulated quality-focused goals and a high degree of alignment of functional and divisional goals with corporate-level goals. Our research confirmed that the corporate finance goals in the study companies are consistent with the goals of the company as a whole and are also explicitly, and usually clearly, articulated in mission statements, quality policies, and similar statements.

Figure 4.1 contains three phrases used to describe goals that are consistent with tqm. The three phrases build on the discussion of goals in Chapters 2 and 3 and pick up five possible aspects of goals that would be consistent with tqm: customers, the long term, quality, continuous improvement, and stakeholders.

Customers and Long-Term Survival

The goal of satisfying internal and external customers is clear in each of the finance functions in the study, as is the commitment to the long-term survival of the company. However, there is an interesting aspect to the long-term survival dimension. Although each finance function is clearly committed to the long-term survival of the company as a whole, the finance functions do not appear to be committed to defending their own survival in their traditional, hierarchical form. Rather than defending a centralized corporate finance empire, they seem to be embarked on a quest for achieving financial excellence in the entire company. As

FIGURE 4.1 **Tqm Goals**

Customer and long-term	"To stay in business forever by exceeding customer expectations."
Quality and continuous improvement	"To improve continuously and forever the quality of the organization's products and services (by continuously improving the processes that produce those products and services)."
Stakeholders	"To exceed stakeholder expectations."

part of that quest, they seem willing to accept whatever size and shape corporate finance function that eventually emerges. Survival of excellence in finance is sought, but a particular form of corporate finance structure is not. (We see no conflict between a commitment to organizational survival and a willingness to let corporate finance become whatever it becomes, as long as financial excellence is achieved. In fact, as barriers among all functions and all business units are broken down, such flexibility about functional unit structure and willingness to allow functional empires to whither away may be the very things required to give organizations a chance "to stay in business forever.")

In the corporate finance functions of the study companies, the goal of exceeding customer expectations is clear for both internal and external customers. However, it comes up in finance people's daily work most frequently in the context of internal customers and in particular in the context of establishing collaborative customer-supplier relationships. For example, Federal Express' Customer-Supplier Alignment process is used extensively by finance members and is one of the parts of the company's tqm processes most highly valued by the finance function. Both as a formal process—there is a written process guide with instructions and short forms to use—and as a way of thinking about relationships with other units, Customer-Supplier Alignment captures much of the new spirit of finance at Federal Express. At the heart of the process are three questions:

- What do you need from me?

- What do you do with what I give you?

- Are there any gaps between what I give you and what you need?

Based upon the answers to these questions, a Customer-Supplier Agreement is drawn up, specifying what actions will be taken, how they will be taken, who will take them, and a date by which they will be taken. The final phase of the formal process includes an alignment progress report, for following up on the action items. The Finance Quality Policy captures this customer commitment, reading in part: "It is our policy to continuously strive to improve services to our customers (both internal and external), to meet/exceed their expectations . . . ." An indication of the long-term perspective is also picked up in the last sentence of the Policy: "It is our objective to build and perpetuate a quality organization that supports our corporate goals."

Quality and Continuous Improvement

Each of the finance functions has a set of goals for improved quality and continuous improvement in its corporate finance activities. Corning, for example, has a set of Key Results Indicators for each Treasury activity and is searching for a single indicator that will capture the unit's separate activities and tie them together in such a way that the success of the entire unit will require collaboration of all the separate parts. Motorola's finance function, like the rest of the company, has embarked on a program to achieve six sigma levels of excellence in all finance activities and will now be seeking a ten-times cycle time reduction in all its activities by 1997. It has created a series of "Finance Councils" to study new technologies for incorporation into its continuous improvement efforts. Federal Express' Finance Quality Policy includes this commitment: "It is our policy to continuously strive . . . to control/reduce costs, and to improve the efficiency and quality of our operating environment." Solectron, like all the study companies, has committed to increasing the time and diversity of training offered to all employees. Training hours, targeted at 95 per person in Fiscal Year 1992, are scheduled to rise to 150 per person by FY 95. At Southern Pacific, a relative newcomer to tqm, the finance organization joined the rest of the company in committing to continuous improvement as the quality program was rolled out.

Stakeholders

In addition to seeking to exceed the expectations of external customers, the companies in the study seek to satisfy a variety of other stakeholders: internal customers, employees, shareholders, suppliers, and the community. The finance functions in these companies see themselves playing a leading or supporting role in each of these areas and see advantages for all groups in their own tqm progress.

The shareholders of the company, the traditional stakeholders of Conventional Corporate Finance, obviously are not neglected. They are seen as benefiting from the health of the company and its ability to grow, be profitable, and pay dividends. The goal of satisfying investors is clearly apparent in each of the finance functions in the study, but the emphasis has also shifted to a more balanced view of how the investor-stakeholder is to be served: balanced both in terms of time horizon and in terms of shareholders' relationships to other stakeholders. The goal is to satisfy shareholders, or even exceed their expectations if such a thing is possible, over a reasonable period of time. For example, the Investor Relations group in Corning's finance function has a target price earnings multiple for the company's stock as one of its Key Results Indicators. Keeping the P/E above a target figure is a necessary success factor, as are other KRIs associated with the services provided by that function to all shareholders.

Employees, including people who work in finance, are also very important stakeholders in these companies. Goals of adding to their ability to contribute and enjoyment of work are both clearly visible. These are also areas where the successes of tqm efforts are most clear. A major objective of the teams working to improve financial processes is to make finance easier to work with; the customer-supplier alignment processes in place under a variety of names in the various companies are directed explicitly at satisfying internal as well as external customers.

A number of companies in the study are very articulate in their commitment to the community. In addition to the usual ways in which companies seek to benefit their communities, the companies in this study put particular emphasis on global competitiveness as a necessary condition for community health. Two of the most explicit on this point are Motorola and Solectron. Bob Galvin, retired Chairman of the Board of Motorola, has long been one of the country's leading quality champions and has taken the lead in sponsoring the "Tqm University Challenge," an attempt to increase quality management teaching and research in business and engineering schools. Solectron sees a major part of its mission as demonstrating, by its performance, that American companies can regain global manufacturing leadership. It also sees its role as aiding other companies by sharing how it achieves manufacturing excellence.

Solectron's Baldrige Award application notes, with no exaggeration, that its Chairman and co-CEO, Winston Chen, "is a crusader for US manufacturing excellence . . . . He makes the point repeatedly that America must return to a first-rank position in manufacturing capability. The path back to a leadership position must be grounded in missionary zeal for quality and customer satisfaction."

Other Goals

Two additional goals are consistently stated by the study companies and their finance functions, but were not clearly stated above. They relate to people and ethics. With regard to people, the goal is most frequently articulated by the phrases: "Respect for People" or "Respect for the Individual." With regard to ethics, they are clearly stated by phrases such as "Uncompromising Integrity" used, for example, by Motorola and Solectron. Both of these goals are consistent with the preceding five. For example, respect for people is a necessary part of exceeding the expectations of employees as stakeholders, and ethical behavior is required for long-term survival and for exceeding customer and other stakeholders' expectations. Although it could be argued that these two goals are implicit in the other five, their prominence in the companies' statements of beliefs, purposes, and missions and in the companies' actions leads us to note them specifically.

Management Methods

The finance functions in the study companies have added three sets of quality management methods (or tools) to the well-established financial analysis, planning, and control tools used by essentially all well-managed companies. The three sets of management methods are

- numerical and analytical methods,

- behavioral methods, and

- competitive benchmarking.

Numerical and Analytical Methods (Tools)

The finance functions of the five case study companies differ in the extent to which the basic tools of statistical process control have been incorporated in daily work and mastered by all members. But in each company, finance members have received training in the basic tools, and at least some of the tools are used to display data and monitor progress in improving processes. Eight of the more widely used tools are described briefly in Figure 4.2.

The comfort with numbers that most finance people have makes learning and using these tools relatively easy for financial staff, and they frequently play teaching roles on the quality improvement teams they join. However, even winning the Baldrige award does not guarantee that an organization has mastered all of these tools. One of the Baldrige winners was informed in its site visit feedback that it needed considerable improvement in its use of statistical process control and benchmarking.

Although the eight "classical tools of statistical process control (SPC)" were used fairly widely in the finance functions, much less progress appears to have been made in using a set of more complex and more specialized tools called the "seven new management and planning tools." This other set of tools is relatively infrequently used in leading American quality companies. And when these tools are used, they tend to be used by relatively few individuals and teams rather than being mastered and used by individuals throughout the organization in the way that the "classical SPC tools" are used. The new tools are called affinity/K.J. diagram, interrelationship diagraph, systems flow/tree diagram, matrix data analysis, matrix diagram, PDPC chart, and arrow diagram.

Although not widely used at present, these tools are likely to become more frequently used in the future. Because of their affinity for such tools and their wide organizational involvements, finance members in these and other companies may well play a significant role in their adoption.

Behavioral Methods (Tools)

There is considerable agreement about the necessity of using the classical numerical tools of SPC if an organization is "really doing tqm," and also a reasonably high level of agreement that the seven new management tools are becoming part of the tqm package. However, there is less agreement about which behavioral methods are inherent parts of tqm as a management system. Figure 4.3 describes briefly some team-based and some individual-based methods or tools that are frequently considered tqm behavioral tools. These tools were widely used in the study companies' finance functions and were a part of the tqm training

FIGURE 4.2 **Numerical and Analytical Methods (Tools)**

Data check sheets	For recording and keeping track of data
Bar charts	For showing the frequency with which events occur
Pareto charts	For separating more frequent events and items from less frequent ones
Run charts	For tracking how something varies over time
Control charts	For investigating the stability of a process
Scatter diagrams	For investigating the relationship between two variables
Flowcharts	For showing how events occur in a sequence over time and relate to each other
Cause and effect diagrams	For collecting and organizing possible causes of an event

FIGURE 4.3 **Behavioral Methods (Tools)**

Brainstorming	A process (usually group-based) for generating ideas
Nominal group technique	A group process that combines individual and group brainstorming with methods for sharing and prioritizing ideas
Task forces	Project teams which tackle specific problems and opportunities
Self-managing work teams	Team-based techniques for managing the on-going work of an organizational unit
Quality improvement teams	Team-based techniques for defining, analyzing, and improving organizational work processes
Active listening	A set of techniques for listening to others effectively
Imagineering	A process for describing a "perfectly" functioning organizational process

of finance members, although they are called by a variety of names. For example, the nominal group technique is so frequently and incorrectly called brainstorming that the erroneous label may well replace the correct one. Although these tools do not come as easily to some finance people as do the quantitative tools, our evidence is that many finance people embrace them avidly and quickly.

In each of the companies, we found abundant evidence that the behavioral tools were being used to empower employees to increase their contributions to the firm. Ko Nishimura of Solectron remarked, only half jokingly, "Companies used to hire only their employees' bodies—when they came to work, people were told to check their brains at the door." This is certainly not the case for our study companies. At Corning, tqm has enabled finance employees at all levels to be much more confident, acting on their own without "endless rounds of approvals."

Competitive Benchmarking

Benchmarking is widely used in the finance functions of the companies in the study in at least two ways: for prioritizing and for improvement. In the first use, benchmarking helps select processes on which to focus improvement. In the second use, it energizes and guides improvement efforts.

Prioritizing: Benchmarking financial and other processes of leading companies is used to determine where particularly large and valuable improvements in processes may be made. For example, if the accounts payable process of a comparable company is conducted with many fewer errors or with a much lower head count than one's own, payables may be an attractive place to focus attention. Southern Pacific began benchmarking the processes of comparable railroads early in its formal adoption of tqm systems. Using the Interstate Commerce Commission's "R1 reports," annual summaries of U.S. railroad operations, Southern Pacific identified areas where its costs were out of line with other major western railroads. These differences signaled high priority areas for cost reduction through quality improvements. The Finance Department compared detailed operating and financial information from the R1 reports with Southern Pacific's own data. Calculated in the comparisons were the potential savings in each line item that would be achieved if Southern Pacific matched the average performance of its competitors and also the savings if it reached a "world class" status—matching the performance of its best competitor at each activity. This led Southern Pacific to conclude that at least $400 million dollars could be saved annually by bringing current operations in each activity up to the standards of the best competitor.

Improvement: Benchmarking is also widely used in the more traditional quality manner of selecting a process to be improved, determining at least one world class example of that process in some other organization, and using that example as a goal to be matched or exceeded and perhaps also as a model process to be understood and improved upon. The finance functions of these companies are also frequently invited to participate in multi-company benchmarking studies conducted by their peers and by consultants. Motorola's finance function, for example, is often asked to take part in such studies because of the recognition that many of its processes are world class in terms of defect rate and cycle time. Motorola finance is also particularly comfortable talking in the language of benchmarking, as indicated by the comment that opens the Motorola case: "I think we have moved the benchmark in the auditing process."

Ways of Managing

Three ways in which these management methods, or tools, are used in pursuit of finance's and the organization's goals are:

- in a total organizational context of teamwork and participation,

- in project teams focused on quality improvements, and

- in a day-by-day (or "moment-by-moment") manner, in which the attempt is made to integrate quality and continuous improvement into as many aspects of the daily work routine as possible—"to make quality a way of life" at work every day.

Although all of these ways of managing are clear and visible in the companies, their progress on each dimension varies. The dimensions themselves do not seem to have agreed labels—either among the companies or in the quality management literature. In the absence of accepted labels, we shall provide examples of each under these titles: team-oriented participation and empowerment, project-by-project basis, and moment-by-moment basis.

Team-Oriented Participation and Empowerment

The commitment to and practice of teamwork, participation, and empowerment are cornerstones of tqm and are clear in all of the companies and in their finance functions. The tqm goals and management methods discussed previously require such a context to be effective, and their sustained use over time creates such an environment. Teamwork, participation, and empowerment are also aspects of tqm widely regarded as major personal benefits for finance members. This way of working is appreciated as an alternative to finance's traditional police, judge, and evaluator roles and as a way of making greater contributions to the organization.

For Federal Express and Solectron—the two youngest companies in the study—this way of managing, especially the participative dimension, has been embedded in the company from the very beginning, and the formal use of tqm approaches has extended and deepened its use. For example, at Federal Express the commitment to utilizing the contribution of everyone in the organization and helping everyone grow has been captured by the core belief, "People First," and by the commitments to training, the highly regarded "Guaranteed Fair Treatment Procedure," and the encouragement for risk taking that support that belief. The "People First" phrase captures at least two aspects of the key role of participation and empowerment: the recognition that "customer satisfaction begins with employee satisfaction," and the belief that a major purpose of the organization is to provide empowering work experiences and attractive career opportunities for employees—that the organization is at least as much a means for employees as the employees are a means for the organization.

For a longer established company like Motorola, this way of managing was formalized and built into the management system under the label PMP—"Participative Management Process."

Project-by-Project Basis

Quality improvement teams are a hallmark of tqm. Although the famous management thinker Joseph Juran puts great stress on planning, designing, and leading for quality, he has often stated that all quality improvement occurs on a project-by-project basis. Quality improvement team projects are numerous in the finance departments and were frequently one of the earliest involvements of finance in adopting tqm. For example, Motorola's pilot application of quality management to finance processes was a very successful project to speed up closing the books at the end of each month. And the first application in the internal audit department was the successful attempt to apply the six sigma approach to the internal audit process. Both projects subsequently won Motorola's internal quality award.

At Federal Express, finance members regularly work on project teams, both cross-functional teams, such as the team which designed and implemented the ASTRA package labeling system, and also within the Finance Division, such as the teams which worked to reduce the cycle time for paying accounts payable and for processing employee travel and expense reports. At Southern Pacific, members from the controller's office have joined marketing people on several teams to improve billing accuracy. Teams at each of the companies include customer and supplier members to define requirements and resolve problems.

Moment-by-Moment Basis

Quality as a way of life in finance's daily work shows up in a variety of ways:

- At Corning, outside Treasurer Sandy Helton's office where colorful up-to-date graphs are posted on a bulletin board. The graphs plot the progress of each of Treasury's six major groups in improving quality as measured by their Key Results Indicators.

- At Federal Express, part of the variable compensation of certain individual contributors and all management is dependent (in part) on the satisfaction of internal customers and leads to an intense awareness of how well those customers are being served on a daily basis.

- At Motorola, where quality results are the leading numbers in "financial" reports to top management.

- At Solectron, where division controllers report revenue performance by customer and P+L by division at a meeting each week, and identify the quality initiatives they are supporting to remedy any concerns which surface.

- At Southern Pacific, in the way the Finance Department relates to its suppliers of funds. After a presentation to the company's bankers that described how the company had adopted the tqm management technology, how it was starting to be managed through a fully integrated strategic/operational/financial/quality plan, and how it had implemented specific quality initiatives that had already produced dramatic improvements and promised more, Southern Pacific's CFO observed "Quality made all the difference in our credibility with the banks—in our being able to convince the bankers to proceed with the financing we needed."

Some of the many ways these companies and their finance functions are keeping a day-to-day focus on quality and continuous improvement are by integrating the quality planning process with the strategic planning process, building specific targets for quality success into performance review systems, and linking bonuses and other compensation to performance against quality objectives.

5

Integrating Corporate Finance into the Organization's Tqm Efforts

Federal Express' finance function is developing financial information systems to support financial analysis and decision-making throughout the company. One such system, playfully named ELVIS, supports budget preparation and financial reporting. ELVIS is intended to increase dramatically the amount of financial analysis being performed by individuals and teams outside the Finance Division.

Solectron's finance function is working to change where finance is done in the company structure—"distributing financial work" so that it is performed closer to the customer and sometimes performed by non-finance people. For example, finance's traditional task of analyzing the creditworthiness of potential customers and determining the amount of credit the prospects would be eligible to receive is now performed not by finance people, but by members of the sales force.

Southern Pacific's finance function is playing a major role in the company's efforts to change how strategy is made and how it is integrated with other planning efforts. One of the more important innovations at Southern Pacific is a new planning process that yields an improvement-focused plan integrating strategy, quality, operations, and finance.

Systems, structure, strategy—all are changing as these companies move forward on their tqm journeys. These organizational elements are becoming more aligned with tqm practices, and in each case finance is playing an important role. In the process, the work of finance is becoming more closely integrated with the work of other organizational units, and barriers between them and finance are being broken down. This chapter looks at the role finance plays in integrating tqm into the rest of the organization and the way finance's work becomes more consistent with tqm and more integrated with the work of other organizational units. We will emphasize one theme for each of the seven organizational elements introduced in Chapters 2 and 3 and illustrate the theme with findings from our six case study companies. These themes are listed in Figure 5.1.

We will start with corporate finance's emerging management style—the way finance sees and plays its role in the organization. This theme touches on many aspects of the changes that tqm is bringing to corporate finance and the changes that corporate finance is bringing to these companies. And in starting with style, we will connect this study with a prior study also sponsored by the Financial Executives Research Foundation.

Corporate Finance's Style and the Competitive-Team Orientation

In *Changing Roles of Financial Management*, Patrick J. Keating and Stephen F. Jablonsky identified three distinct "orientations" of financial work: the command and control orientation, the conformance orientation, and the competitive-team orientation—each reflecting the company's management philosophy. In all three, finance retains responsibility for financial market relationships and the acquisition of funds, and for internal reporting and financial analysis. However, within each orientation the finance function has its own distinct character, positioning in the company, and ways of operating.

The Command-and-Control Orientation

This orientation is consistent with the Traditional Management systems discussed in Chapters 2 and 3 and is the way in which Conventional Corporate Finance is organized. It is based on the military model of management with a clear top-down chain of command. The role of top management is traditional: to plan, organize, lead, and control the work of subordinates. Management acquires and allocates resources, and takes responsibility for their conservation and efficient use. The primary role of finance is to be an arm of management, providing detached analyses, criticisms, and recommendations about various business plans, and reporting the results of operations.

FIGURE 5.1 **Integrating Finance and Tqm into the Organization**

Style	Adopting a competitive-team orientation
Shared values	Seeing the purpose of the firm as more than maximizing share price
Skills	Integrating traditional financial tools and skills with tqm tools and skills
Staff	Experiencing the personal changes associated with working in a tqm manner
Systems	Bringing non-financial information into the management information system and placing it on a par with financial information
Structure	Distributing corporate financial resources, skills, and tasks away from headquarters and closer to the customer
Strategy	Developing a single quality/strategic planning system and document that integrates quality strategy with other plans

The Conformance Orientation

This orientation is characteristic of firms which operate in a regulated environment or for which government is a major customer. Management's role is similar to that within the command-and-control orientation with the addition that it must satisfy its regulators if it is to remain in business and grow. Finance serves as an expert organization, assuring compliance with regulations. It tends to be a bureaucracy of specialists in regulatory rules and the keeper of the required records.

The Competitive-Team Orientation

This orientation is a feature of companies which are market focused. Management's primary role is to support company members in their efforts to serve customers. In these firms, finance tends to be integrated with other organizational units and sees its role as bringing financial skills and business knowledge to the support of those units and to customer service. Finance people are often part of a matrix organization, or they report directly to the various business units rather than being physically and organizationally concentrated near senior management.

Keating and Jablonsky make effective use of a sports analogy to point out that in the competitive-team orientation, finance, like every other unit of a company, adds value by "getting close to the business," being a participant and not merely an observer:

> Getting close to the business means getting on the field as part of the management team. As a player, you are involved in the game. As a coach, you are on the sidelines or in the coaching booth to support the players. In either case you are not a commentator hired by the news media to provide an independent view of the game, nor are you locked in a back office counting gate receipts. You are a player or coach directly participating in the outcome of the game.

> Within the competitive-team orientation, members of the financial organization are committed first and foremost to help create value in the marketplace, not simply conserving or counting the value created by other members of the organization. To do so, financial managers must become players and committed students of the business. Detached financial analysis carries no credibility with those spilling their guts on the field. When owners of sports teams forget that championships are won on the field, or that success is determined in the marketplace, fans lose interest and customers go elsewhere.[*]

We see the competitive-team orientation as consistent with total quality management, and, as it applies to the finance organization, as fully consistent with what we have referred to as total quality finance. In a customer-focused organization, finance cannot be distinct from the remainder of the business, since finance affects customers, both directly through billing and other customer contact, and indirectly by providing important inputs to others within the firm. In a process-focused organization, finance must work closely with others as processes cut across organizational boundaries.

All five of the companies of this study are using or moving toward the competitive-team orientation in their finance operations. Four of the five companies—Corning, Federal Express, Motorola, and Solectron have operated using the competitive-team orientation for a decade or more. Southern Pacific is moving from the conformance orientation it adopted as a railroad when it was more highly regulated than it is today.

---

[*] *Patrick J. Keating and Stephen F. Jablonsky,* Changing Roles of Financial Management: Getting Close to the Business. (*Morristown, N. J. : Financial Executives Research Foundation, 1990): 16.*

Shared Values about Customers, Tqm, and Profits

OUR FUNDAMENTAL OBJECTIVE
(Everyone's Overriding Responsibility)

Total Customer Satisfaction

 **MOTOROLA**

Motorola's corporate purpose is printed succinctly on a small plastic card given to every employee and carried by each person we talked with. This fundamental objective is consistent with the purpose of the other four companies in the study. In each company, members of finance seem to be at least as emphatic as anyone else in stressing that profits are the result of putting customers first. This widely shared value does not demean the importance of profits in any way—no one we talked with indicated that profits were not valued as necessary for organizational survival, for meeting or exceeding shareholder expectations, or as part of the longer term scorecard of how well the company is doing. But it is clear that finance people in these companies share with each other and with others in the organization a belief that a focus on day-to-day efforts to maximize share price is not a management focus that will work.

In the finance functions of the study companies, a commitment to tqm as a necessary means for satisfying customers, and thus for long-term survival, seemed to us to replace the talk of day-to-day stock-price maximization we might have heard in organizations that have not yet progressed far on the quality journey. And in talking of tqm's role in satisfying customers and strengthening the company for the long term, the link from tqm to profitability seems clear. As Alan Graf, Federal Express' CFO said,

> The great thing for the CFOs of the world is that every single time [the work of Quality Action Teams] boils down to something that benefits the bottom line. It either increases the revenue, or engineers some cost problem out, or puts enough quality in that you get fewer failures on the backside. When

you get specific and draw that bottom line, it helps every single time. And people really feel great about that.

If we were to try to capture in six phrases the values that we heard from the finance people we interviewed, they would look like the following list:

- Customer commitment—seeing the customer as the reason for all organizational activities.

- Quality, excellence, and continuous improvement—using quality, excellence, and continuous improvement to translate customer commitment into customer satisfaction.

- Being data driven—managing by fact rather than opinion or by reacting to the "squeaky wheel."

- Respect for the individual—realizing that people, both inside and outside the corporation, are its most important resource, and maybe even its most important "product."

- Ethics and integrity—deriving "uncompromising integrity" from the values of all organizational members made real by open communications and processes, and excellent management practices.

- Profit—accepting profit as a prerequisite for survival, a natural outcome of pursuing customer satisfaction, and an indicator of success rather than a goal in itself.

Integrating Financial and Tqm Skills

Federal Express' Business Case Approach (BCA), described briefly in Chapter 4, provides a vehicle for sharing financial skills throughout the company. This development of financial skills is also encouraged by ELVIS, an on-line financial information system developed by finance. ELVIS (Electronic Large Variance Information System) permits people in other parts of the company to track their financial position and perform their own financial analyses by accessing Federal Express' financial database to extract financial or manpower data, or the status of internal paperwork (such as personnel and capital expenditure requests) relevant to their part of the business. ELVIS provides faster and more user-friendly access to real time financial data, and the finance staff now encourages other divisions to initiate and conduct their own financial analyses rather than waiting for leadership or assistance from finance. The finance function believes ELVIS may be increasing dramatically the amount of financial analysis being performed by individuals and teams outside the Finance Division.

Federal Express' Business Case Approach also supports finance members in developing skills they traditionally have not considered important for doing finance work. As Debra Gray noted in discussing a typical project, "the financial role became a real coordination and communication function for the whole process." In the Business Case Approach, success is dependent upon people in finance using such classic tqm skills as listening, acknowledging, coaching, teaching, sharing, empowering, enabling, and celebrating.

Corning's ability to operate its lean, high value-added treasury function depends heavily on finance professionals and non-professionals developing and using non-traditional skills. There is a lean support staff, and most people who do secretarial tasks have responsibility for some treasury function.

These companies are investing heavily in training members for the skills they need. For example, as part of its quality program Corning set increasing targets for training over the last five years, reaching its goal of devoting 5 percent of total working hours to training in 1991. Solectron has targeted for 150 training hours per employee by 1995. Motorola has long been recognized as a leader in training; its in-house education program, Motorola University, has become the prototype for many other companies.

For effective performance, members of the finance functions in the study companies are working to become effective at tqm skills:

- Skills focused outside the company such as listening to the customer and competitive benchmarking

- Skills needed for working in teams, like task force management skills and quality improvement team skills, and needed for working one-on-one like the skills noted earlier: listening, acknowledging, coaching, teaching, sharing, empowering, enabling, and celebrating

- Skills needed for analyzing and improving work processes, like quantitative skills, process analysis skills, opportunity finding skills, problem finding skills, and problem analysis and solving skills

Finance Staff as "Quality Champions"

The finance people we interviewed see themselves and are seen by others in their companies as being fully committed to their organizations' quality efforts—as committed as any other group in the company. In the process of learning about quality and becoming committed to it, many of the people with whom we talked had clearly become quality champions in their companies and outside. They had found a way of managing that worked better than previous ways, not only for customers, suppliers, and shareholders, but also for themselves and their co-workers as people.

The characteristics we saw in the finance people in these companies are consistent with the characteristics to be found in other organizations that have achieved significant progress on the quality journey. They include the following:

- A high level of education and training relative to other companies in their industry—these companies devote a significant number of hours per year to formal training and education, not only in the job people are currently doing, but in "cross training" for other jobs as well.

- Broad organizational experience and perspective—having a good sense of the entire organization and how the pieces fit together. In many cases this is supported by a job rotation process connected to cross training.

- A positive framing of the world—being constructive, optimistic, and trusting; seeing opportunities instead of problems; and relying on others to act in good faith and with a similar high degree of commitment.

- A solid understanding of tqm concepts and tools and a habit of using them regularly—using widely understood and shared concepts of quality, natural variation, process and process capability, control and breakthrough, and cost of poor quality as mental filters to frame issues in ways amenable to improvement and solution using the tools of quality management.

Aligning Financial and Other Systems with Tqm

A number of the companies studied are working to build quality and customer data into their information systems on a par with financial data. In one company four key financial processes have been defined—planning and estimating, executing and recording, measurements, and control—composed of a total of 10 sub-processes. Each process is evaluated on a process maturity scale, indicating how well it is understood and what progress is being made documenting and improving it. The owner of each process is clearly stated, and goals for improvement and progress on improvement are publicly reported and tracked.

At Corning, key Treasury processes have been identified and are starting to be rated as being in one of six sequential categories: process mapped, process documented, key control points identified, process benchmarked, continuous improvement in place, or process under tqm management. At Federal Express a company-wide system called Service Quality Indicators (SQIs) measures the company's and the individual functions' progress in quality improvement. SQIs capture the level of customer satisfaction by counting the number of times the company fails to satisfy a customer. In finance, the purchasing group, for example, developed a set of 10 SQIs for procurement. These 10 quantified measures are supplemented by a set of qualitative inputs including comments from buyers, supplier responsiveness and attitude, and the availability of needed materials. Later in this chapter we note Southern Pacific's efforts to integrate their quality planning system with the strategic, operations, and budgeting systems.

In addition to improving their own systems and contributing to the improvement of production and operations systems and processes, finance is a participant in improving a variety of other organizational processes such as people-focused systems for recruiting, training, utilizing, retaining, and rewarding staff.

As they work to improve financial systems, the finance functions attempt to reduce their complexity, integrate them with other organizational systems, and assure that they have clear ownership—with specific individuals responsible for assuring complete documentation and regular reviews for improving the systems.

Organizational Structure and Inverted Frisbees: Distributing Finance Throughout the Organization

Solectron's finance function is working to change where finance is done in the company structure—"distributing financial work" so that it is performed closer to the customer and sometimes performed by non-finance people. As a company, Solectron seeks the same thing from customers that many companies committed to quality want—solid, long term relationships. In identifying promising prospects, finance plays an important role in an effective team-based process, supporting sales, marketing, and other personnel in evaluating the potential and suitability of each prospective customer. A step that originally came relatively late in the process—the decision on the credit-worthiness of the prospect and the amount of credit the prospect would be eligible to receive—is now being performed very early in the process. And rather than being performed by someone in finance it is now done by people in sales. In "distributing" this financial task closer to the customer and "giving away" this piece of financial work, finance has improved considerably its contribution to the entire process. Finance staffers are now seen as a support system—coaches and teachers—and no longer as the "bad guys" who interfere with sales. By distributing some of his skills to the sales force, Myron Lee, Solectron's Financial Manager with credit responsibility, has eliminated much of his routine work and can now devote more time to supporting strategic marketing decisions.

Solectron's attempts to distribute financial skills, tasks, and responsibilities are representative of efforts in the other companies in the study—and Solectron's successes with credit analysis, self-audits, and other distributed financial processes are also mirrored by successes at the other companies, such as Federal Express' ELVIS system, which permits non-finance members to do their own financial analysis. As the organizational structures of these companies come more into alignment with tqm, financial work is defined more in collaboration with other parts of the organization rather than by finance in relative isolation. Efforts are made to move that work closer to the customer, to make finance more of a team member, and to make the financial skills available to members of other functions. Typical changes in finance include:

- Defining and simplifying work processes. Increasing effort is directed toward precise definition of work tasks and the processes for accomplishing them, simplifying the processes, and then documenting the processes explicitly. The documentation is readily shared and revised promptly as the processes are improved.

- Allocating work to teams, especially cross-functional teams, and in some cases self-directed work teams.

- Re-aggregating work tasks that had been too finely subdivided. When the work units assigned to people in finance were too small, they could not see how it served the internal and external customers for whom it was being performed, and the sense of task accomplishment was lost.

- Avoiding steep pyramids and growing numbers of financial staff. Some of the finance functions in the study have reduced the number of people in the corporate finance function while accomplishing greater volumes of work. In doing so they have also reduced the number of middle managers inspecting the work of others, thus flattening and shrinking the hierarchical pyramid in classic tqm fashion. Others have tended to do increasing amounts of work without adding personnel or have tended to accomplish the increased work with the same number or fewer middle managers. For example, the Motorola internal audit department now audits a company with nearly 1 3/4 times the sales of five years ago yet with only 2/3 of the staff used five years ago.

Integrating Tqm and Finance with Company Strategy and the Strategy-Making Process

Southern Pacific's finance function is playing a major role in the company's efforts to change how strategy is made and how it is integrated with other planning processes. One of the more important innovations at Southern Pacific to derive from the company's quality efforts is the development of a management system focused on change using a variety of elements all coordinated with only one document—an improvement-focused plan integrating strategy, quality, operations, and finance. The new planning process has already changed the receptiveness of operating managers to the budget, and increased commitment to operate according to the plan. As a by-product of the new process, the capital budget is much better understood by both finance and the operating departments. Joe Doherty, Southern Pacific's Assistant VP–Finance, who leads the budgeting process, observes, "The new budget process has pretty much eliminated the games people were playing with the budget such as inflating their capital requests in anticipation of cutbacks. The process is no longer seen as quite so arbitrary, and there is much greater buy-in and commitment to meeting the budget targets."

The need to integrate quality into the organization's total strategic process is well recognized by quality experts. In most companies, finance is a key player in the strategy-making process, so finance has much to contribute in establishing the common thread or theme which gives an organization its direction, guides the raising and allocation of resources, and communicates the organization's intent and commitment to its members and others.

Tqm shows up in the strategic thrusts and themes of these companies in such ways as being:

- Customer driven, placing a strong emphasis on exceeding customer expectations by focusing on innovative and high-quality products and services.

- Flexibility-seeking, in terms of the organization and in terms of the organization's products and services. For the organization as a whole, the strategies attempt to increase the ability of the organization to respond quickly and effectively to unanticipated changes in its competitive environment. In terms of products and services, the strategies frequently seek to enable the organization to provide customized products and services—permitting the company to respond uniquely to the needs of each customer.

- Attuned to cycle-time reduction, recognizing that it is extremely competitive and cost-effective to complete work of all kinds in a shorter time, and that the process and design improvements that make shorter cycle time possible can also improve quality dramatically.

- Open to strategic alliances, allowing the firm to pool its expertise with others.

- Focused on developing core competencies, developing skill and technology platforms to support short-run plans and provide a bridge to the long run.

6

Lessons Learned

I have been at Solectron since 1984 and I'm still having a blast. I still enjoy the work here. It's not work; it's almost a vacation. It is a group of very committed people who are dedicated to managing businesses the right way by delivering quality and excellence.

–Susan Wang
Senior VP and CFO, Solectron

You have to be disciplined, lean, dedicated, rigorous, sensitive, but you improve the process. So yes, it is more fun.

–Len Zanoni
Treasurer, Solectron

The people in Solectron's finance function are representative of the finance members of the other companies in the study. They have learned that the tools and philosophy of tqm apply in finance just as they do in other parts of the company; that finance people are willing and frequently eager to use tqm tools and find their work more rewarding when they do; and that there are opportunities for finance, like other areas, to take a leadership role in bringing tqm to their own function and to the rest of the organization. In this chapter we discuss some of these lessons learned and their implications for financial executives.

Tqm Is Applicable to Corporate Finance

The experiences of the companies in the study make it clear that quality management approaches work in corporate finance, just as they work in a wide variety of countries, industries, and other corporate functions. Finance achieves the same types of improvements in its own processes that other parts of the company achieve. Finance members become full partners on quality improvement teams, learn to speak the same language of quality and continuous improvement, establish the same type of customer-supplier partnerships, and get the same satisfaction out of working in an organizational system—and a functional department—committed to supporting them in delighting customers.

As in other parts of their organizations, some finance people are quick learners and embrace tqm approaches rapidly. Others are slow to get the message, seeing many problems in the new approaches and few opportunities.

Some Things Come Easily

Finance people bring some special characteristics and skills to the tqm implementation process that make it easy for them to grasp tqm approaches and techniques. Three of these relate to numbers, skills, and perspective.

Numbers: Finance people are usually comfortable with quantitative tools and measures. Some are already familiar with simple quality management tools, such as run charts and scatter diagrams, and are quick to grasp the less familiar, but also simple, tools such as control charts and Pareto diagrams. Many also quickly learn the more advanced quantitative techniques like experimental design.

Skills: The quantitative interests and analytical skills most finance people have, and which frequently attracted them to finance as a profession, fit well with the data gathering and analysis aspects of tqm. For many, the commitment to making decisions based on data, reflected in tqm mottos like "in God we trust; all others must provide data" appeals to more than their love for numbers (and sense of humor)—it appeals to a way of working and managing that finance people have frequently advocated but have not previously had the tools to achieve.

Perspective: The ability to see "the big picture" through the integrative lens of finance also predisposes finance people to embrace the systems-oriented, total organizational perspective of tqm. Finance people are accustomed to combining the elements of an activity into a comprehensive, integrated whole, such as net present value and net income. They often welcome the opportunity and challenges offered by tqm's attempts to bring in additional dimensions, such as customer satisfaction, cycle time reduction, and defect reduction. In a similar vein, finance people are frequently called upon to estimate the financial implications of an action taken in one area on another (for example, the additional recruitment and sales training costs to be borne by the human resource function when a company decides to reorganize one division into two, each with its own sales force). The opportunity to expand the analysis to include additional dimensions adds richness and excitement to finance's work.

And Some Things Do Not Come As Easily

While some of the skills finance people have facilitated their adoption of tqm, other skills and mind-sets inhibit their ability to grasp tqm approaches and techniques. Three changes that can be particularly difficult for finance people to make involve their roles, how they are evaluated, and the reality of continuous change.

Roles: Traditionally, finance has been positioned to perform impartial, detached analysis and enforce financial control. In response, finance people have developed a high degree of comfort with numerical work and often believe that companies can be managed solely "by the numbers." With a change to tqm, they are asked to work more closely with other organizational members and devote more attention to relationships and interpersonal skills. Finance people can have a difficult time adjusting to the team-oriented approach to work. They may also struggle with their new roles as coach, facilitator, and teacher.

Evaluation: Finance has long viewed the "bottom line" and stock price as a company's measure of success and as the basis for evaluating performance. In a tqm organization, however, promotions, salary, and incentive pay may be based on success in meeting the expectations of external and internal customers, improving processes, and contributing to team efforts. Finance people can be uncomfortable evaluating others and being evaluated along these new dimensions, especially when such attempts may be relatively new and not yet fully effective.

Change: Economic optimization and maximization rules underlie much of finance theory and typically lead finance people to search for "the best answer." Tqm goals, by contrast, do not represent a final destination that will be stable once attained. The phrase "quality journey" is used frequently in tqm companies. Improvement in processes and in the quality of products and services is never ending—there will always be changes in customer preferences, technology, and processes. Also, tqm as a way of managing—as a technology of managing—will continue to evolve and change. This change of mind-set may be difficult for finance people to become comfortable with.

The Important Thing Is to Start

> Many financial executives ask me for the name of the best consulting firm to hire or the best program to buy to get them started in quality management. I tell every one of them that there is no need for any of that. Quality management has to do with simplifying work—with eliminating non-value added activities. If we just look around us, its easy to find activities that can be simplified or eliminated altogether. The important thing is to select a process to improve, improve it, and then go after the next one.
>
> –Ken Johnson
> VP and Corporate Controller, Motorola

Ken Johnson's observation captures a theme we heard repeatedly from our study firms: the important thing is to get started. Although outside quality experts were often useful, there is no requirement for companies—or their finance organizations—to make elaborate investments in outside professional resources to get started in quality management. Quality may or may not be free, but the cost of starting is no reason to delay the quality journey. Ken's observation also suggests one of the alternatives available to any company—rely heavily on internal resources to address basic questions.

Finance members from the study companies reported that many of the early benefits from their quality management efforts came from simply asking whether their work was useful to their customers and eliminating the activities that were not. Several financial executives remarked that in some ways, this was nothing more than using some "good common sense."

On the other hand, the systematic practice of quality management requires important skills—both behavioral, such as teamwork and group problem solving, and technical, such as process analysis, statistical process control, and experimental design. Mastery of these skills is unlikely to emerge spontaneously and quickly within an organization, and outside experts may have much to contribute. Tqm also requires extensive and universal training in which outsiders may play an important role. Each study company currently devotes a significant portion of its personnel budget to training and is systematically extending the number of hours and type of training provided to employees at all levels.

Southern Pacific, the study's "second generation" tqm company, provides a counterpoint. In order to move much more quickly than its first generation counterparts, Southern Pacific recruited a staff of quality professionals to design and implement a tqm program at an accelerated rate. For a company of that scale, the profit possibilities from a rapid and intensive transition to quality management clearly exceeded the additional costs.

There Is a Great Yearning for Quality

Our interviews repeatedly reminded us that people desire a high level of quality in their organizations. They simply don't want to produce junk. They don't want to see their work time devoted to non-value added activities. They would rather get things done faster than slower. As a result, they are willing to take chances and work harder when they believe their organization is committed to excellence and to finding better ways to manage. The finance people we interviewed were acutely aware of this desire for quality in themselves and the people they work with.

As the organization's commitment to quality grows, people's enjoyment of their work also grows. We heard again and again that total quality finance is simply more fun than the old ways of Conventional Corporate Finance. Most case study participants felt it was more rewarding to be a team player than an outsider or judge, and to be more actively engaged in contributing to the business than enforcing rules from the sidelines and keeping score on others' performance. Finance people took pride in improving their own processes and having their own quality improvement successes to share. They liked feeling that they were learning and growing.

Although people did at times talk about "driving" quality through the organization, as though it were something that had to be forced on others, we more frequently heard people emphasize how they and others were learning to get out of people's way, allowing them to do quality work. We heard "enabling" and "empowering" more than "motivating" or "directing." We do not believe the people we talked with thought that, if they simply got out of people's way, six sigma improvements would magically appear from a liberated workforce. However, there was a strong recognition that when people are given the tools to do good work and are not blocked from doing so, they will do their very best, in quite creative ways. This trust in the commitment and capabilities of others was something many finance people recognized had been discouraged by their own previous training and by the ways they were rewarded for their work.

Resistance To Change Can Be Exaggerated

Through training we were able to move away from a passive stance of "you tell me what to do, and I'll do it" and shift toward a more active role. And, we found out that resistance to change was not really resistance at all—but just lack of knowledge on how to move forward.

–Robert Sorakubo
Operations Controller, Solectron

Robert Sorakubo reports a situation in which organization members were eager to move forward, but did not know how—a situation that might well have been mislabeled "resistance to change." One of the strongest messages picked up in our interviews was that the eagerness to embrace quality management was much greater than any resistance to it. People were sometimes too busy to lay aside high-priority projects to attend a training program; they sometimes got discouraged and frustrated with the quality improvement project their team tackled; and some did not find the quality tools and approaches useful in their work. But more often, people were willing to work still longer hours to flowchart a financial process after an already full work day; to substitute reading an article or book on quality for a popular novel; or to cover for someone attending a training program.

People embrace change:

- when they initiate it themselves and feel they can control its progress and outcomes,

- when they understand its desirability and can predict many of its implications,

- when they value the new benefits they, their co-workers, and organizations will receive with the new state of affairs and are willing to bear the costs arising from the change, and

- when they see how they can contribute to the change and increase the likelihood of successful change.

Conversely, people tend to resist change:

- when they are unclear about the implications of the change for them and their work,

- when they see the costs to them in terms of lost benefits and forgone advantages while not seeing the new benefits that will arise and the old disadvantages that will be removed,

- when they cannot see how to contribute to and control the process of making the change,

- when the proposed change has errors built into it that they can see and are powerless to correct, and

- when decisions about undertaking the change and how it will be implemented are made in ways that exclude, disempower, and devalue them.

Tqm has many characteristics that support people in embracing it. One factor for supporting the ready acceptance of tqm is that it is more consistent with "human nature" than Traditional Management systems. The trusting, empowering, customer-committed, quality-focused, and improvement-oriented ways of tqm are more consistent with human nature than the suspicious, authoritarian, shareholder-oriented, quantity-focused, and status-quo-preserving ways of Traditional Management. Thus, the replacement of Traditional Management practices by tqm systems is in many ways a process of giving people what they want rather than imposing still another quick management fix on them. To a much larger extent than with other management changes of the past, we can expect people to embrace tqm as they come to understand what it is and what it means for them.

Many of us are well trained in identifying and overcoming resistance to change. For the transition to tqm, a more powerful skill may turn out to be the ability to identify and support people's willingness to embrace change.

Financial Managers Can Be Quality Leaders

People in finance don't have to wait for others to take leadership in pursuing tqm. There are so many ways finance contributes to the tqm transformation that there is no reason why someone in finance cannot be the key trigger in stimulating their company's quality revolution.

Although no one in finance was the very first quality champion in our case studies, finance supplied many strong tqm advocates. They facilitated acceptance in a number of ways:

- aligning financial and quality information systems,

- integrating quality planning with financial and strategic planning,

- breaking down barriers between the finance function and the rest of the organization,

- leading and supporting quality improvement teams, and

- empowering members of other functions and divisions to do some of their own finance work.

At Corning and Southern Pacific, finance people were involved from the beginning in planning and executing a company-wide tqm program.

Senior management must eventually provide strong leadership for tqm to be implemented and sustained over time. For some companies, like Federal Express and Solectron, commitment to systematic quality management comes from the top at an early stage in the company's life. For others, quality champions arise spontaneously anywhere in the company. Most companies with no formal commitment to tqm have a number of quality champions who move their own organizational units and the rest of the organization toward tqm while trying to convince senior management to take a leadership role. In Corning, Motorola, and Southern Pacific the leadership of senior managers was initially stimulated and then strongly supported by quality champions throughout the organization.

Implications for Financial Executives

The lessons learned by the financial executives in this study suggest four implications for other financial executives and members of corporate finance functions interested in adding similar value to their own organizations.

Just Start

In an organization which has already embarked on some type of tqm effort, there is considerable payoff for finance members joining in if they have not already done so. They should look for opportunities to support existing tqm efforts and to add the many special contributions finance can make. In a company that has not yet embarked on such an effort, finance members have an opportunity to become quality champions and lead senior management to begin the journey.

Build on Existing Resources

The adoption of tqm does not require complex nor expensive programs brought in from the outside. It is typically possible to get started, and to make much progress in adopting quality management, using resources already within the organization. Additional resources from outside can speed the journey and increase the benefits.

Expect Full Results and Expect It to Be Fun

Finance members can expect to achieve improvements in their own processes and to make contributions to the rest of the organization at least as great as those made by any other unit of the organization. And they can expect to have a lot more fun in their work and to be a lot more fun for others to work with.

Don't Over-Emphasize Resistance to Change

Anticipate that, as finance members make the personal changes associated with tqm and support others in doing the same, they will embrace the changes. People leading the transformation should spend at least as much time and energy looking for and building on the factors and conditions that support people in embracing tqm as they devote to anticipating and overcoming the factors that encourage people to resist it.

7
What's Next?
The Continuing Evolution of
Corporate Finance

Quality can be profitable too!

–Winston Chen
Chairman and Co-CEO, Solectron

The quality management phenomenon is bringing important new insights to financial executives. Among other observations, they are discovering that total quality management can be very financially rewarding. When a business concentrates on exceeding customer expectations and continuously improving its processes, revenue opportunities increase at the same time that costs decline. It is quite possible to be the lowest cost producer of the product or service which is also most highly preferred by customers.

In our research we have discovered many examples of how the practice of corporate finance has changed, and continues to change, as companies move from Traditional Management (TM) toward total quality management (tqm). In Chapter 4 we identified how the philosophy and tools of quality management are modifying the way finance is practiced in our study companies. Then in Chapter 5 we summarized how tqm is permitting the viewpoints and skills of finance to be better woven throughout the fabric of organizations.

In this concluding chapter, we speculate about the future. How might financial practice continue to evolve as companies learn more about tqm? What might be the directions in which corporate finance theory moves to comprehend and attempt to reconcile itself with tqm? Will corporate finance emerge as a strengthened discipline, with new tools and approaches to problem solving and analysis? Or, might the diffusion of financial people and skills throughout tqm organizations point to the end of corporate finance as a recognizable function? While we cannot know the answers, we find it useful, and fascinating, to pose several of the questions.

Evolving Finance Practice

As tqm becomes the norm for companies around the world, financial practice will naturally evolve. Looking through today's glasses, it is difficult to foresee all, or even many, of the changes tqm will bring. However, the three discussed below are among those under active consideration by financial executives of the study companies: (1) the diffusion of specialization, (2) rethinking the "bottom line," and (3) extending quality measurements.

The Diffusion of Specialization

In the Traditional Management system it has been common to maintain a large staff group, expert in their various disciplines, to perform detailed analyses, handle special projects, and make recommendations to senior management. The tqm firm, however, tends to be a flatter organization with far less staff, in part because it finds the cost of a specialized staff high in terms of dollars and in terms of slowing organizational decision making. Specialist skills are more fully distributed throughout the tqm organization. How will firms capture the value that was added by sophisticated staff specialists in a flattened organization? Is it possible to have the benefits of specialization without paying the costs? How can a tqm firm protect itself so that distribution of previously specialized responsibilities does not translate to loss of sophisticated abilities?

Rethinking the "Bottom Line"

For many years it has been considered good practice to set targets for profitability and growth and to manage the business to reach those numbers, somewhat independent of how they are achieved. By contrast, tqm companies fear that attempts to manage profits directly are rarely sustainable and very often involve tampering—destabilizing consistent, well-functioning systems. They have learned that profits derive from delighted customers purchasing high-quality products produced by well-functioning processes. Will tqm persuade companies to cease their attempts to "manage profits" and manage processes instead? For that matter, is it possible to manage profits at all, or is "managing profits" an oxymoron in that direct attempts to change profits imply lack of management?

If profits come from processes, it would be desirable to establish empirically verifiable links between process drivers and customers, and profitability. What form will these linkages take? Will an understanding of them lead to better internal financial analysis? Will external financial analysts look less at profits and more at process performance and improvement to value a company's prospects? Will these newly uncovered relationships help external analysts become more comfortable evaluating the firm through the tqm lens?

Extending Quality Measurements

Management thinker W. Edwards Deming has remarked that the most important information needed to manage a firm is unknown and unknowable. In this comment, he refers to such things as the costs of not fully serving the customer or not having well-functioning processes in place, costs which are not part of traditional accounting systems. Yet, because these items might be unmeasurable today, will they remain unmeasurable tomorrow?

At least one of the companies studied is attempting to move to a third stage of comprehending their customers and markets. Beyond understanding existing customers, and beyond understanding potential customers who looked at their wares but chose a competitor's product, they are now thinking about those potential customers who never looked at their products at all. How might a company begin to measure this systematically?

Within the firm, expert judgment has been such a major component of some finance activities that these activities have not been seen as processes amenable to definition and continuous improvement. An example is establishing goals for a company's annual or multi-year plan. How can the establishment of these goals be more fully connected to the company's measurement system and made explicit for study? And how can a company measure its success against the plan? As one finance executive asks: "Have we done well if we perform according to the plan? Maybe the plan was not bold enough and we could have done better. What if the plan was chosen to challenge the company? Perhaps then we would be doing well even if we fell short of the targets."

Evolving Finance Theory

As discussed in the preceding chapters, our research confirms that contemporary business is making a transition from Traditional Management to total quality management, from Conventional Corporate Finance to total quality finance. With business conditions and practice changing, we can anticipate that finance theory will change as well, as it has done in the past when comparable transformations have taken place.

There is some question as to whether the traditional finance model was useful as a guide to Traditional Management. There are many more questions as to whether it is a valid guide for a tqm firm.

The Traditional Finance Model

The traditional model of corporate finance derives from Adam Smith's model of a perfectly competitive firm developed during the industrial revolution over 200 years ago. Each small owner-managed business, maximizing profits in its own interest, contributes to an overall efficiency of resource use and production which maximizes benefits to all of society—the famous "invisible hand." Over the years, changing conditions have added complexity to the model: the firm has grown to be a corporation owned by non-manager shareholders, insights into risk and time value of money have led to the replacement of profit maximization with owners' wealth maximization, and efficient capital markets have made owners' wealth visible for many companies as a stock price.

Figure 7.1 summarizes the model's logic. The goal of the firm is to maximize its share price. Led by management, the firm takes a series of actions which are communicated to investors and analysts. They in turn use the information to price the firm's stock. Management, reading the signals from changes in the firm's market value, adjusts its actions doing more of the same if the company's stock price rose, and changing its actions if the stock price fell—and we go around the loop again. Should management's actions not be directed at maximum stock price, there is an agency problem. The board of directors must then more closely align managers' incentives with those of the shareholders, or the board and management will be evicted, victims of the "market for corporate control."

Note that the traditional model does not include the firm's customers, employees, nor any other stakeholders of the firm (other than the equity holders), nor does it incorporate processes. It is interesting to contrast this model with the Baldrige application model of Chapter 2, Figure 2.2.

FIGURE 7.1 **The Traditional Finance Model of Shareholder Wealth Maximization**

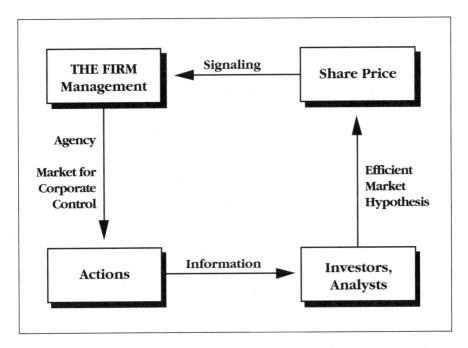

For this model to be an accurate guide for management, its premises must be true, and each of its four legs must work flawlessly. But the business environment changes continuously. Are the global changes that are contributing to and part of tqm chipping away at the conditions necessary for the model to be valid?

Signaling: A tqm firm is characterized by many simultaneous initiatives, some large and some small, to improve the firm's many processes. Is it possible in such a company, or in any company for that matter, to connect stock price movements to specific management actions so as to know precisely what made the firm's stock price change?

Financial market efficiency: The efficient market hypothesis, that stock prices fully contain all public information about a firm, has been a staple of finance theory since the early 1970s. However, since that time, the equity markets have been characterized by an increasing concentration of economic power due to economies of scale of fund management, the theoretical imperative for investment diversification, and regulatory pressure for fully funding pension and insurance plans.

There has also been increasing evidence of pricing inefficiencies as "anomalies" in stock market pricing have been observed and documented. And we have seen that tqm companies are expanding the data set they consider relevant for management well beyond financial metrics. How efficient are the capital markets today? Do they capture the meaning of all the data relevant to the company's worth? Are they efficient enough to be a good measure of the existing value of the firm and therefore a confirmation of "good management"? Are they efficient enough to be a good predictor of the firm's long-run value and therefore a valid guide to future management actions?

Information: In the traditional model, money is considered the common denominator, a universal measure of worth. Tqm directs management to look at a new and expanded data set containing far more than financial and managerial accounting numbers. What is the importance of these other numbers for the firm's value? Does the information flow from a firm to the financial markets capture the key variables needed to value the firm? Is the new information now, and will it be, in the public domain so financial analysts can include it in their evaluations, or will market efficiency further decline as analysts realize that more of the relevant information required to understand a company is private?

Agency theory: Agency theory is premised on a legalistic definition of the relationship of manager to owner. Yet tqm asks the firm to concentrate its efforts on customers, processes, and stakeholders. Does the framing of management as agent of the shareholder accurately capture the relationship as it is evolving in these firms? Is it best to view the shareholders as the firm's owners, and therefore deserving of management's highest obligation, or should they be seen simply as investors and risk bearers? Said another way, is it valuable for the firm's long-run viability (or even possible) to align management's interests solely with those of the shareholders? Does the agency viewpoint contribute to a manager-owner relationship which is beneficial to the firm, leading managers to make the best decisions for the firm (and its shareholders), or does it discourage management from establishing necessary relationships with other stakeholders?

In some other countries, most notably Japan with its many tqm companies, where there is less investment risk created by structural mistrust between investor and business, the cost of capital is consistently lower than elsewhere. How is it possible to create new relationships between businesses and their financial suppliers which mirror the progress tqm firms have made in their relationships with other suppliers?

In a quality management system the responsibilities of management are diffused throughout the organization. How does agency theory apply in a non-hierarchial organization where everyone is a manager?

The purpose of the firm: Unlike TM, tqm places its attention on customers and processes. This raises the most fundamental of corporate finance questions: is the purpose of the firm to maximize shareholder wealth, or is this simply one result of good management? With the growing awareness that changing technology has made human capital the most important input in many firms, does it make sense to measure, and manage the company to maximize, only the return to financial capital? More broadly, could financial capital be simply one input to the firm, not significantly different from, and particularly not more important than, any other input in terms of its value to the firm's success?

The Next Finance Model

The prospect that the transition to quality management is just starting, and that even today's quality leaders are but a short distance into a long and continuing journey, suggests that many more changes to business theory and practice lie ahead. With respect to finance theory, two "macro-level" questions emerge. What will the "next theory of finance" look like? Will it be a model which is not based on the primacy of the stockholder but instead balances the positions of the firm's various suppliers and customers and guides management in making trade-offs among them? What will the "next theory of the firm" look like? Will it be a model which will integrate economic and finance theory with systems and organizational theory?

Toward the Long Term

In addition to speculating about current issues in finance theory and practice prompted by the transition from TM to tqm, it is equally fascinating to ask about the much longer term—what might happen after tqm becomes fully ingrained in the management systems of many companies.

The End of Corporate Finance?

The companies in this study seem to be moving functional experts to the furthest reaches of the organization so they will be routinely and immediately available to serve their customers. We have borrowed the language of data processing and characterized this trend as "distributed finance." Rather than expanding a central finance organization, tqm firms are physically relocating their finance people throughout the organization: examples are Federal Express, which places financial analysts worldwide with various departments they support, and Solectron with its divisional controllers.

We have also identified examples of what may well be another wave of distributed finance, distributing not people but finance skills throughout the organization. Solectron's internal auditor is an example of a finance professional changing his role to that of teacher and internal consultant so that "self-audits" by many more organization members can start replacing the traditional internal audit conducted by a few specialists.

If these trends are representative of the future, what does this mean for the notion of a "finance department"? Is the finance department as we know it doomed to extinction, or will it be reborn in a very different guise? Taking the trend further, if other skills are broadly distributed, will every organizational unit effectively become a little business? Some evidence, such as Solectron's internal divisions, suggests that this might already be happening.

The End of Management . . . or the Beginning?

In many ways, tqm eliminates the concept of a manager as we know it. The military model characteristics of the TM system which created the distinction between the manager and the managed are no longer relevant for personal or corporate success. In a tqm company, the traditional jobs ascribed to management—planning, organizing, leading, and controlling—become everybody's job, an inherent part of the corporate system. Our study companies are already experiencing a blurring of responsibilities between what were formally considered "managers" and "workers." Will this trend continue? What will "management" jobs look like as tqm continues to evolve? What should we be teaching about management in business schools? How should company members at all levels be trained?

Finally, will we reach the point where diffusion of responsibilities has progressed so far that, in the words of some companies, "every manager will become a CEO? . . . and every non-manager will become a CEO as well"?

Section II

Corning Incorporated

One of the more striking aspects of Corning Incorporated's global Treasury function is how lean it is. The 33,000 person company has a treasury staff of only 54. Yet, a number of its groups are recognized as "world class." Corning's progress in implementing tqm in the Treasury function—and throughout the company—is a vital element in its ability to operate a lean, high value-added function.

Although Corning has long been known for high-quality products and innovation, its pursuit of systematic quality management systems began in 1983 when CEO Jamie Houghton announced his intent to back a company-wide commitment to quality with a $5 million investment in quality training and related activities. Finance was an active participant from the very beginning; Treasury's manager of customer financial services was appointed as one of the 12 members of the first Quality Council that designed and guided Corning's approach.

Treasury is characterized by multiple individual initiatives. Many members have little interaction on a day-to-day basis. Tqm is seen as a linking factor across Treasury and as critical to its success. It has alerted staff members to their customers inside and outside the Treasury Division, empowered staff members to act on their own, and created a shared language. It has opened staffers' eyes to the benefits of teamwork and focused efforts on defining and improving processes for serving the external customer. People's attention has shifted from an activity-based orientation to a results-based orientation, and voluntary resource sharing has increased as barriers labeling resources as "mine" or "yours" have broken down.

Treasury's Key Results Indicators (KRIs) play an important role in creating teamwork in the division. KRIs are chosen to join individual responsibilities, with the goal of making it impossible for Treasury members to meet their KRI targets without cooperating.

Each of Treasury's six groups—cash management and corporate finance, international treasury, risk management and prevention, investor relations, investment management, and economic planning and research—has made significant progress in implementing tqm into its day-to-day operations. That progress has translated to direct bottom-line results.

A

Corning Incorporated

People feel a lot better about their jobs. Because they listen to their customers so well, they know what they are supposed to do, they measure it, and they find out how well they are doing—over and over and over again. They find out directly from their customers when they are adding value. They don't have to stand around and wait for somebody else to say "attaboy."

                                        –Van Campbell, Vice Chairman

Corning Incorporated's global Treasury function is remarkably lean. The 33,000 person company has a treasury staff of only 54: 32 in the U.S. and 22 in Europe. The ability to operate with so few people arises neither from a simple organizational structure nor from low standards for Treasury's performance. To the contrary, Corning has extensive international operations including more than 20 subsidiaries and equity ventures. A number of its treasury functions are recognized as "world class," among them risk management and investor relations.

Sandy Helton, Vice President and Treasurer, and Van Campbell, Vice Chairman, believe the company's quality processes are the key to the group's ability to run a very lean, yet high performing treasury function. Treasury listens carefully to its customers to eliminate non-value added activities. It establishes partnerships inside and outside the company to get important tasks accomplished. It develops and continuously adjusts its Key Results Indicators (KRIs) to keep its members focused on the highest priority tasks. And it studies and improves Treasury's processes to simplify work, increase reliability, and reduce cycle time. As Sandy says:

The secret sounds mundane: understanding our customers and suppliers, keeping focused on what we are trying to achieve, identifying and eliminating unnecessary work, and so on. But we could not do what we do with the few people we have if we did not use our quality processes—plus, of course, a lot of hard work.

Corning Adopts a Tqm Approach

Corning Glass Works, as the company was called from 1875 until 1989, has long been known for high-quality consumer and industrial products and for innovation in "glass-related" technologies. There are few consumers who have never heard of Steuben™ crystal, a classic artisan product, or Corelle™ dinnerware, which quickly became a dominant product based upon a break-through in glass technology. Known today as Corning Incorporated, the company has gone well beyond its beginnings in glass products to become an international corporation operating in four broad market sectors: specialty materials, telecommunications, laboratory services, and consumer housewares. A supplier of more than 60,000 products, plus advanced laboratory and engineering services, Corning is active in every major world industry. As a family-led organization since Amory Houghton purchased an interest in a small Cambridge, Massachusetts, glass company in 1851, Corning has always valued pride in workmanship and pride in company. But, as is true of many U.S. companies, for years quality products were achieved through hard work, repeated inspections, and considerable rework.

In 1983, Jamie Houghton, great-great-grandson of the founder, was named chairman and chief executive officer. One of his first actions was to declare that Corning would transform itself into a "Total Quality" organization dedicated to meeting the requirements of customers. The impetus to focus on total quality came from the company's customers who were increasingly demanding products that met the quality standards of manufacturers in Japan and Taiwan. Profitability also motivated the company; the new standards held promise of locating and correcting wasteful practices. In addition, trying to improve quality offered challenge and responsibility to employees who wanted to use their heads as well as their hands.

At the time Corning committed to becoming a Total Quality organization, there were not many American companies to learn from. While Corning did benefit from the experiences of other companies, to a considerable extent it tended to discover and invent many of its approaches by itself or with the help of quality consultants. Its journey had the following characteristics:

- strong, visible, and consistent support from the top of the organization led by Jamie Houghton,

- an early decision to draw heavily on Philip Crosby's approach to quality management,

- a heavy emphasis on developing and delivering quality management courses to every employee in the company—domestic and foreign—as well as marketing the courses to other organizations,

- a tendency for the quality effort to become internally focused in the mid-1980s with a re-emphasis on the importance of external customers in the late 1980s, stimulated in part by a visit to the company and speech on the subject in 1987 by Tom Peters,

- an early emphasis on cost of quality as a key concept and metric followed by the gradual replacement of that concept with KRIs and Motorola's six sigma approach,

- increasing use of Baldrige Award criteria as guidelines for the quality process, and

- increasing use of self-directed work teams throughout the company.

Initiating Quality Management

Jamie Houghton's October 1983 announcement of his commitment to quality management was backed by a commitment to invest $5 million in quality training and related activities. One of Jamie's first acts was to appoint Forrest E. Behm, a senior vice president, as the company's first director of quality. A Quality Council was created and given responsibility and broad guidelines for defining and implementing a corporate-wide quality approach. By November, statements on the quality goal, policy, and implementation approach were issued. Corning's current quality policy, consistent with its initial statement, reads:

> It is the policy of Corning to achieve Total Quality performance in meeting the requirements of external and internal customers. Total Quality performance means understanding who the customer is, what the requirements are, and meeting those requirements, without error, on time, every time.

In December 1983, the Corning Quality Institute was established and the company's quality symbol chosen, a combination of an apple with a "Q" for quality called the "quapple."

In early 1984, consistent with Crosby's approach to quality management, Corning adopted "Four Quality Principles" and "Ten Actions" as key elements of its plan. The Four Principles are:

1. Meeting customer requirements
2. Achieving error-free work
3. Managing by prevention
4. Measuring by cost of quality

The Ten Actions are:

1. Making a personal commitment to quality
2. Working in teams
3. Providing education in quality awareness and skills
4. Measuring and displaying performance data
5. Identifying the dollar cost of poor quality
6. Communicating about quality progress and needs
7. Establishing a corrective action system
8. Recognizing contributions
9. Celebrating successes
10. Establishing error reduction goals for everyone

By the end of 1984, significant progress had been made on each of the Ten Actions. The first quality training program, Phase I of the Quality Awareness Seminar, had been translated into six languages and taught to 4000 employees worldwide, with the Management Committee attending in January and the first overseas offering the same month. One hundred fifty quality improvement steering teams had been formed and hundreds of Corrective Action Teams (CATs) were in operation. The first company-wide employee climate survey had been conducted, including questions on how employees felt the company was doing on quality. The first "Quality Milestone Meeting" was held, a celebration of quality progress in which eight teams shared the success of their projects.

By the end of 1985, 80 percent of all employees had completed Phase I training and the second phase of quality training programs, which focused on skills, was under development. The company's quality efforts were recognized in 1986 when Jamie Houghton was selected by the American Society for Quality Control to chair the following year's

National Quality Month. More than 8000 employees attended at least one of three Phase II Quality Skills training courses on communications and group dynamics, problem solving skills, or statistical tools. More than 7700 Corrective Action suggestions were submitted, an 18 times increase from the previous year, and 4700 implemented. Some 40 percent of employees participated on a quality team and/or submitted a Corrective Action suggestion. The company also started its monthly Visitor Quality Orientation, a day-long program for customers, suppliers, and others interested in learning about Corning's quality approach.

In the following years, a series of new training courses was developed, and Corning's Quality Institute attracted a growing number of outside customers. Annual hours devoted to job-related training rose steadily as Corning pursued a goal of devoting 5 percent of employee time to such training by 1991. The number of Corrective Action suggestions and teams rose steadily, and a Union-Management Quality Review Committee was formed and became an active contributor to the quality effort.

In 1987 the company became aware, in part from Tom Peters' participation in that year's Quality Milestone celebration, that some of its quality efforts were acquiring an element of "going through the motions" and were losing sight of quality's ultimate purpose: better serving the external customer. To shift its focus outward, Corning increased the number and frequency of customer surveys, developed and introduced the Customer Action Planning System—a new tool for measuring customers' expectations and perceptions, and began to develop Key Results Indicators (KRIs) to tie quality efforts more directly to outcomes that would add value for customers. Although cost of quality remained one of the 10 Actions, and a quality tool based upon it—"Problem-Based Cost of Quality"—was developed, Corning experienced the same troubles other companies have had in translating the cost of quality concept into a useful management tool for guiding and measuring day-to-day actions.

In addition to receiving growing numbers of customer quality awards, Corning's quality progress received a special recognition in 1988 when Corning was one of two companies selected as models for the U.S. Government's new Federal Quality Institute. Government representatives spent four days in Corning, NY, learning about the company's quality management system. In that year, quality management performance became a formal part of the performance development and review process for salaried employees.

A major step in Corning's quality efforts occurred when the Telecommunications Products Division submitted an application for the Baldrige Award in May 1989 and was one of nine organizations to receive a site visit. The following year, the division received the first Houghton Quality Award, Corning's newly established internal quality prize based on the Baldrige Award categories and assessment system. During 1990, the company adopted the seven Baldrige application categories as its framework for guiding the next stage of its Total Quality efforts.

Other major steps in the evolution of the quality management system occurred in benchmarking, quality metrics, and training. Increased awareness of the importance of learning from other quality leaders was signaled by the Quality Institute's development of a benchmarking course and intensified company efforts to benchmark other companies' processes. After the Management Committee visited Motorola in August 1990, a shift in quality metrics occurred, and Corning began emphasizing the six sigma measurement system. In 1991, Corning reached its goal of devoting 5 percent of employee time to job-related training.

As the Fall of 1992 approached, Corning considered whether to prepare a corporate-wide application for the 1993 Baldrige Award. The company desired the valuable parts of the process: improvements arising from the company-wide focus, hard work and excitement involved in preparing the application, and feedback from the examiners. However, there were concerns over total corporate readiness in all Baldrige categories and the significant effort it would take to prepare the application. Corning decided to postpone applying for the Baldrige Award as a corporation. Rather, it focused on internal improvement using the Baldrige criteria as a template and periodic self-assessments as the measurement of the corporation's drive to become world class. Corning also initiated an internal quality award based on the Baldrige criteria to recognize the achievement of superior performance in pursuit of World-Class Quality by a division or business unit. While the Treasury Division has not yet applied for this internal award, the corporate process of self-assessment has become a critical part of the drive toward quality in finance.

Finance's Role in Corning's Quality Approach

Finance was an active participant from the very beginning of Corning's adoption of systematic quality management processes. As Van Campbell recalls:

We all jumped in together. The whole company worked together to develop a common language, to find a common approach, and to create the Quality Institute. We all went through the courses together. So we were all learning at the same time.

Sandy Helton, at that time the treasury function's manager of customer financial services, was one of the 12 members of the Quality Council appointed by Jamie Houghton in October 1983. She recalls three early initiatives for the Council:

- Selecting the form the program would take and how the various approaches of Crosby, Deming, Juran, and others would be used and integrated.

- Beginning the internal education program for all employees "post haste": increasing awareness of the need for systematic quality systems and commitments, establishing the Corning Quality Institute, determining quality knowledge and skill needs, and starting to deliver training. Top management took the training first, both to demonstrate their commitment and to be in a position to support others.

- Translating the concept of quality for each division. In addition to defining and leading the overall corporate approach to quality, Quality Council members were also responsible for bringing quality to their own parts of the company. As a representative of Finance, Treasury, and the administrative functions reporting to Van Campbell, much of Sandy's time was devoted to helping those areas get started on the new approaches that were emerging.

Bringing Quality into Finance

In addition to continuing her normal work activities and participating in the Council's corporate level quality work, Sandy started her divisional quality work by looking for a project for a Corrective Action Team and for ways to measure the cost of quality in finance.

The first team she worked with focused on improving an information book prepared quarterly for the Board's Finance Committee. The goal was to prepare the report right the first time, to do it with zero errors. She recalls the project as a reasonable place to start in learning the new methods and that it went "fairly well," but was concerned that it was "a bit artificial"—it succeeded in involving many Treasury members, but was not Finance's most critical activity.

Simultaneously, the team responsible for managing the quality process in the division was working on the Ten Actions and efforts to measure and use the cost of quality to guide improvement efforts. Two of the Ten Actions received particular attention in Finance's early efforts: teamwork and recognition. The fact that Finance has many specialists with advanced professional training and professional pride was a barrier to both. Much of the department's work was specialized and involved little interaction with others. For considerable numbers of department members, the need to work in teams to get their day-to-day work accomplished did not come up regularly. Thus, recognizing when it is important to work as part of a team and learning how to work effectively in teams when it is necessary was more difficult than for others whose work requires frequent team-based collaboration.

In the same way, for those in finance whose work was specialized and professionally sophisticated, Sandy and others were concerned about finding ways to recognize the quality improvements accomplished. The problem was to avoid the danger of recognizing people in ways that might trivialize their contributions. The solution was to have people in the division design their own recognition system.

As part of her work, Sandy prepared a reference guide ("QIT Reference Manual for S&A Groups") dealing with the meaning of quality processes for staff and administrative groups, how quality processes would impact them, and how they could get started on implementing quality. She also encouraged individuals and groups in Finance to begin measuring and displaying the results of their activities. A formal tracking system for quality improvements was set up, entitled FINS (Finance Improvement Never Stops). FINS is similar to tracking systems elsewhere in Corning, but Treasury believes it averages more improvement items than any other division: 14–15 per person on average in 1991, with 90 percent acted upon by the end of the year. By making quality issues visible, it has encouraged people to think about quality and empowered them to do something about it. Employees have the freedom to act on their quality ideas without formal approval. Quality improvement has become such a way of life that Jim Wheat, assistant treasurer, International, believes the FINS system is no longer necessary—people correct processes without needing to track improvement opportunities and the actions taken.

Both as a member of the Quality Council and as a quality leader in the finance area, Sandy was involved in attempts to translate the cost of quality concept from a useful way of increasing awareness of the importance of quality at a conceptual level into an effective metric for guiding specific quality initiatives. Early in the Quality Council's work,

Sandy recognized and reported that existing financial and accounting measurement and recording systems were inadequate to capture the information needed to measure quality costs, opportunity costs, and the value of improvements. In spite of the limitations of the existing data, she recalls "thrashing mightily" with the cost of quality concept and achieving some moderate successes. However, as time passed, the efforts to make cost of quality the key metric in Corning's quality process decreased and it was recognized as more valuable as a concept rather than as a day-to-day measure.

As efforts to develop useful cost of quality based measures declined, Finance—like the rest of the company—started relying more and more on KRIs to focus and guide its quality improvement efforts and then supplemented them with use of the Baldrige criteria.

Total Quality in the Lean Finance Organization

Corning's Treasury has found Total Quality to be a vital element in its ability to operate a lean, high value-added function. It is staffed by a cadre of independent professionals. The traditional boundary between "managers" and "support staff" is breaking down: all traditional "secretarial" positions have been transformed to include quantitative, report writing, and specific project responsibilities, while "managers" are inclined to do more and more of their own word processing, calendar maintenance, and so on.

Since the staff is so lean, Treasury members and the quality teams they serve on tend to look at broad issues. Process boundaries are drawn widely and processes throughout the organization are relatively visible, with more and more being documented. As an example, Sandy Helton describes how Corning's Total Quality philosophy supported a recent internal reorganization. In 1992, Treasury reorganized its European operations, which created new lines of reporting and required some staff to relocate. The changes in responsibilities and locations required changes in processes. Without its quality culture, staff members might have continued working as before, not easily adapting to the changes. But the existence of the Total Quality culture meant staff could see the process implications of reorganization, recognize the benefits from the change, identify process modifications required, and take the actions necessary to put the revised processes in place.

Total Quality as a Linking Factor

Treasury is characterized by multiple individual initiatives. While the U.S. staff shares a common physical location, members often do not have significant interaction in their day-to-day work. Each manages an area of responsibility, drawing on the others as needed.

Sandy talks eloquently of how Total Quality acts as a linking factor across Treasury and is critical to its success. In her view, quality emphasizes how each staff member has customers and suppliers outside the Treasury Division and is a customer and supplier of other Treasury and Finance members. It empowers staff members to act on their own and avoid endless rounds of approvals. It creates a shared language. It opens staffers' eyes to the benefits of teamwork, especially in an environment in which people tend to do much work alone and can easily lose sight of the company's larger goals. Focusing on the ultimate customer and on defining and improving the processes for serving that customer shifts people's attention from an activity-based orientation to a results-based orientation. It makes possible voluntary resource sharing by breaking down the barriers that label resources "mine" or "yours." By challenging and changing people's thinking patterns, it leads to and supports creativity.

Because Treasury members spend so much of their time working individually, Sandy emphasizes training and awareness as important factors to help insure that all staffers continue to share a common language, goals, and technologies. Defining processes and taking the time to work with teams are additional work. It is important to make it clearly visible that these efforts produce better results than individual work under a non-Total Quality system.

The Treasury Mission Statement

To create a vision for the staff to work toward, in 1991 Sandy wrote the first draft of a mission statement for the Treasury Division. It derived from her cumulative experience in quality management, but, in the spirit of continuous improvement, Sandy points out that it is open to regular revision to increase its applicability, focus, and comprehensibility. Titled "Quality Statement," the current version reads:

The Treasury Division's strategy is to be perceived as a World Class provider of Quality Services, evidenced by:

- Feedback from customers on their satisfaction and their perception of value we add;

- Employee satisfaction and motivation;

- Benchmark comparisons with other World Class Treasury operations; and

- The outside world seeking us out as the best in Quality Treasury Operations.

We shall accomplish this through the following tactical plan:

- Customer requirements mutually agreed upon;

- Customer satisfaction assessed at least annually through surveys, interviews, focus groups, etc. Results used to improve processes and outcomes;

- All key processes documented. Control points established to assess quality prior to process completion;

- Key processes continually revised to improve cycle times, costs, and quality of results;

- KRIs track results and process variables. Other data (such as process control data) are tracked to identify trends and opportunities for improvement; and

- Our people are empowered, trained, developed, and motivated to contribute to their full potential. They are recognized and rewarded accordingly.

The Role of KRIs

Key Results Indicators play an important role in the linkage process within Corning's Treasury. KRIs are chosen to couple individual responsibilities: the intent is for it to be impossible for Treasury members to meet the KRI targets without cooperation. The KRIs must be broad enough measures to impact the company, yet narrow enough to direct individual actions.

There was no master plan in the development of Treasury's KRIs. Instead they were motivated by the requirement of the Ten Actions to measure and display performance data, and were originally derived about two years ago from the Baldrige Award criteria. Treasury's first goal was simply to measure process results. But as they examined possible candidates for KRIs, the staff found most to be narrow and trivial. Thinking back, Sandy says, "The KRIs became obvious when the alternatives were considered." Treasury settled on indices that directly measured each group's larger goals. However, the KRIs are still evolving, and the measures and their goals are "tweaked" quarterly.

Within Treasury, each group has its own KRIs, which are further detailed later in this case study. Cash Management and Corporate Finance measure net borrowing cost and failure to deliver cash. International Treasury's KRI is foreign exchange gains or losses. Risk Management and Prevention captures risk management costs and avoidable litigation expenses. Archives and Records Management tracks the cost of records maintenance and uses the six sigma system to measure on-time, error-free records delivery. Investor relations has two KRIs: number of institutional stockholders and Corning's price/earnings ratio. Investment Management uses investment performance and the funding of pension fund liabilities. Economic Planning and Research tracks forecast accuracy.

In 1992, Corning's Treasury began a move toward division-wide KRIs, numbers that could further integrate and summarize the entire treasury function's activities. Treasury is initiating a division-wide customer satisfaction KRI to measure, on an overall basis, how well its groups are meeting customer needs. This will be an aggregate of existing customer surveys throughout the Division, normalized to a 1–10 scale, and then averaged. Also under development is a division-wide process management KRI to capture how well Treasury processes have been brought "under management." Jim Chambers, assistant treasurer, has developed a worksheet listing key Treasury processes on one dimension and a scale showing the degree of Total Quality process management on the other. As now planned, each process will be rated as having achieved one of the following levels of Total Quality management:

- process mapped,

- process documented,

- key control points identified,

- process benchmarked,

- continuous improvement in place, and

- process under Total Quality management.

Treasury's goal is to have 90 percent of its processes "under management" by 1995.

Sandy Helton sees the desirability of a third division-wide KRI: a measure of the total impact of treasury operations on the company, perhaps the net cost of treasury activities. Her objective is to create a measure that goes beyond the concept of Treasury as a cost center, and captures, instead, the ability of the treasury function to contribute to Corning's profitability. As she currently conceives it, this index would aggregate four measures:

- Net borrowing costs: combining borrowing costs, earnings on short-term investments, and the cost of under-utilizing cash within the company by deploying it at rates of return below the cost of borrowing,

- Risk management costs: the total cost of managing the company's risk exposure, including direct insurance and hedging costs and also costs avoided by good risk management,

- Pension investment: the amount by which high portfolio earnings lowers the company's required current funding contribution, and

- The cost of the administrative staff.

Quality Initiatives in Finance

Each of the six groups reporting to Sandy Helton, Corning's treasurer, is deeply involved in the company's quality efforts. Each has learned to identify suppliers and customers and to view its work in process terms. Each is involved in the continuous improvement of those processes, the better to meet customer requirements. And each group uses one or more Key Results Indicators to capture its progress in increasing the quality of its operations.

Jim Chambers relates how the treasury function is changing under quality management.

> Previously the treasury group was a monopoly. The rest of the company had to take what we gave them. Now, we've moved from taking customers for granted to working with them to understand and fulfill their requirements.

One payoff: as Corning continues its strategy to create equity ventures, Treasury has begun providing consulting services to the subsidiaries, advice that yields financial benefits to the entity as well as to the parent company. SIECOR, a 50-50 equity venture with Siemens to produce fiber optic cable, provides an example. Although SIECOR has its own CFO and treasury staff, it turned to Jim and his group for analysis and advice that allowed it to reduce the cost and covenant requirements of its revolving credit line.

Cash Management

Corning now defines its requirements to banks in the same terms used for other suppliers. The company invites bankers to its Visitor Quality Orientation (VQO), where they learn of Corning's approach to Total Quality and what Corning expects from product and service providers. As Jim says, "It is resulting in 'bells going off.' Now they are using quality terminology and beginning to get some customer focus." The banks are invited to become partners in Corning's treasury processes to improve their service. For example, Citibank and Wachovia are now tailoring their cash management systems to tie into Corning's general ledger system. Corning gets the data in a form immediately useful, saving considerable rework. As a by-product, the banks are developing a heightened level of customer awareness and an expanded product line that they can sell to others.

Cash forecasting is an area in which Total Quality has enabled the treasury group to refocus its efforts. Previously a static reporting tool providing quarterly statements of cash balance, the cash forecast is changing to a proactive tool permitting Treasury to get better day-to-day guidance on cash needs. Jim's group is working to fold additional company activities into the model and says Total Quality's emphasis on breaking down barriers is making it easier to get information from sources not used to providing it. The cash forecast has now become accurate enough to be used as input to questions of commercial paper maturity and when borrowing maturities should be lengthened into long-term debt.

Shelf registration is one illustration of the progress Jim's group has made in framing their work in process terms. The number of people and organizations whose input and cooperation is required—internal counsel, controller, treasury, external auditors, outside counsel, investment bankers, underwriters' counsel—makes shelf registration a complex and time-consuming process. Some six years ago, Jim's (then Sandy's) staff began to work on defining and understanding the process steps; tasks, due dates, information flow, and critical path elements were studied. The result was a re-engineering of the flow, which eliminated many process steps, reduced cycle time, and eliminated last minute "chaos" in preparing materials. Both Corning and its outside advisors saved time and money while significantly shortening the process. Jim relates that investment bankers at Goldman, Sachs are impressed with the smoothness and efficiency of the process and report that they've "never seen anyone do this like you do."

Lindsay Brown, now director, Investment Services, describes a CAT to improve the accounting for cash operations on which he participated when he had responsibility for cash management. The old system was manually intensive, and focused the accounting staff on transactions processing instead of funding needs. Poor instructions led to many errors in data entry. There was too much rework. Yet the number of transactions was increasing with the growing complexity of

Corning's businesses. The team identified the impact of the existing system on each affected party, developed requirements, and purchased a new system that automated some 90 percent of daily transactions. The net result was sufficient work reduction to eliminate the equivalent of one person-job and permit staff members to be reassigned to more value-adding work. Where previously Lindsay had to meet with accounting every month to reconcile the cash accounts, this is no longer necessary. "These problems have gone away."

Cash Management has two KRIs to measure its objective: on-time delivery of cash at a world class cost. Cost is net borrowing cost as a percent of net borrowings based on a rolling four quarter average of interest expense less interest income. On-time delivery is captured by counting the number of times Treasury fails to deliver cash where and when needed. The cost goal is to be better than the average of the top quartile of Fortune 500 Single A companies; the on-time delivery goal is to have zero missed deliveries. Jim points out that the borrowing cost measure is a high impact index; it provides an external reference point in comparison to companies with similar bond ratings.

Jim observes that Total Quality has helped change the Treasury staff's thinking. Corning has traditionally been a conservative company, primarily financing long-term. As a result, it was slow to reduce the interest it was paying as rates declined over the last several years. Now, Treasury is more willing and able to be proactive in interest expense management. Longer term, Jim sees the need to refine the borrowing cost KRI to improve the way it joins Treasury activities, since some members find it difficult to relate their individual jobs to net borrowing cost. "We need to find out how to get more 'emotional attachment' to the KRI."

International Treasury

The work of Jim Wheat, assistant treasurer, International, provides an excellent example of how a process focus can drastically simplify activities and reduce costs. An important part of Jim's work is the foreign exchange payments mechanism, a process he has studied intensively. By reducing the frequency of purchasing foreign exchange to once per month, Corning now buys less currency in larger amounts on fewer occasions, saving from $1 million to $1.3 million per year in commissions.

Jim has identified that his group works on some 25–30 processes, has determined that 6 of those processes are key activities that should be documented, and has documented 3 of the 6 in the last year. He observes, "The more efficient you get, the more process documentation is needed because you leave less of an audit trail." He warns about limits to documentation: "Continuous improvement means our processes are changing regularly." And, "It's hard to document everything; we can document mechanical processes but often not thought processes, and expert systems are just too costly." In addition, like many successful executives, he has a predilection for action. "I'd prefer to do it rather than document it."

International Treasury has one KRI: foreign exchange gains or losses. Since Corning has chosen not to profit from its foreign exchange exposure, the goal is to have zero gain or loss after hedging costs. Through the first two quarters of 1992, foreign exchange gain/loss ran very close to zero.

Jim Wheat identifies that simplification of the foreign currency process has drastically simplified his job, permitting him to contribute to many more company activities. In a company with hundreds of millions of dollars of foreign transactions, Jim handles all the currency buys himself—taking only two to three hours each month.

Risk Management and Prevention

Peter Maier, director, Risk Management and Prevention, has largely redefined his job since Corning began to pursue Total Quality. Previously, his role was a buyer of insurance; today Peter defines his role and the service he directs as "risk management."

Peter's customers are Corning's operating units, each of which has its own risk profile. To gain a better understanding of the operating units' needs, his group has instituted routine meetings and other communication with its customers, jointly working to identify, clarify, and update their requirements. The group conducts systematic surveys to measure customer satisfaction and to identify opportunities for improvement.

Peter's team has worked equally hard to sensitize its suppliers to Corning's needs and to move them toward higher quality. The team arranges for the company's insurers and brokers to attend the Visitor Quality Orientation. They work with insurers to define Corning's requirements in terms of risk management and not just in terms of the product the insurer wishes to sell. Peter believes that without Total Quality, Corning would be far more vulnerable to its competition, and urges suppliers to join Corning in adopting quality management so they can "survive with us." Interestingly, he finds insurance brokers more adaptable to quality than the insurers themselves, perhaps because the brokers are more used to interacting with the insured as a customer.

Since 1990, the risk management and prevention team has identified and inventoried its key processes: risk identification, risk assessment, records management, and product liability management. Peter talks about "climbing inside processes" to understand and improve them. Among his group's successes are completely rebuilding their administrative data flow to eliminate duplicate files and installing process measurements, such as control logs, to reduce the cycle time from first awareness of a product liability claim to contacting the relevant attorneys, insurers, and plaintiffs. They are currently benchmarking how other companies handle workers' compensation and property insurance with a group of 30 risk managers.

Risk Management and Prevention has two KRIs: risk management costs, and avoidable litigation expenses. Risk management costs, including insurance premiums and self-insured losses, are measured as a percentage of sales. Avoidable litigation expenses are those on cases over $5,000 that would not have happened if all had gone 100 percent right. The goal is to reduce each over time. Currently, the risk management cost target is well below 1 percent of sales, and the goal is to push avoidable litigation expenses to nil.

Archives and Records Management, Peter's second function, has two KRIs of its own: on-time, error-free delivery of records, and the cost of records maintenance. Corning has applied Motorola's six sigma measurement system to records delivery and has set six sigma performance as its goal—no more than 3.4 errors per million deliveries of requested records. The goal for costs, including records creation, storage, retrieval, and final disposition, is a downward trend over time.

In reflecting on the impact of Total Quality on his area, Peter Maier points especially to the value of the risk management KRIs. By capturing key goals, they have led to a far more meaningful dialogue with Corning's insurance suppliers. Since these KRIs are not FASB or SEC focused, they have shifted the mindset of his staff away from rigid rules and toward their operating unit customers. As Peter observes,

> All too often, we measure the things that are easy, not the things that matter. The KRIs are useful in focusing our attention, communicating our goals and successes, and integrating the various activities of the department.

Investor Relations

Investor Relations conveys both strategic and financial information to financial analysts so they can accurately assess the company's market value. Steve Albertalli, vice president and director, Investor Relations,

identifies a good investor relations program as one marked by availability, listening, preparation, and credibility. While he constantly deals
with how much he can tell his customers—given the availability of
information, and legal and ethical boundaries—he wants to "leave
them all feeling they got the best information available."

For Steve, seeing his role in customer/supplier terms was natural.
He describes his work as "all customer contact," and treats not only the
analyst community as customers, but also Corning's top management as
he helps them represent the company. He works closely with Corning's
Corporate Communication division to coordinate the amount, kind, and
timing of information, as well as to share contacts and establish mutual
goals, so one group does not accidentally undercut the other. He main-
tains both formal and informal communication channels with his suppliers, the Corning operating units that provide the data and insights
necessary to tell the full story. He surveys his customers—both infor-
mally throughout the year and formally after the annual analysts meeting—to identify opportunities for better meeting their needs.

Consistent with the Total Quality focus on long-term survival, Steve
works to move the analyst community away from a short-term valuation
approach. He does this by putting events in strategic context and by acting as a teacher, helping analysts perform better analyses. For example,
he credits Corning's open lines of communication with investors and its
strategic contextualizing with supporting its stock price when the con-
troversy regarding the Dow Corning breast implant failures unfolded.
Institutional investors were well aware that Dow Corning was a distinct-
ly different company than Corning Incorporated. Although initially
Corning's stock price fell severely, the fall was only temporary due to
the effective communications network Steve had put in place.

In addition to his long-established customer orientation, Steve has
begun to see his work in process terms. He has documented the process
of writing and approving a press release. He conceptualizes the annual
analysts meeting as another process, has begun to document it, and uses
past meeting analyst surveys for improving the meeting from year to
year. He is part of a team documenting and improving the preparation
of the annual report, in which he has become the "tone-setter."

Investor relations has two KRIs: number of institutional stockholders and Corning's price/earnings ratio. Corning wishes to ensure a
diverse ownership that will support the company's long-term quality
focus. The initial goal was for more than 200 institutional investors to
own not more than 55 percent of outstanding shares and to increase

the number of institutional owners over time. Today, nearly 350 institutions include Corning common in their portfolios. The P/E target is measured relative to the P/E ratio of the S+P 500. Corning's goal is to maintain a P/E ratio that is aggressive when compared with the company's peer group and competitive companies. Originally the target was a P/E equal to that of the index, but Corning achieved that level easily, saw it as being only average, and "raised the bar" for the company's performance. The P/E target is not static, but is regularly revised to reflect changes in market and peer company conditions.

Steve Albertalli identifies the need to continue to refine his KRIs and customer surveys as Corning learns more about itself and how to implement Total Quality. He is looking to increase the frequency of formal measurement of analysts' satisfaction from once per year after the annual meeting. With his colleagues, he is rethinking the institutional stockholder KRI, wondering if his ability to stay in close contact with key investors might be enhanced if Corning's stock were held by a more moderate number of institutions with somewhat larger holdings. He is also studying how to connect the P/E KRI to Corning's growth rate and other underlying fundamental variables, rather than target for a fixed percentage over the S+P 500.

Investment Management

Lindsay Brown, director, Investment Services, can see the change in his group's suppliers since Corning began to bring them into its quality processes. Now, he says,

> The investment managers are more willing to give Corning what we want rather than what they have to sell. They are asking us if we would be interested in their designing new fund options. They are much more prone to figure out how to solve a problem than simply say "I can't do it."

An important current area for Lindsay's group is asset allocation—the desire to move toward a more proactive investment approach using real-time data. At present, they typically get month-end master trustee information that arrives one-half month later. They are working with their suppliers to ask what they must know or have to make the shift toward real-time reporting.

Investment Services is applying Total Quality to the difficult decision of how to select, evaluate, and, if necessary, terminate a fund manager. Lindsay points out that, as the funds' customer, Corning makes the decision about investment management style (value, growth, small cap, nifty-50, etc.). Accordingly, he begins manager selection with an analysis of the fund's ability to respond to Corning's needs. Measurement requires good data and consistency in its application. "It's important not to change rules during the game," he observes. Lindsay's staff measures managers according to the managers' own goals and against others in the same market sector. Corning will not terminate a manager for one or two bad quarters. And, as he has found, "Good manager selection criteria make termination decisions easier." He is now enhancing the data base on manager performance to improve the fund manager rating process.

Investment Management has two KRIs to capture investment performance and the funding of pension fund liabilities. Funding is measured by the ratio of the market value of pension assets to actuarial pension liabilities. The performance measure is the rate of return on the investment portfolio. Corning's long-term goals are to fund its pension liabilities fully and to generate returns in the top quartile of large pension funds over a three-to-five year period.

Like other Treasury members, Lindsay is working to improve his KRIs. He is testing several alternative performance measures over various time horizons using both gross returns and returns net of fees. The funding KRI's original target was 75 percent, but was raised when the 75 percent coverage ratio was reached. Rather than pick a specific number as the next target, he is looking to integrate pension funding with cash management to prevent optimizing pension funding at the expense of a higher cost of corporate cash.

Economic Planning and Research

Satinder Mullick, director, Economic Planning and Research, sees his role as providing insights into the future to improve decision making. His forecasts help to identify opportunities for strategic repositioning and profit improvement.

Satinder identifies three groups of customers. For senior management, he forecasts sales and profit margins. For purchasing, he forecasts commodities prices and advises on the timing of purchases. For Treasury, he forecasts interest rates. He spends only about 10 percent of his time forecasting overall company performance; the remaining 90 percent is devoted to special projects.

Satinder regularly surveys his customers to learn how he can better serve them with different data, different presentations, etc. He uses Total Quality to understand the process of forecasting so he can leverage his work by systematically applying his forecasting knowledge from one area to another. He is also active nationally with other professional economists. As a benchmarking activity, he recently participated in a study sponsored by AT&T to identify the state-of-the-art in business forecasting.

Prior to Corning's use of quality management, Satinder's forecasts were not a part of the MIS system. They were driven by accounting and finance needs. His reports were kept in those areas, and his forecasts were easily ignored. Today, his forecasts and analyses are part of the corporate data system and are available to all users in both numerical and graphical form.

Economic Planning and Research currently has one KRI: the accuracy of sales and operating margin forecasts. Actual sales and margins are compared with Satinder's prior year's December forecast. The goal is to forecast sales within 2 percent of actual and operating profit margin within 7.5 percent of actual. Since 1985, when this KRI was started, Satinder has been within these ranges. Satinder realizes that his KRI is only tested once a year and is working on ways to increase the measurement frequency.

Results for the Finance Function and the Company

A major pay-off for Treasury's, and the rest of Finance's, commitments to systematic quality improvement has been the change in how finance members see themselves and their roles in the company: how they do their day-to-day work. Although still separated by individual work responsibilities, finance members now understand they are part of a larger team, with common goals and the need to collaborate in reaching them. Their extensive quality training has enabled them to work together through the sharing of a language, work methodology, and common concerns. They have developed a "can do" attitude that has translated directly into higher levels of performance and considerably more "joy in work." As Van Campbell says:

> The quality process makes people think about staff and other activities as businesses. They recognize that error-free work is everybody's job. Everyone in the company comes to believe his or her input can make a difference. People think and, in particular, work together differently.

> The approach in finance does not look any different from the approach anywhere else. But in finance it is a big mental shift. We really are a supplier. We really do have customers. We are not here just doing whatever we do because we think it is the right thing to do. We do it because our customers tell us it helps them do their jobs. And we keep making

significant improvements as we focus on processes and ask who are we doing it for, map the processes, find where the errors take place, set performance goals, and measure the results. It is a big shift, yet now that we do it, it seems pretty straight-forward. It is hard to imagine not doing our work this way.

Quality has become a way of life for Corning Finance. Staff members have learned to see their work as a set of processes targeted toward customer needs to be continually improved through better definition, documentation, and measurement. They are actively looking at new ways to do their jobs and are developing new quality measurements as they better understand the company's capabilities and the linkages among people and processes. The increased customer awareness of the Finance staff is also being picked up by Finance's suppliers. Bankers, insurance brokers, Corning divisions, and others are enabling Finance to do its job better, faster, and more economically by being more willing and able to understand and meet Finance's needs.

Although attempts to use the cost of quality as a measure and tool are less frequent than a decade ago when Corning embarked on this part of its quality journey, the concept is still used at times to estimate the pay-off from the company's quality efforts. Tom Blumer, previously director, quality management, estimated that in the early 1980s, cost of quality was running about 35 percent of all costs. In September 1991, he estimated that it had been reduced to 20–25 percent. Sandy Helton expects the next wave of improvements will be more difficult to achieve as systematic Total Quality is further applied to knowledge-based activities such as judgment, decision-making, and strategic thinking to produce an "organizational expert system."

The lean Treasury function, and similar efficiencies elsewhere in finance, are direct bottom-line payoffs for Corning's investments in quality. By working to improve its financial processes, Corning has understood them, simplified them, sped them up, and increased their reliability. Treasury is better able to measure the performance of its functions and, through its benchmarking activities, compare itself to the best in the world. This has included progress in reducing financing costs and maintaining independence from stock market vagaries and hostile investors. Improved processes in each of Treasury's major areas of activity allow high quality work to be accomplished with low administrative costs. Increased earnings come directly from better cash management, lower risk management costs, better forecasting, and so on.

As Sandy Helton observes,

> Quality is now an essential part of managing Treasury. It is neither easy to conceptualize nor to implement at many junctures. But the payoffs are very real, and have gone directly to the bottom line. Quality helped focus us on the things that allow us to contribute more to the organization: net borrowing costs, risk management costs, and especially people management—empowerment and skills development. It created a language and approach for talking with outsiders—bankers and insurance brokers—that has brought value back to the company. We'll never know if the financial benefits we see are directly due to quality, or would have happened anyway, but there is a feeling around here that we got there much faster through our quality programs.

People Interviewed

Steve Albertalli, Vice President and Director of Investor Relations
Lindsay Brown, Director, Investment Services
Van Campbell, Vice Chairman
Jim Chambers, Assistant Treasurer
Bill Felthousen, Manager of Quality Management
Carol Griffith, Quality Manager–Finance and Administration
Sandy Helton, Vice President and Treasurer
Peter Maier, Director, Risk Management and Prevention
Satinder Mullick, Director, Economic Planning and Research
Jim Wheat, Assistant Treasurer, International

Fordham Student Research Team

Cathy Borzon, case assistant

"Corelle" and "Steuben" are registered trademarks of Corning Incorporated.

Federal Express

Federal Express is making significant progress in finding new ways for corporate finance to support other parts of the company. In doing so, the roles of finance members are changing—from judge and police to team member and coach. Corporate finance has developed its Business Case Approach into a broad and holistic method of project analysis and evaluation that improves the quality of decision-making, brings finance members into the project analysis process at the beginning, and provides a vehicle for assuming finance's new roles.

A new financial information system, nicknamed ELVIS, empowers individuals throughout the company to get more involved in financial analysis and frees up the finance staff to make additional contributions. Both the Business Case Approach and ELVIS are part of Finance's efforts to distribute financial skills throughout the company to bring financial analysis and decision-making closer to the data—and closer to both internal and external customers.

Federal Express's quality management system goes back to the beginning of the company and its emphasis on three pillars of tqm: people, customers, and measurement. Although elements of tqm can be traced to earlier activities, a good dating of the start of systematic quality efforts in finance is 1983. That year, financial managers visited Intel and then led a team that applied Intel's fast cycle approach to improving the efficiency of their building's mail room. Success with this test of a team-based quality improvement approach led to a variety of other initiatives including extensive use of service quality indicators to measure finance's success in meeting customer expectations and improving its processes.

Like the CFOs of many companies that are quality leaders, Federal Express' CFO is convinced that quality in its various manifestations (reliability, short cycle time, customer satisfaction, etc.) has been the key to Federal Express' survival and success. For Federal Express, well-recognized payoffs include major competitive advantages, significant improvements in internal processes, an enhanced ability of finance "to do its job" of contributing to the organization, and the increasing ability of the rest of the organization "to do finance's job."

B

Federal Express

We went into elaborate detail—trying to understand what a mis-sort costs us. In the process of this investigation, the finance staff started to move from saying "We will only count it if you can prove it," to putting much more devotion into quantifying soft benefits. And, today you are much more likely to hear a finance person say: "I can't prove it, but I think it is the right thing to do."

—Debra Gray, Managing Director,
Financial Planning Customer/Systems Support

Federal Express has worked on a variety of approaches to prevent the routing of packages to the wrong location, an event called a "mis-sort." In 1988 the company initiated a project to eliminate mis-sorts 100 percent by providing each package with an optically readable label at the point of pickup. The label would contain key address, routing, and other information to be used as the package moved from the "sending customer" to the "receiving customer." A new technique, called the Business Case Approach (BCA), was used to analyze this otherwise traditional type of quality improvement project.

Debra Gray, managing director, Financial Planning Customer/Systems Support, describes the business case approach as a way to build continuing financial analysis into a project rather than merely doing it at the end and to uncover the project's

. . . ramifications on the whole organization. We have been able to use BCA to help us focus on the important issues, to quantify not only costs but also benefits, and to force the company to look, look, look, and look again at what is going to happen with a given project or system. And we can use that to mold what we are going to do in the future.

The project led to the decision to implement a new labeling system, called "ASTRA." Significant improvements in the mis-sort situation were realized even before ASTRA could be implemented due to the findings in the process. Perhaps as important, it continued a trend in the finance organization of working with the rest of the company more as consultants, partners, and facilitators rather than as judges, controllers, and police officers. It also led to a new ability and willingness to quantify the value of improvements in quality.

Federal Express' attempts to eliminate mis-sorts in the late 1980s were consistent with its commitment to customer satisfaction from the company's beginnings in 1973. In perhaps the best known "low quality" Yale term paper ever, Frederick W. Smith outlined a concept for a new company and a new industry. Although the 1965 paper earned only a "C," the company Smith subsequently founded earned $115 million and the Malcolm Baldrige National Quality Award in 1990. Along the way it created a new industry, achieved sales of over $7.5 billion in 1992 and created jobs for more than 90,000 employees.

Federal Express' pioneering of the overnight air-express package industry and its success in achieving on-time delivery has made "Fedex" an everyday name in the business world. When Federal Express became the first service company winner of the Malcolm Baldrige National Quality Award in 1990, attention was called to the company's commitment to quality and the systems that made the commitment a reality.

In this case profile we start by describing how the company formalized and improved its quality systems, and how the finance function adopted the company's quality initiatives, is being changed by them, and is adding its own flavor and ingredients to the total mix. We describe three aspects of finance's work in quality: the use of Service Quality Indicators (SQIs) in finance, the development of a method of financial analysis that attempts to take a broader and more holistic view of a project and its total impact on the organization than traditional project analysis, and the development of a financial information system to encourage and support individuals anywhere in the organization in analyzing the financial and business implications of current performance, proposed actions, or changes in business situations. Finally, we report the benefits Federal Express is earning on its investments in quality.

Federal Express' Quality Journey

Federal Express' quality journey can be seen as having had two phases: first, the pursuit of a quality management system without calling it by that name, and second, a more formal and conscious attempt to build upon, extend, and systematize the company's quality efforts. In this perspective, Federal Express built much of its quality system without a formal plan, simply by seeking to be excellent. It then added the rest "by design" as it attempted to achieve consistency and integration among the elements of a quality system that had emerged in various parts of the company, to incorporate into that system the emerging discoveries and tools of the quality management movement, and to use the language of quality management to describe and communicate its quality system.

The Foundations of Federal Express' Quality Management System

Federal Express' quality management system rests on three premises relating to people, customers, and measurement. All three can be traced back to the company's earliest days and to Fred Smith's personal beliefs and commitments. In pursuing those premises, Federal Express built up the key elements of a strong quality management system well before starting to call it by such a name.

People: Federal Express' early emphasis on people is picked up in three closely related themes connecting employees to customer service. One theme is caught in the phrases "people-service-profit (P-S-P)" and "putting people first." In the "people-service-profit" phrase, the company recognizes that revenues and profits are the result of excellence in service, which in turn comes from committed, trained people—properly supported and motivated. Profit is recognized as necessary for survival, as a way of measuring successful performance, and as the means for rewarding investors. But the causal chain is seen as starting with the people in the company. People come first because they create the service, which in turn creates the profits necessary for survival.

"People come first" in still another, and perhaps more important, way: Federal Express' commitments to personal growth and training, to fair treatment of all employees, and to providing secure employment mean that its employees are treated as ends in themselves and not just as means to an end. For example, call center agents are given six weeks of intensive training before they take customer calls. Every year, couriers, service agents, and customer service agents are reexamined on their job knowledge, with retraining or updating immediately provided to those who could benefit from it.

A second people-related theme emphasizes that employees need to be treated well if they are to treat customers well. It is caught in the phrase "satisfied customers come from satisfied employees."

The third theme, "quality is everybody's business," captures the reality that poor customer service can result from a failure anywhere throughout the company. Providing high quality service to customers is a company-wide process, not something just for managers and not just for part of the company to pursue and achieve.

Customers: From the beginning, Fred Smith and other company leaders emphasized the need to achieve the "impossible objective" of on-time delivery every time. The phrase "absolutely, positively" emerged later (in 1978), but the commitment to seek error-free operations in all aspects of the business was present from the start. This commitment, and goal, has been phrased repeatedly as "100 percent customer satisfaction."

Measurement: A popular company saying has long been "If you can't measure it, you can't manage it." Over the years, Federal Express developed a series of measurements of its success in treating its people well and in satisfying customers. In 1980, Federal Express took a major step in measuring the people dimension by developing the leadership section of the Survey-Feedback-Action (SFA) process. In 1988 it took a similar step on the customer side with its Service Quality Indicator (SQI).

Survey-Feedback-Action: In 1978 Federal Express started surveying its employees to measure how well they felt they were being managed. Once a year each employee is asked to complete a survey-feedback-action scale, a 29 item questionnaire in which each employee rates the company as a place to work, its top management, and the employee's immediate manager. Employees' ratings of their managers are aggregated anonymously and fed back to their managers in the SFA process.

Over the years, SFA has come to be used in three ways to improve the quality of managerial leadership and, in turn, employee performance and satisfaction: organizational diagnosis, organizational and individual manager improvement, and compensation. As a tool of organizational diagnosis, the scale is analyzed to identify areas of managerial weakness, either in Federal Express as a whole or in a specific unit of the company. To encourage organizational and managerial improvement, individual managers also receive the overall company and divisional results of the survey, including the aggregated results of the ratings of their own leadership. They then meet with their work groups to develop action plans for improving any problem areas with their own leadership or with organizational issues the group can deal with. As a compensation tool, the first ten questions of the survey comprise a measure called the "Leadership Index" which is tied to incentive compensation through the company's management by objectives (MBO) goal setting process.

Measuring Service Quality: In support of the PSP philosophy, the Federal Express management system has developed a single company-wide "Service Quality Indicator" to assist in measuring and improving its performance for external customers. The SQI is a summary of twelve indices of company performance that is calculated and reported every day and is built into all bonus systems. This very important service measurement and its offspring for measuring service to internal customers are discussed in detail in the section on "Service Quality Indicators" below.

The people–customer–measurement foundations of Federal Express' quality management system were supported by a variety of consultants, training programs, cross-functional management meetings, and by the use of sophisticated information technology, in both running the business and for communications within the company. An early use of consultants was to support Federal Express' efforts to improve productivity and quality. The consulting organizations introduced several different ways of approaching the pursuit of quality and a number of different terminologies for basic quality concepts. Among the influential consultants were Deming, Crosby, and ODI (Organizational Dynamics Incorporated) whose program was known as "Making Things Better."

In 1984 statistical process control (SPC) was first introduced into the emerging quality training programs with a series of one- to-three day sessions for top managers and others. This program turned out to be useful for a few managers who had strong grounding in a variety of quality concepts, but for most who had not had sufficient exposure to quality concepts, it was premature and too theoretically oriented. Some top managers left the program with serious doubts about the applicability of SPC, a conclusion that probably slowed adoption of those techniques by a number of years.

Cross-functional management emerged in a number of ways, particularly visible at the daily 8:30 A.M. operations meeting in which division representatives discuss major operational problems from the previous 24 hours. In a worldwide conference call, the group determines who will attack each problem and how it will be done. Action plans are due by the next day's meeting.

Federal Express became a leader in using computer-based information technology to run its business and to communicate throughout the company. It later developed a satellite-linked television network, FXTV, for training, sharing major meetings, and phone-in question and answer sessions with top officers and experts on special topics.

Formalizing the Process: A Quality System "by Design"

By the mid-1980s most of the elements of Federal Express' current quality system were in place as part of its overall management approach. Some pieces were initially driven by the pursuit of productivity, but by 1986 the connection between quality and productivity started to become clear. This connection was recognized in a new phrase: "Q equals P"—quality equals productivity. Looking back, Chauncey Burton, Senior Quality Administrator, Finance, suggests the Q=P equation is a good benchmark for the start of the formalization phase of Federal Express' quality journey. In that phase, Federal Express started to formalize, integrate, and re-label what it was doing in the mid-1980s.

One of the first steps was to select one major consultant to standardize the company's framework for defining its quality system, the language it would use in defining and communicating about quality, and the techniques and training programs it would implement. The company selected ODI to help it carry the work to the next stage, in part because of its past successful experiences with ODI, and perhaps in part because ODI was perceived as having a strong "people orientation" that fit well with Federal Express' philosophy.

Training programs were extended and focused more specifically and formally around classic quality concepts like quality improvement teams (which became known as Quality Action Teams (QATs), pronounced "kwats"), quality improvement processes, and building customer/supplier relationships (which evolved into a widely used process called "customer/supplier alignment").

The organization structure to support the quality efforts was augmented by forming an Executive Quality Board and a Quality Advisory Board, by staffing full-time quality professionals in all divisions of the company, and by developing a group of part-time facilitators (quality champions) to work with the growing number of QATs. The Quality Advisory Board consists of full-time quality administrators and facilitators, and the Executive Quality Board is composed of corporate vice presidents and managing directors representing all divisions.

When Federal Express received its site visit by the Baldrige examiners in 1990, one of the examiners' strongest impressions was how much of Federal Express' winning quality management system had been in place for many years, well grounded in the 1973 roots of the company.

Finance Begins to Do Quality Management

Federal Express' initial tqm efforts within the Finance Division involved clerical activities and financial operations such as invoicing and collecting receivables. In 1981, ODI initiated its "Making Things Better" program in the vendor services, customer service, and credit and collections areas. The intent was to involve employees in examining their work processes by grouping them into teams. This was the first time members of the finance staff had been asked to study business processes in a systematic way. By today's standards, the program was rudimentary: although processes were studied, no particular attention was paid to the customers of those processes. The focus was on productivity—how to speed up paying bills, collections, payroll, etc. The program was somewhat successful, reducing the time to do routine tasks. A second, and perhaps more important outcome was the leadership training and experience gained by team members, many of whom subsequently earned promotion to the professional ranks. Chauncey Burton identifies the Making Things Better project as the first use of QATs in the finance division.

In 1983 Mike Dale, then senior manager of productivity improvement, and Martha Thomas, then a newly appointed manager in vendor services (accounts payable), attended a presentation at Intel, at the time a recognized leader in employee involvement activities. Upon their return, Mike and Martha worked with a team to improve efficiency in her department's mail room based on the "fast cycle" concept they learned at Intel. Using flowcharts to diagram the mail sorting and delivery process, the team discovered that while sorting the mail was relatively efficient, mail delivery took an excessive amount of time. The team relocated the mail room near the rest rooms and break room; with staff members passing the mail room several times each day, mail delivery was no longer necessary. As a result, the mail room staff could be reduced from four full-time employees to one person working four hours per day.

Relative to the clerical and operations staff, finance's professional staff members were much slower to get involved in systematic quality improvement efforts. The finance professionals, feeling pressure to work longer hours, concluded there was no extra time available to pursue quality, let alone be trained in it. But there were other, equally important reasons for their initial reluctance. The professional staff had a deeply ingrained culture that defined how they saw themselves and therefore how they responded to change. Better educated than the clerical and operations staffs, they were more skeptical by nature, saying: "What do you mean quality training? I know about quality. I'm already well trained." "Prove it to me." "Let me see it work somewhere else, then I'll try it." They were also skeptical about the worth of "structured" quality, unwilling to endorse a program in which the costs stood out but benefits were difficult to quantify. This reluctance was reinforced by the perception that quality in the Finance Division was high already—they were already doing a high-quality job.

Perhaps the greatest cultural barrier was a feeling shared by professional finance staff members that they played a very special role in the organization. Because of their responsibility for assuring that funds were allocated properly and the exposure to other parts of the organization their work provided, many felt they played a key role in seeing "the big picture" for the company and assuring responsible action. Tqm, different in approach from the traditional finance methods used by the staff, was therefore automatically suspect, especially since it talked of pushing decision-making authority "down" to "lower levels" of the organization. As Martha Thomas remarked, "Like finance people in other organizations at that time, we thought we were the only adults in the company."

Reasons for Successful Implementation

The success of the quality program in the Finance Division was based upon five factors: leadership, training, focusing on "small wins," focusing on processes, and recognition.

First, the leadership of Fred Smith and other senior officers sent a clear signal that finance members were expected to be active players in the quality movement. This leadership was supported by the company's emerging quality culture. As Alan Graf, now Senior Vice President and CFO, said about his arrival in the company in January 1980,

> From the first day I came into this company, I was inundated with quality. We did not call it that. What we said was that we cannot have any failures; we have got to have 100% reliability in everything we do. Nobody ever said 99; nobody ever said 98.

Second, it became mandatory that all finance members be trained in the concepts and tools of quality. Training was done from the top of the organization chart down, with senior management first training middle managers, and then middle managers training their staff. While professional quality facilitators were available at times, this was considered a luxury; most training was on a one-to-one, manager-to-employee basis. Thus, middle management became the division's change agents, converting their staff to the quality concept. All managers at every level were expected to "walk and talk quality every day."

The third success factor was a focus on small, incremental successes. There was no push to solve all the company's problems overnight. In recounting this approach, Debra Gray uses a baseball metaphor: "We were taught to attempt base hits rather than home runs because you are less likely to strike out that way."

Fourth, management, and the quality training, made it clear that staff were to focus on processes, rather than specific outcomes, or the "fire of the moment." Some processes became apparent immediately, such as the processing of a travel expense report, the paying of an account payable, or the cutting of a paycheck. Other processes, such as capital expense approval, became visible much later. Looking at processes made it clear that quality efforts would have to be cross functional, and this perspective began to break down the barriers that had separated the finance staff from the rest of the organization.

Finally, finance management quickly understood that successes had to be recognized and shared if the program were to succeed. Appropriate recognition and rewards would raise and maintain the level of motivation to pursue tqm. The staff would see quality success as a legitimate, and perhaps *the*, path to promotion and salary increases.

Service Quality Indicators

As noted above, Federal Express has developed a company-wide system called service quality indicators (SQIs) for measuring its progress in quality improvement. SQIs measure the number of times the company fails to satisfy a customer. Federal Express' goal is to approach an SQI of zero, as indicated by Fred Smith's charge to the company:

> Our service standard is 100% plus. 98% or 99% may be fine for other human endeavors. Our chosen profession is not among them. Our customers expect faultless service . . . all the time.

Unlike companies that measure defects as a percentage of opportunities for error—such as Motorola with its six sigma system—Federal Express measures the absolute number of errors it makes. Debra Gray relates why:

> We deliver over 1.5 million packages a night. Even a one% failure rate is a big deal, so we started measuring in absolute points.

In 1983, the Customer Service department began to compile its "hierarchy of horrors," a list of the service failures most critical to Federal Express' customers. As quality became more organized throughout the company, the hierarchy of horrors was updated to become a numerical index of customer satisfaction. Known as the company-wide Service Quality Indicator, it begins with the twelve most critical failures, each with a point score indicating its importance to customers. (Table B.1)

Each day, the total number of service failures is compiled into the SQI score, in which each failure is multiplied by its customer importance weight, and the weighted failures are then summed. The previous day's score and its trend are posted prominently throughout the company so all employees can see Federal Express' latest performance,

TABLE B.1 **Components of the Company-Wide Service Quality Indicator**

Indicator	Weight
Abandoned calls	1
Complaints reopened	5
Damaged packages	10
International	1
Invoice adjustments requested	1
Lost packages	10
Missed pick-ups	10
Missing proofs of delivery	1
Overgoods (lost and found)	5
Right day late deliveries	1
Traces	1
Wrong day late deliveries	5

as well as its progress toward reducing the SQI over time. Company-wide goals for the SQI are set on a semiannual basis, and Federal Express has established an intermediate term goal to cut the average daily SQI by a factor of 10. Ultimately the company is aiming for Fred Smith's goal of zero failures.

Service Quality Indicators for Finance

Soon after the implementation of the primary SQI for external customers, top management asked each area of the company to develop comparable measures of failure to meet the requirements of their customers. In response, various finance division units have developed their own SQIs using the company-wide SQI process as a model. As in the rest of Federal Express, these SQIs are used to maintain a focus on satisfying one's customers, to set goals for quality improvements, to encourage the formation and focus the work of QATs, to monitor progress on improvement efforts, and to provide a quality-based metric for incentive compensation and other rewards.

Michael Babineaux, senior procurement specialist, relates how his area began with a 12 question survey given to internal customers for whom purchasing buys. The results were eye opening, as purchasing's customers identified areas of poor performance, and led to a set of 10 SQIs for procurement:

- On-time delivery—receipt of materials on the correct dock on the correct date.

- Error-free receipts—zero discrepancies at the receiving location.

- Zero invoice discrepancies—every invoice payable upon receipt.

- Quality assurance compliance—all documents covered by the company's quality assurance program.

- Zero upward pricing actions—no unjustified materials price increases.

- Inventory requisition turn time—number of days for order placement on repetitive buys.

- Non-inventory requisition turn time—number of days for order placement on non-repetitive buys.

- Invoice discrepancy aging—number of days discrepant invoices remain unpaid.

- Annual negotiated cost savings—negotiated price reductions times annual usage.

- Purchase order documentation/authorization compliance—percentage of purchase orders authorized and documented.

These 10 quantified measures are supplemented by a set of subjective inputs including comments from buyers, supplier responsiveness and attitude, and the availability of needed materials and supplier representatives.

Don Daniell, manager, International Financial Controls, identified how his area produces a monthly international financial quality indicator report consisting of three groups of SQIs:

- SQIs that quantify and score accounting errors, such as out of balance inter- or intracompany accounts, out-of-period adjustments, post-close journal vouchers, and unexplained variances,

- SQIs that measure performance of cash collections activities, and

- SQIs that measure noncompliance with internal control systems.

Don reports that a QAT recently developed an online "variance explanation system" in which finance personnel can enter the reasons for trend and budget variances and can receive feedback from corporate headquarters much faster than when the analysis of variances was transmitted on paper.

Martha Thomas, now senior manager, Vendor Services/Finance, has a similar set of SQIs based on surveys of her customers. These include:

- Lack of prompt response time to suppliers' phone inquiries,

- Turnaround longer than one day on properly prepared expense reports, check requests, petty cash requests, and cash advances, and

- Failure to process supplier payments promptly or without error.

Other SQIs have been formulated by the controller's area, in particular with respect to book closing time, errors in journal entries, etc.

Mis-sorts, The Business Case Approach, and Quantifying Soft Benefits

The Federal Express project to eliminate mis-sorts and the business case approach applied to the project illustrate at least five aspects of tqm's increasing influence on how business is conducted in Federal Express' finance function—and how the finance function is influencing the company's pursuit of quality and customer satisfaction.

First, it illustrates how finance is becoming part of problem-solving teams from the beginning of the work, and is adding the financial dimension during the design of a project rather than merely quantifying the project's implications after the design is complete.

Second, in the same vein, it illustrates ways in which the work and roles of finance people are becoming more consultative, facilitative, and team oriented, and less judge, controller, and police officer oriented.

Third, it provides an example of how the company is seeking to make its financial analysis and decision-making processes less narrowly finance-focused and more effective in capturing the total corporate impact of a project.

Fourth, it shows how the finance division is "distributing" its skills throughout the organization. In the business case approach, finance is working to improve the ability of other organization members to make two of finance's historically particularly valuable contributions: the taking of a broad organizational view in analyzing projects and the use of the "tool box" of financial analytical techniques to conduct logical and organized analyses.

Fifth, it illustrates some of finance's attempts to move forward in learning how to quantify previously unquantified data, especially data related to quality, and to provide a means to address unquantifiable impacts during the decision-making process.

The Business Case Approach

The Business Case Approach (BCA) is a process for analyzing projects likely to have an impact throughout the company. The approach emphasizes a broad company-wide focus rather than a narrow financial or departmental one and the building of a team bringing diverse perspectives, including the financial perspective, into the analysis at early stages. Most of the financial analysis takes place during a series of iterations as the project concept and design evolve rather than at the end when the project design has been completed. Along the way, financial models of the project and its implications are assembled, so that the iterations may be analyzed as alternative approaches. The BCA process does not end when a completed proposal is presented to senior management or when senior management makes its decision on the project. Instead, the modeling and documentation developed during the design process are retained. If the project is accepted, implementation alternatives can then be reconsidered at key decision points. For example, procedural steps can be modified based on test results or contracts can be restructured before execution as information on equipment reliability becomes available. If, on the other hand, the project is rejected, the BCA modeling provides a means to reconsider the original proposal or other ones as new technological and market information becomes available.

The Business Case Approach to the ASTRA Project

ASTRA (Advanced Sorting Tracking Routing Assistance), the new package labeling system, grew out of a study to eliminate mis-sorts, the accidental sending of packages to the wrong location. This study provided one of the first opportunities to apply the BCA to a large quality improvement project.

In discussing finance's role in the ASTRA project, Debra Gray remarked:

> One of the things we are most proud of is our role in the project. I would guess there were 50 or 60 people who worked on ASTRA at one point or another. We had one financial person leading, and had some supporting analysts involved. To gather the information we needed from other divisions we would go out and selectively involve financial analysts to help us with certain pieces. But frankly, the financial role became a real coordination and communication function for the whole process. Everybody's information was an input to some parts of the analysis and an output to others. We coordinated the data gathering, data simulation, financial projections, and then communication of those results outward. We really became a central point for the total process.

In the business case approach there are six processes that must occur to bring a project into being. The team assembled to perform the analysis must:

- identify the objective of the expenditure,

- test the technical feasibility of the project,

- design the details of the project,

- develop financial projections,

- gain approval, and

- support implementation.

Identifying the objective: In describing the process, Phil King, then manager, information systems and telecommunications-finance, began by observing that,

> Identifying the objective of the project may seem obvious, but it is very important to the rest of the process, particularly at the point of selecting alternatives. The ASTRA project was one part of a series of iterative processes to remove all delivery errors.
>
> In the case of ASTRA, we were trying to address how to prevent a mis-sorted package. What are the various types of mis-sorts and how can we eliminate all of them?

In the existing process, the courier would enter the zip code and type of package into the "Supertracker," a small hand held electronic scanner that contained an algorithm to determine the optimal route from package origin to destination.

> The Supertracker would designate "the package needs to go to the OLV station." The courier would then take out a black magic marker and write OLV on the box. As you might imagine, when he has 20 packages to pick up before customers close, and has to get back to the station to meet the truck that meets the airplane bound for Memphis, his writing can get sloppy and his OLV may look like an OLU to someone else. All of a sudden this package can be off to another part of the country because the courier was a little rushed with his penmanship.

The ASTRA proposal involved having the first person to handle the shipment apply a machine-generated label to the package. The label would contain machine and person-readable destination, routing, and other information. These data would reduce sorting errors by allowing the label to be scanned at various decision points in the routing process. For example, a package would be scanned prior to placing it in a shipping container bound for a specific destination.

> If a courier or loader is about to put a package in the wrong container bound for the wrong destination, the scanner will beep to say "you are about to make a mistake." The only way we can prevent a mis-sort is to highlight the error before the mistake is made. We wanted to be sure that 100% of the time, every time a package changes hands, it goes in the right direction to the right destination.

Testing technical feasibility: Once the objective is clearly defined, the project team looks at the technical feasibility of alternative solutions. Federal Express had been looking at the possibility of applying address labels for quite some time, but the technology was not available.

We had to have the capability for the courier to put a machine-generated and machine-readable label on every package. We had to have the bar code technology, the thermal printing technology, and the battery technology all in a light, portable package. A few years ago, a printer with all those features would have been so cumbersome that the couriers couldn't have carried it.

We consider the feasibility of different technologies. We design the system, design the hardware, and design the process. We look at how it is going to operate. What does it do for the company? What do the couriers have to do differently? Concurrently, we develop financial projections. The financial projections can change the technical solution; they can change the design; they can change the operating procedures. Through this iterative process, we try to get the best technical solutions. In the next stage we can try to "tweak" the way we implement the system to get the best benefit for all involved. This is more of an iterative process (than a linear one) and it sometimes takes months.

Designing the details:

Once we have a technology that is feasible, we have to do a detailed design. What is the best bar code to use? What is the best way to present it on the package so that it is easily readable? What is the best way to orient the label? What is going to look best to our customers? How does the Supertracker talk to the printer? We even looked at how the printer should be shaped to make it easiest to use for the couriers.

As these things are being worked out in the design process, the financial projections and the operating scenario typically change. We get back into that iterative process asking: "What is the impact of each change, and what is the best solution?"

In ASTRA we asked about the impact on couriers' productivity. We have roughly 30,000 couriers. When you start adding even one or two minutes per stop for every courier you have a strong impact on your bottom line just from that productivity hit. How do we train the 30,000 couriers who will be receiving these printers? What do we do when a printer breaks? All of these things have to be evaluated to understand the total corporate impact of implementing this new technology.

Debra Gray noted that

what should not be lost in discussing this process is that much of the benefit of the approach does not come out merely in the final document. The benefits are felt throughout the process as our integrated approach to the whole business case analysis yields input and learning across departmental lines. The end product that is given to management therefore carries with it greater reliability because the expertise of the operating groups is merged with the tools and analysis provided by the financial staff.

Developing financial projections: Financial projections are made and revised throughout each stage of the project. As the design and operating scenario become clear with successive iterations, the capital cost of the technology can be factored in with increasing certainty. In addition, the operating projections become firm.

> We look at the courier productivity impact, the impact on customers—all the things we can possibly conceive. Finally, after we go through this iterative process, we end up with a business case that tells senior management: "this is the best solution and its impact."

Estimating "soft benefits": Since its founding, Federal Express has understood that satisfied customers are a critical determinant of revenues. By reducing mis-sorts, ASTRA promised to increase customer satisfaction, but this benefit was not easy to quantify. During the ASTRA project, the finance staff made progress in estimating these "soft benefits." As Debra Gray observed,

> Years ago, the capital expenditure process would have lamented the frustration of the customer whose package was mis-sorted and proceeded to ignore this customer when making financial projections. One of the contributions of the Business Case Approach is the learning about hard-to-quantify benefits that takes place across departments as they build toward a solution to the problem. In a traditional analysis, the same questions may be asked, but they are asked by only a few people after the project is designed. With BCA, the technical feasibility, design, and projections are constantly revisited through an iterative process that is constantly asking "what is the impact, and what is the best solution?"

In their attempt "to combine hard, reliable numbers with softer projections that include variables that were always there but never quantified," the analysts found "the most difficult of these numbers to quantify is the cost of a lost customer, or the cost of poor quality." For the ASTRA project, they tried to visualize what a dissatisfied customer could do to Federal Express' business: for example, stop using the company or tell other customers or potential customers about the unacceptable service. The team did not come up with a single number for the cost of a dissatisfied customer, in part because the answer would depend on who, and how dissatisfied, the customer would be. But the team did attempt to assess the costs of dissatisfaction for various types of customers and engaged in "what if?" explorations in which various ranges of estimates were tried out to see how well they fit the team members' sense of what reasonable numbers might look like. These estimates of "soft benefits and costs" influenced the team members on "hard" dimensions like design of equipment and procedures to be followed.

Parametric analysis: In the business case approach, financial analysis is supported with a form of risk and sensitivity analysis that also attempts to include the impact of "soft data."

The finance division's description of parametric analysis captures the traditional sensitivity analysis theme: "a quantified definition of the relationship between financial indices and key variables (cost, revenue, capital, etc.) across a reasonable range of possible values." Phil King elaborates:

> We try to define the financial relationship between the key drivers of the project and overall project value to find out what impact they have. In ASTRA we looked at capital investment as one variable and productivity gains or costs as another.

The results are presented in tables showing the different returns associated with alternative values of the key drivers selected for analysis.

To assist senior management in estimating the soft benefits, the final project report identified possible ranges of values for the soft benefits the team considered.

> Once we present executive management with a project and a set of intangible returns we have tried to quantify, we are now able to say, "based on hard savings you should receive this return." Then we elaborate some of the softer benefits. Executive management may determine what they think the reasonable ranges of these soft variables are using the scenario we presented.

Gaining approval: Gaining approval for a project has two major elements: building a project worthy of support by the team members who develop it and presenting the project in a formal report that contains recommendations upper management will want to accept.

The BCA process is intended to bring all major players into the project development early and keep them in the process long enough either to build a strong project that deserves their support or to reach agreement that the project should not be recommended to senior management.

To communicate the work of the team to senior management, BCA seeks to develop an actionable document that contains clear recommendations and a thorough, yet reasonably brief, analysis of the company-wide implications of the proposed project. Phil King describes the document's purpose as

> To present executive management with a proposal effectively presenting a recommendation that has evaluated available alternatives and achieves the

objective in a manner that supports the best interests of customers, employees, and shareholders.

Supporting implementation: If the work of the team results in a proposal to senior management, and if the proposal is accepted, the modeling performed throughout the BCA continues to be useful as the project proceeds. In discussing the implementation of ASTRA, Debra Gray pointed out how,

> We are still recommending operational changes although we are well under way. The financial work we are doing and the updates we are making are definitely having an impact on how we roll this out and what stages we implement and when. There is an ongoing benefit from the analytical work we did; it's not just a one time decision. If package growth is high, the model will reflect one thing, and it will tell another story if growth is low. So, for example, two years from now we can update the analysis for new volume assumptions.

The Business Case Approach provides a vehicle for cross-functional learning and for the sharing of financial tools and expertise throughout the company. This sharing of financial tools is also encouraged by the financial information system described next.

ELVIS

In a number of divisions at Federal Express, budget preparation and financial reporting are done through an online system developed by the finance staff to make work more efficient and effective. The Electronic Large Variance Information System, or ELVIS, is a computerized system that accesses Federal Express' financial database permitting users to extract financial or human resource data, or the status of internal paperwork (such as personnel and capital expenditure requests) relevant to their part of the business.

Before ELVIS, Federal Express produced paper-based reports in standard formats, as most companies still do. But many of the reports went unread for a variety of reasons. Managers had to wait for reports until month-end, often long after they needed the information. They had to wade through pages of numbers that were irrelevant to them before finding what they were looking for. Even when they located the relevant information, it was rarely in the form needed, requiring considerable effort at respreading the numbers. Managers routinely came to the finance staff asking for special reports that would require a large amount of manual preparation or programming time. Eventually, Phil King took the lead in asking how to construct a better process.

Phil was attempting to recast the role of his staff from reporting past results and controlling current decisions to acting as consultants to the operating units. He reasoned that if his staff did not have to spend so much time preparing reports, they could be more available to their "customers." Phil and his staff set several goals for the new system:

- it had to use the company's central database, to ensure a common set of numbers would be seen by all users,

- it had to provide direct access to any needed financial data without forcing users to wade through irrelevant information,

- it had to present information in the form most useful to its users,

- it had to permit the elimination of printed reports, and

- it had to be available to everyone throughout the organization, permit multiple simultaneous users, and support different terminals and personal computers.

The group studied existing executive information systems, but concluded they tended to be laden with too many expensive features of limited utility, such as beautiful graphical interfaces, or infrared remote controls. As a result, the group recommended that it would be more cost effective for the finance staff to write its own package. Phil King calls ELVIS "a poor man's executive information system."

How ELVIS Works

ELVIS is designed so that users can access financial information sliced in many ways. For example, a divisional vice president can use the system to compare actual staff costs versus plan. Or an analyst can call up the telecommunications or travel costs in each area of the business, showing variances against budget and against last year's numbers or trends over the past six quarters.

The system can be set to highlight differences between budget and actual, or between prior years' and the current year's figures, ordering the differences by absolute or percentage deviation. In this way, the system works like a pointer, helping managers identify the largest financial issues in their units. For example, a manager can go into the system, learn that personnel costs or purchases in a certain unit are higher than expected, and contact the manager of the unit. (A planned enhancement will speed up the process by allowing the manager with such an inquiry to send an electronic mail message to the supervisor of that unit.) According to Debra Gray, this use of ELVIS has led to an important change in management style.

> I think some of the best results we've received from ELVIS have not come from the finance staff. Suppose I'm sitting at my desk and I get a note from my vice president that says, "why did this happen?" One, I'm going to have to do some research and find out, and this [ELVIS] is the way I'm going to do it; and two, next month I'm going to be looking at it before he asks me. So, we've generated a lot of usage that way, where questions have prompted people to be a little bit more proactive in monitoring their status.

The online nature of the system means there is no waiting for reports to arrive, no need to wait until the end of the month to learn of a problem or opportunity.

ELVIS has made a significant change in the amount, cost, and quality of financial analysis done by the Finance Division. Phil King was able to reduce the number of analysts on his staff from 10 to six over two years. Yet the amount of relevant analysis actually increased because it was no longer necessary to produce specific manual reports for managers throughout the company. Analysts are now able to address problems in real time, not simply research what happened some months ago. As Phil says,

> Without the system, it was difficult to ask the finance staff to spend more time being consultants to the various departments. ELVIS changes this. When you give people the tools to work more efficiently and have more impact on decisions, not only does output go up, but morale skyrockets.

Perhaps equally or even more important, ELVIS may be dramatically increasing the amount of financial analysis being performed by individuals and teams outside the Finance Division. ELVIS provides faster and more user-friendly access to real-time financial data, and the finance staff now encourages other divisions to initiate and conduct their own financial analyses rather than waiting for leadership or assistance from finance. In this sense, ELVIS's sharing the tools of financial analysis is another example of finance's move toward "distributed finance."

The benefits of ELVIS are not simply that financial reporting is done more quickly and effectively or that additional tools are provided to the organization. The system has been set up to eliminate paper where not needed, and thereby eliminate delays created by waiting for paper to move from point A to point B. Debra Gray uses the example of hiring to point out how ELVIS has eliminated unnecessary process steps and reduced cycle time:

We started focusing in on all of the steps it takes to hire somebody in the company and were amazed at how much time we were spending just keeping managers informed about the status of their personnel requisitions. They would call in regularly, and we spent a lot of time locating the paperwork so we could respond. Today the status of the requisition is put into the computer which tracks it directly. The result is that there are no more phone calls. That is where the quality process fits into our way of thinking.

Offspring of ELVIS

The success of ELVIS led Phil King's group to interconnect it to BRAVO (Budget Reporting And Variances Online), a budgeting tool that had been in use at Federal Express for the prior five to six years. BRAVO, designed to facilitate budget planning within the operating departments, was an early success in reducing the finance staff's involvement in the details of budget preparation. With BRAVO, budgets are individually keyed in by each cost center manager and are then automatically aggregated to produce budget summaries at each level of the organization. Debra Gray reports how simple BRAVO is to use:

> For example, when you're doing your budget, BRAVO can pull up the monthly amounts you spent last year. BRAVO can also call up your budget from last year. It will ask, 'Do you want to use one of these past numbers for this year?' Answer yes and you're done—with no calculating required. Another field will show your actuals from last year or the year before, so you will have a little more information as you develop your budget. There is added value here that you would never have if you were doing things in a nonautomated fashion. I would say 90% of the nonfield organizations now use the BRAVO system to do their budget. And once you have them schooled on that, ELVIS is second nature.

The success of ELVIS also has led to the development of related systems that are having similar impacts on the company. One is ZULU, a compliment to BRAVO that adds forecasting to the system. ("Bravo Zulu" is the U.S. Navy semaphore signal for a job well done. It is used extensively at Federal Express in the same manner. While ZULU is not an acronym, it seemed the logical name to compliment BRAVO.) The ZULU system permits operating groups to forecast their performance each month to support expenditure decision making.

The operating groups enter recent expenditures and updated forecasts into ZULU, which then provides current estimates of future expenditures to divisional management. The finance staff refers to ZULU as the "guesstimate system."

Repeating the theme of giving employees throughout the company the financial tools to do work traditionally reserved for financial staff members, Debra says, "If you give them a tool box, they'll use it."

Payoffs from Investments in Quality

> I don't see how you can compete in the long run without embracing these (quality approaches). They are proven; there is no question about it anymore. It's a given fact. You had better get on board on these things or you are going to get left behind, and you are not going to be able to catch up.
>
> —Alan Graf
> Senior VP and CFO

Like many CFOs of companies that are quality leaders, Alan Graf is a credible and articulate judge of his company's payoffs from its investments in quality in general, and in finance in particular. For Federal Express, well-recognized payoffs include major competitive advantages, significant improvements in internal processes, an enhanced ability of finance "to do its job" of contributing to the organization, and increasing ability of the rest of the organization "to do finance's job."

Major Competitive Advantages

From its beginnings, quality in its various manifestations (reliability, short cycle time, customer satisfaction, etc.) has been the key to Federal Express' survival and success. Without its commitment to and achievements in quality management, Federal Express would not have started and would not have stayed in business.

Alan Graf's favorite example of the payoff for investment in quality, and the absolute business necessity of high quality systems, is the comparison of the cost of poor quality in time definite, overnight package delivery versus the cost of poor quality in passenger airline travel.

> We have a very high cost maintenance organization for our aircraft, and there is a very good reason for that. The cost of quality that we engineer into our aviation operations gives us an extremely high return on our investment. It is one of the major reasons for our brand name recognition—for the fact that everyone knows that if it has to be there by 10:30 tomorrow, there really is only one choice and that is Federal Express.
>
> We sell reliability—and information about the movement of the items we transport. A perfect example of the cost of not achieving high reliability in our industry is to contrast our situation with the airlines. The comparison

is a logical one because a major part of how we achieve express delivery, if there is distance involved, is by using an airplane.

We have a very interactive system in this company—many interfaces— two national and four regional hubs—a twenty-four hour defined schedule. Things have to go precisely like clockwork—they cannot be a minute late or ten minutes late or the whole system is thrown off. When you have three million customers every day—that's one and a half million shippers and one and a half million consignees—it has to work like clockwork.

Take one of our DC-10s, for example. It will hold approximately 150,000 pounds of freight. Our average weight per piece these days is in the 6 pound range. So on any given day, a DC-10 may have as many as 25,000 pieces, while our friends in the airlines will have 385 passengers on one of their fully loaded DC-10s.

If the passenger plane is late, maybe they misconnect 385 people. But the airline has the ability to say we are going to cancel the flight, or maybe we will be two hours late, or maybe it is the air traffic controllers, or maybe we had a part break, or the maintenance boys are working on it. And once they get you in the air they give you a complimentary cocktail and forget about it. There is a minimum effect on their operations when they have a "one off" failure.

For us, with 25,000 packages, we have 50,000 customers on one airplane and we simply cannot afford to have that plane 10 minutes late because of what happens to us if we "miss the sort" (fail to reach a hub in time to sort and transfer the packages to outgoing flights before they depart). First of all, we have 25,000 service failures and we want zero service failures. 25,000 people who paid for reliability are disappointed—actually, 50,000 are disappointed.

But, missing the sort has all kinds of other ramifications to it. We have a money back guarantee if we don't deliver on time, so we lose revenue—the average revenue per piece is about $14 so we could lose $14 times 25,000 pieces. Then there are the added costs. The next day the phones at our call centers are tied up. We have 25,000 people asking "Where the heck is my package? What happened?" We take orders there but we also disseminate information, and now our phone bill is up and other customers have a harder time getting through. We also expedited those pieces because on-time service is so important to us. We put them on passenger airplanes or maybe did a double turn of our own aircraft depending upon where the packages were headed. We got them out to a station after the initial packages arrived, so the station manager had to send out more couriers, pay them overtime, and have them drive more miles than they would have. And on and on and on. It will take a number of days for things to settle down fully out in the field. The cost of that failure outweighs by a thousand times the cost of the initial heavy investment in quality on the front end.

And one other thing. There may be a "golden package" in that 25,000—this has happened to our competition and we benefited from it. There may be a CEO who is sending something to his wife. He is out of town, and has forgotten her birthday. He is sending something to his wife and it does not get there. He certainly has the power to get mad at Fedex and come back to his transportation department and say "stop using those [people]." We would pay a terrible penalty for that golden package, so we treat every single package as though it is that golden package—as something that can cost us more than just that one failure.

We finance people are great at calculating what things cost. The point of that whole story is that when we realize and understand all the benefits on the back end arising from our front-end investments in quality, we begin to see there is a tremendous return on investment in quality.

Significant Improvements in Internal Processes

The great thing for the CFOs of the world is that every single time [the work of quality action teams] boils down to something that benefits the bottom line. It either increases the revenue, or engineers some cost problem out, or puts enough quality in that you get fewer failures on the back side. When you get specific and draw that bottom line, it helps every single time. And people really feel great about that.

—Alan Graf

Two examples of quality success stories in the Finance Division are the automated refund system known as CAVIAR (Cash Application to Vendors Interface Account Refund) and the international reporting system named SCORPIO (Systematic Country-level Omnifarious Reporting of Performance of International Operations).

CAVIAR was developed by a QAT from U.S. remittance operations and vendor services concerned that the time to refund money to employees and customers was too long—creating confusion and dissatisfaction. Refunds under the existing system took from two to six weeks, and insufficient or illegible information frequently went to the customer and to vendor services. The new CAVIAR system, by contrast, automatically generates and mails refund checks within one day. By simplifying the work in processing a refund to only three steps, CAVIAR has reduced the staffing need to only one person, eliminated 70 percent of customer phone calls inquiring about refunds, improved accounting accuracy, and generated an annual savings of over $200,000.

Following the acquisition of Flying Tigers, new products, different cost structures, and an extensive worldwide dedicated line-haul operation were quickly integrated into Federal Express' existing operations.

SCORPIO was developed in response to difficulties in understanding and analyzing the resulting changes in international business activity. The new system collects international operations and cost data that are used for regular reports and financial analyses. SCORPIO feeds information into the International General Ledger and produces monthly management reports by product, country, and region. It contains extensive cost information that is used for analysis of pricing, line-haul decisions, new products, new country service, and global service partnerships, as well as both short-term and long-range forecasting. Up and running for about a year, SCORPIO has eliminated much manual compiling of data and ensured management and analysts quick access to consistent information.

The Enhanced Ability of Finance to "Do Its Job"

There are significant differences today in the nature of finance staff members' jobs at Federal Express. Many of these changes were made possible by current technologies that free up the staff to do what they were hired to do. In 1980, finance employees were working with columnar pads and calculators, and work with reports was centered around editing and verifying data. The tasks had a very heavy accounting focus, with reporting and gathering information demanding more than half of the staff's time. Finance Division's role was much like a controller, judge, and police officer.

Today this has been turned inside out. Computers now capture information and produce reports. The focus of the finance staff has shifted away from accounting and moved toward analysis. In line with this shift, attention is focused forward upon projections rather than backward upon reporting. The police officer's role has been shed and transformed into a consultative role through the implementation of a matrix organizational reporting relationship that integrates the finance staff with each operational department.

The matrix system is set up with a customer focus, where each department has its own finance staff member to serve all of its financial needs. Through this approach, staff members become more involved in the business of the departments they work with. The benefits are twofold. By being closer to the operating departments, finance staff members can facilitate projects and plans as they are being developed rather than sit in judgment from a removed position. Conversely, the finance division benefits from its integration throughout the company as it develops a collective knowledge of the total organization and breaks down barriers between departments. This position has put the finance division in a much stronger position to contribute to the company.

In recognition of this new role, the finance division has written a "Mission Statement" and a "Quality Policy":

Mission Statement

To be the driver for Global Corporate Quality decisions in the control, measurement and allocation of scarce capital and expense resources, carefully balancing the tradeoffs among our customers/suppliers, shareholders, regulatory compliance agencies and employees through empowering well-trained, highly motivated people to exercise sound judgments while continuously striving to be the world leader in financial management.

Quality Policy

The Finance Division is committed to The Quality Advantage. It is our policy to continuously strive to improve services to our customers (both internal and external), to meet/exceed their expectations, to control/reduce costs, and to improve the efficiency and quality of our operating environment. It is our objective to build and perpetuate a quality organization that supports our corporate goals.

Company-Wide Benefits of "Distributed Finance": The Enhanced Ability of the Rest of the Company "to Do Finance's Job"

At least three factors have been increasing the ability of Federal Express' "nonfinancial" members to initiate and complete the types of analyses that used to be reserved for "financial types." Finance has worked to make the "tool kit" of traditional financial tools and the newly developed computer based financial information and analytical systems available to all company members. Simultaneously, the company's quality training programs have been increasing individuals' knowledge of the traditional tqm tools for data collection and analysis. And, the physical location of financial people out in the business unit locations and their matrix reporting relationships provides sharing of financial skills and coaching in their use.

As a result, more Federal Express members in "nonfinancial" jobs are able to see the appropriateness of framing issues in financial ways and to carry out useful analyses with or without the help of their local financial people. Because of this work performed in the field, individuals in finance are finding more time to perform new types of analyses and to develop still more tools to be shared throughout the company.

The finance division at Federal Express continues to search for innovative methods and systems to support operations personnel and operations management. Debra Gray summarizes the division's, and the company's, philosophy:

> Continuous improvement in all aspects of our job will be key to a more efficient and competitive organization.

People Interviewed

Mike Babineaux, Senior Procurement Specialist

Chauncey Burton, Senior Quality Administrator, Finance

Mike Craig, Managing Director, U.S. Credit and Collections

Harry Dalton, VP, Technology Planning & Services

Don Daniell, Manager, International Financial Controls

Alan Graf, Senior VP and CFO

Debra Gray, Managing Director,
    Financial Planning Customer/Systems Support

Edith Kelly, VP, Internal Audit and Quality Assurance

Phil King, Manager, Information Systems
    and Telecommunications-Finance

Martha Thomas, Senior Manager, Vendor Services/Finance

Jean Ward-Jones, Manager, Quality Planning

John West, Manager, Corporate Quality Improvement

Fordham Student Research Team

Jeff Deiss, case assistant

Dave Susswein, case assistant

Andrea Baker

Mirco Bianchi

Andrew Goldner

Ann Hardy

Victor Tan

Motorola

Motorola, one of the earliest U.S. quality pioneers, demonstrates the payoffs from a sustained quality focus. The company was a winner of the Malcolm Baldrige National Quality Award in 1988, the first year it was offered, and remains one of the few large companies to have won the award for company-wide activities.

Motorola's pilot application of tqm to finance processes was to speed up closing the books at the end of each month. Book closing time has been reduced from nine working days in the early 1980s to two days as of July 1992 producing some $30 million in annual savings. Another early success was in payroll where a tqm analysis led to the installation of a new system that significantly reduced errors and increased Motorola's ability to comply with government reporting requirements.

From the beginning, Motorola recognized the importance of systems to measure defects and time. Its six sigma defects measurement system—representing a defect rate of only 3.4 errors per million opportunities—is now used widely by many tqm companies, including several others in this study. Its assiduous attention to shortening process cycle time has made the company more flexible and responsive and has reduced the opportunity to make errors.

While the six sigma measurement system readily lends itself to processes with millions of repetitions, Motorola has found a way to apply it to "soft" processes as well, those with less obvious process steps or that infrequently repeat. An excellent example is Motorola's internal audit function, which is operating at world-class levels. Beginning with a task force in October 1987, internal audit identified its "customers," defined its "products," defined the "audit process," defined what would be considered a "defective product," and established measures of the department's performance. This led to improvements in audit scheduling, planning, fieldwork, reporting, and post-audit activities. The payoffs have been significant. From 1983 to 1991, Motorola's revenues grew from $4.8 billion to $11.3 billion, yet annual domestic audit hours fell from 24,000 hours to 12,000, external audit cycle time was cut in half, and some $1.8 million in external audit fees was avoided.

C
Motorola

I think we have moved the benchmark in the auditing process.
—Larry Grow, Senior Manager of Internal Audit

When the corporate audit department started improving its internal audit process in 1987, it took an average of 20 days to complete a draft report, and 51 days to issue a final report. Within 2 1/2 years, final reports were being completed in five days, and draft reports were so rarely issued that their cycle times were no longer worth tracking. The department's measurements showed that quality improved 25 times, a 33 percent reduction in management and clerical staff saved $1.1 million a year over a three-year period, and a 26 percent increase in audit staff productivity saved $1.5 million per year over a three-year period.

Motorola, widely recognized as a national leader in total quality management, is raising the benchmark in many of its processes. The company was a winner of the Malcolm Baldrige National Quality Award in 1988, the first year it was offered, and remains one of the few large companies to have won the award for company-wide activities. Tqm is pursued actively at all levels of the organization.

Early in its journey to tqm, Motorola recognized the importance of measurement systems and the need for a common measurement language throughout the company. It adopted the "sigma system," a statistically based tool that measures defects in relation to opportunities for error. "Six sigma," representing a defect rate of only 3.4 errors per million opportunities, has become the company's target in everything it does, and the company is already looking toward its next target once six sigma is achieved.

While the six sigma measurement system readily lends itself to processes with millions of repetitions, Motorola has found a way to apply it to "soft" processes as well, those with less obvious process steps or that infrequently repeat. An excellent example is Motorola's internal audit function, which is operating at world-class levels and on which we report in this case study.

On a par with the measurement of defects at Motorola is the measurement of time. Motorola assiduously studies its activities to reduce process cycle time. By speeding up its operations, the company has become more flexible and responsive to customer needs and to the changing environment. Also, the quest for shorter cycle time requires that new and simplified methods be found, further reducing the opportunity to make errors.

How Motorola has used six sigma measurement and cycle time reduction to drive quality throughout its finance organization makes up the core of this case profile.

Motorola's Entry into Quality Management

According to company lore, Motorola recognized the need for tqm during an all-officers meeting in 1978. The meeting was proceeding as planned when Art Sundry, national sales manager of Motorola's largest business, stood up and said,

> The agenda is going fine and we seem to be addressing the subjects that we want to talk about, but we are missing the most important subject of all—our quality stinks.

At the time, Sundry's business unit had a large share of its market and was growing at a double digit rate, not an experience which typically leads to the feeling that something is wrong. Yet Sundry recognized that Motorola could easily lose its customers and profitability unless quality were significantly improved. Bob Galvin, Motorola's CEO at the time, recollects that in one action Sundry turned the meeting "right side up" and changed the direction of the company. Everything at the meeting, and at Motorola from that point forward, was seeded with the subject of quality.

Like many companies, Motorola had been concerned about quality for a long time and was reasonably confident it understood what quality meant. In 1958 Motorola had established a Corporate Quality Council to strengthen and cross-fertilize the quality process and culture among its divisions. As a natural extension, quality had been one of Motorola's top ten goals since the early 1970s. After the 1978 meeting, however, Motorola executives began to understand that quality in a tqm sense was something well above their use of the word. Looking back, Richard

Buetow, corporate vice president and director of quality, recalls the insight that was emerging:

> We may be the best in the world in what we do, and have the best market share in our business, but if somebody got their act together and did quality management in the way you really could do it, they'd just drive you out of business. A new attitude had to be adopted. Quality had to become a personal expression; the vernacular had to change to "I" and "we" in place of "them" and "you."

People: The Critical Resource

Bob Galvin's initial approach to tqm was framed in his question "How do we become more competitive?" After thought and discussion, Galvin realized people were his critical resource: to stay competitive every member of Motorola had to achieve a high personal level of quality. When addressing this issue Galvin quotes his father (who founded the company), "I don't mind a man who is dumb, I can't stand a man who is numb." To set the example, he began to admit openly "he did not know what he did not know," and began asking "what do you think other people know that I don't know?" Galvin concluded that he would have to become as good as the best CEO in the industry. This would be the same for his vice presidents and so on, for each and every position at Motorola.

Active questioning led Motorola executives to the concepts of humility and listening—humility in the sense that they were willing to admit they did not know or have all the answers, listening in the sense that they were willing to hear how others did similar tasks in the search for the most efficient and effective way.

Motorola's commitment to learning led to a realization that the company had to do much more in training and educating its people. But while training and education received support in concept, many executives were reluctant to release their employees for training or to spend the required funds from their budgets. In response, Galvin mandated an education program that currently requires every employee, at every level of the company including the chairman, to attend a minimum of 40 hours of schooling each year. Today, Motorola has one of the largest training programs in its industry and is closer to its goal of helping all employees be the quality leader in their position compared with their counterparts in other companies. For Galvin, the tens of millions Motorola spends on education is not a cost, but an investment in cost savings.

Galvin began to invite guests, leaders in their particular fields, to speak at Motorola. Employees could listen and learn from these people as part of their education process. Through this program, Westinghouse, whose Commercial Nuclear Fuels Division was another 1988 Baldrige Award winner, taught Motorola how to use quality improvement task forces—teams of employees who leave their regular jobs for two to four months to attack quality and competitiveness problems. A conspicuous success of the task forces was the introduction of competitive benchmarking into Motorola's quality efforts. Manufacturing processes such as warehousing were among the first to be studied. In the finance area, Motorola benchmarked companies that were better at managing their accounts receivable, accounts payable, and invoice processing. Soft processes as well as hard processes were examined.

Bob Galvin's "Marshall Plan"

By 1981, quality at Motorola had taken sufficient shape to provide a glimpse of what it might be like if Motorola were truly a world-class company. To speed up and give further direction to the company's quality efforts, Bob Galvin asked his management team to devise Motorola's version of a "Marshall Plan," beginning with a vision for Motorola's future quality efforts. Today, this vision is carried by every employee on a pocket-sized card so all members of Motorola can work together toward the same goals.

The vision begins with what Motorola calls "our fundamental objective (everyone's overriding responsibility): total customer satisfaction." This is to be achieved by a set of key beliefs, key goals, and key initiatives (Table C.1).

A New Quality Vision

In 1987 Bob Galvin thought Motorola was ready for the next phase of its journey toward total quality management. To "raise the bar" for his company, he developed five challenges:

1. Improve product and service quality 10 times by 1989 (100 times from the base line year of 1981).

2. Further improve product and service quality another 10 times by 1991 (representing a 100 times improvement from 1987 and a 1000 times improvement from 1981).

3. Achieve six sigma error rates throughout the company by 1992.

4. Spread the dedication to quality to every facet of the corporation.

5. Achieve a culture of continual improvement to assure total customer satisfaction.

TABLE C.1 **Key Beliefs, Goals, and Initiatives**

KEY BELIEFS—how we will always act

- • Constant Respect for People

- • Uncompromising Integrity

KEY GOALS—what we must accomplish

- • Best in Class
    People
    Marketing
    Technology
    Product: Software, Hardware, and Systems
    Manufacturing
    Service

- • Increased Global Market Share

- • Superior Financial Results

KEY INITIATIVES—how we will do it

- • Six Sigma Quality

- • Total Cycle Time Reduction

- • Product, Manufacturing and Environmental Leadership

- • Profit Improvement

- • Empowerment for all, in a Participative, Cooperative, and Creative Workplace

Finance Joins Motorola's Quality Movement

The finance arm of Motorola joined the quality movement for much the same reason as many other parts of the company: management's insistence on and support of quality made it difficult for any part of the company not to buy in. Yet Motorola's management rapidly came to understand that applying this new management technology to soft areas or support areas could easily lead to skepticism if not downright rejection. It might be difficult for the support staff to see the relevance of a "production technology" to soft or nonproduction tasks.

To assist these departments in adopting quality management, Motorola laid out a six-step action program:

1. Define the major functions or services performed by a unit of the company.

2. Determine the internal customers and suppliers of these services.

3. Identify the customer's requirements, along with quantitative measures to assess customer satisfaction in meeting such requirements.

4. Identify the requirements and measurement criteria that the supplier to the process must meet.

5. Flowchart or map the process at the macro (interdepartmental) level, and at the micro (intradepartmental) level.

6. Continuously improve the process with respect to effectiveness, quality, cycle time, and cost.

Cycle Time Reduction in Closing the Books

Motorola's pilot application of quality management to finance processes was to speed up closing the books at the end of each month. In the language of quality management, Motorola reduced the cycle time of its closing process—the time from month-end to the completion of financial statements available for management review.

In the early 1980s, prior to the finance organization's adoption of quality management, the monthly close averaged nine working days. As a result, an updated forecast for the coming month was normally not available until 11 or 12 working days of that month had passed, and it was not until the 18th or 19th working day that the monthly operating committee meeting would be held to review the prior month's activities and the current month's plan. Management was getting information for last month with the next already two-thirds over. Motorola finance set a very ambitious goal: closing the books in four days by the first quarter of 1990 and in two days by the end of 1992. As David Hickie, at that time senior vice president and assistant chief financial officer, points out,

> If you tell people to close the books in seven days instead of eight, they will figure out how to do it very easily. They will work a little overtime over the weekend. If you say do it in six days, they will work on Sunday. But they would not change what they were doing. When we told them to do it in 4 days and that we would not let them use the weekend as a crutch, they had to look at a fundamental change in the process.

In examining the closing process, Motorola found that much of the cycle time was due to errors in making journal entries. In the past, the accuracy rate of journal entries—greater than 98.6 percent—had been considered acceptable. However, the company made some 600,000 entries per month worldwide, and, even with 98.6 percent accuracy,

8,000 entries each month were wrong. Correcting and reconciling those entries at month's end were enormously time consuming. Today the journal entry process is approaching six sigma accuracy, eliminating the time and cost of month-end repairs.

A second cause of long cycle time was the number of signoffs required as data originating in factories located abroad made their way to headquarters. Each factory would send its numbers to its sector international headquarters for approval. From there the data would go to Motorola's U.S. international headquarters, then to U.S. sector headquarters, and finally to the corporate offices. At each step, the information would be held up for approval before being sent on. By studying approval rates, Motorola finance concluded it was extremely rare for a report to be modified prior to approval; time was being added but not value. Motorola instructed each local factory to send reports directly to U.S. sector headquarters at the same time they are distributed locally, which vastly improved cycle time by 2.3 days.

Further cycle time delay was caused by a manual data entry system in which Motorola sent accounting information to an outside vendor where it would be keypunched and returned to corporate headquarters. Errors would be flagged and returned to the vendor for reentry. Motorola replaced this process with a system in which Motorola finance personnel enter data directly into company computers that had been reprogrammed to trap input errors. Although the personnel cost increased—the accountants who enter the data are more highly paid than the vendor's keypunch operators—overall cost dropped as efficiency rose and errors virtually disappeared.

Commenting on the improved process, Ken Johnson, vice president and corporate controller, points out the advantages of closing the books quickly.

> In addition to the cost savings, the early close frees up several hundred finance people for each day removed from the process. They can devote their attention to more important things than just preparing the numbers—like helping our people run the business.

Since the early 1980s, Motorola's finance organization has reduced monthly closing time from nine days to two days as of July 1992. By July 1991, Motorola was able to report that speeding up the monthly close from the sixth to fourth day had saved the company $20 million per year. Motorola expects a further $10 million annual savings now that it has reached a two-day close. In September 1991, *Financial World* identified Motorola's accounting department as the U.S. benchmark, partly in recognition for its leadership in reducing book-closing cycle time.

Payroll Accuracy

Another early success was in the area of payroll. Motorola had been using a traditional time card system to assign labor costs to its various activities. However, the system was prone to errors in filling out, keypunching, and processing the cards. This resulted in large payroll suspense balances that had to be traced and manually allocated. In addition, the existing system left Motorola open to exposure for non-compliance in the company's government contracts that require a high level of accuracy in assigning costs.

Motorola studied the time card process and concluded it could not be improved to the desired accuracy level. Instead, two cross-functional teams were formed to study alternative data collection methods and recommend a new system. Government auditors were invited to join the team drawn from the part of the business working on government contracts, both to obtain their input and suggestions and to gain their approval early in the new process design.

One team recommended the installation of an online payroll log, in which employees enter data directly into the central computer through terminals located throughout the company. The second team developed an optical scanning system to read employee identification data directly from their ID badges. Both projects were implemented. Today, employees insert their badges into the terminals and then enter job-specific information that is checked for accuracy and consistency as it is entered. Keypunching has been eliminated, employees are no longer misidentified, and the payroll suspense balances have been driven nearly to zero. The government auditors report a high degree of confidence in the new system.

The Six Sigma Measurement System

Sigma is a term adapted from statistics to measure the number of errors in products or processes. A higher sigma value indicates a lower number of errors, and fewer errors translate to lowered rework and more satisfied customers. As Motorola points out, a "four sigma" manufacturer will spend in excess of 10 percent of its sales dollar on internal and external repairs whereas a "six sigma" manufacturer will spend less than 1 percent. In today's global economy, a four sigma company simply cannot compete and survive against a six sigma company.

Motorola's studies have shown that without the application of systematic quality management, the norm for human processes is to perform at a four sigma level. This translates to 6210 errors per million opportunities, a success rate of 99.38 percent. While this might seem a high enough rate to be acceptable, customers normally demand significantly higher levels of performance. Consider the following, compiled for a success rate of 99.9 percent. At 99.9 percent accuracy:*

- 12 babies will be given to the wrong parents each day,

- 107 incorrect medical procedures will be performed each day, and

- 20,000 incorrect drug prescriptions will be written each year.

Standards are equally high for business products and services. At 99.9 percent accuracy:

- 1,314 phone calls will be misplaced by telecommunication services each minute,

- 18,322 pieces of mail will be mishandled each hour,

- 22,000 checks will be deducted from the wrong account each hour, and

- 268,500 defective tires will be shipped each year.

By contrast, six sigma translates to a success rate of 99.9997 percent.

Motorola measures the error rate in each process using the sigma system and establishes a plan for bringing the quality of that process up to the six sigma level. This often requires a radical rethinking of the process design since moving from four sigma to six sigma requires significant change. At an error rate of 233 per million opportunities, five sigma represents a 27 times improvement over four sigma. Six sigma, only 3.4 errors per million opportunities, represents another 69 times improvement over five sigma.

Measuring defects per opportunity is particularly appropriate for complex products and processes. The failure of only one part or step can cause a complex product or process to fail; the more complex the product or process, the lower the likelihood of overall success. Table C.2 is an excerpt from a table used by Motorola to emphasize the

---

* Natalie Gabel, "Is 99.9% Good Enough?" *Training* (March 1991): 40–41.

TABLE C.2 **Overall Yield vs. Sigma Level**

Number of Parts	Yield at			
	3 sigma	4 sigma	5 sigma	6 sigma
100	0.10%	53.64%	97.70%	99.97%
500	—	4.44	89.02	99.83
1,000	—	0.20	79.24	99.66
17,000	—	—	0.02	94.38

need for six sigma quality. As the table indicates, a product with 100 parts, or a process with 100 steps, will be error free only 0.1 percent of the time if it operates at a three sigma level—in which each part or step has a 93.32 percent chance of being correct. At a four sigma level, the product or process will work 53.64 percent of the time, while at six sigma, the success rate, or yield, will be 99.97 percent. As a product or process becomes more complex, a higher sigma level is required to obtain an acceptable yield. Note that even at five sigma, a product or process with 1000 parts or steps has only a 79.24 percent chance of working; at four sigma it will fail nearly 100 percent of the time.

For Motorola's manufacturing people, six sigma was a natural way to measure defects. Because of the company's engineering roots, many production employees had been trained in statistics and could quickly appreciate the concept. Yet the same was not true in finance. As David Hickie remarked, "I challenge you to find an accountant in the world who wants to work off a log scale. That is absolutely a fundamental change." An important part of Motorola's movement toward total quality in finance was to train every finance employee in the concept and use of six sigma.

Applying Six Sigma to a "Soft" Administrative Activity: The Internal Audit Process

In 1987, the Motorola internal audit department began a series of steps that would soon raise the company's internal audit process to world class levels—and would lead to the department receiving one of two corporate-wide quality awards given to Motorola finance in 1990. The key to this success was a six-person task force working full-time for two weeks—plus many years of hard work by many people improving the audit process before and after the task force did its work.

The Audit Department at Motorola

Motorola's corporate audit department has 59 professionals—43 financial auditors and 16 EDP auditors, operating out of three locations: Schaumburg, Illinois; Phoenix, Arizona; and Slough, in the UK. The clerical staff is only 4 1/2—a very low number to support 59 professionals.

Motorola generally hires experienced auditors, primarily individuals who have been with a Big Six accounting firm for two or three years. Auditors travel about 50 percent of their time; roughly half within and half outside the U.S. A normal tour of duty lasts for twenty-four months, with some individuals choosing to continue for another year before being rotated to one of the business units. The auditing department is considered an entry point into the company that provides valuable training and a rich exposure to the entire organization. Five years after leaving the audit department, 90 percent of audit department graduates are still with the company.

A high quality process for many years: The Motorola audit process was not in bad shape in 1987. Many improvements had been made over the years; some were apparent in the tools provided to the auditors and some were apparent in the audit reports themselves.

Beginning in the fall of 1986, the auditors were equipped with state-of-the-art personal computer tool kits that enabled them to work effectively and efficiently in the field. Each kit included a laptop computer with modem and printer on which was loaded a full range of analytical and presentation software.

Well-established elements of the audit included grading the control environment, preparing concise reports, tracking the audit findings (including responses to issues raised in the audit), and distributing all audit reports to the audit committee of the Board of Directors.

In the upper right-hand corner of each audit report, in 1/2 inch bold red letters, there is a single word describing the control environment: excellent, satisfactory, marginal, or unsatisfactory. Locations with marginal and unsatisfactory grades must report on their corrective action plans every quarter.

The reports are brief, typically 10–12 pages. They consist of a yellow cover page with the grade on it, a 1-page introduction and conclusion, a

3/4 page of introductory background information on what was done in the audit and what type of work is performed by the facility, a short justification of the grade on the front page, and then findings and recommendations.

Repeat audit findings are tracked. Some years ago, the auditors found they were often writing up the same audit findings year after year. They would audit something, discover a problem, report it to the operating manager, and get a commitment to fix it. But when the auditors returned the next year, they would find either the problem had not been fixed, or the person who had committed to fix it had moved on and the replacement did not know that the problem had not been repaired. So, Larry Grow reports, internal audit went to the various divisions and departments and said,

> We can improve the audit department's productivity substantially if we just don't have to write up the same things we flagged last time. If you will simply fix what we ask you to fix, our quality and productivity will go up.

In benchmarking other internal audit departments, Motorola found that many audit departments issue reports and then wait up to 30 days to get a response. By contrast, Motorola issues all audit reports with the responses in them. The auditors tell each department or division what they found, what was broken, and what they want done to fix any problems. And they look for a response in which the division or department agrees the problem exists, identifies what will be done to fix it, and commits to a date by which the fix will be made.

All audit reports are distributed directly to the audit committee of the board of directors in the same form as they are given to the division or department. In this way, the audit committee and the division or department see exactly the same thing. Executive summaries are not prepared—except for a quarterly summary of those audits that earn unsatisfactory grades—nor is there any highlight tracking of unique audit findings or unusual issues. The audit committee receives about 150 audit reports annually, and seems to read every one of them. Since department or division members know board members will be reading their report, there is a great deal of concern that the reports be accurate and factual.

Bringing Six Sigma to the Audit Department

Ken Johnson and Larry Grow report that in the summer of 1987 managers in Motorola's audit department were becoming aware that the company's factories were moving toward six sigma performance much faster than the administrative areas. They felt it was becoming imperative that the audit staff better understand the quality movement and quality initiatives at Motorola. They also thought it important that the audit department have some success stories of its own, something it could relay back to the people on the front lines that communicated administrative groups were also involved in quality. The corporate audit staff seemed to be particularly important people to bear this message because of their role in improving financial and management systems. In addition, they might be the only representatives from the corporate office that people in some locations might see in a year, so they had a potentially critical role in communicating the company's quality commitment to the field.

A quality program focused on cycle time goals had been in place in the department for several years, but progress was slow. Larry Grow noted:

> We seemed to spend more time arguing over whether it was calendar days or work days that we ought to be tracking rather than working on the results we were trying to improve.

The department's managers talked among themselves about how to implement a six sigma program, and many excuses came up: "This is a mushy process." "We don't think it applies here." "We are not a production line." "We are not a transactional kind of department." "We don't know how to do it." In response, Larry recalls

> Somewhat out of frustration, I suggested that we ought to ask the staff how to implement a six sigma program. After all, they are the ones that will have to live with the program. And, that is what we did.

The Audit Department Task Force

In October 1987, a task force composed of four auditors was set up, each with less than 24 months in the audit department, and two managers. All were volunteers. Larry Grow related:

> We pulled them off the staffing schedule and said, "for the next two weeks we are going to sequester you in this conference room. We want you to spend full time trying to define what our quality program ought to look like." In essence, we built a think tank.

> Like all good managers I gave them a set of impossible constraints. I said, "You have to do this in two weeks; you cannot have any longer. You cannot come out in two weeks and say it can't be done. You must come out with a program that is easy to administer, something that will not bureaucratically drag us to our knees. And whatever you come up with must be something that can be implemented in no longer than three months."

The formal mission of the task force was:

> To define what quality is in the internal audit department and develop a measurement system for implementation on January 1, 1988.

A written report of recommendations was also required from the task force, and it was to be their responsibility to train the other members of the department in whatever new processes and procedures they chose to recommend.

In addition to these constraints, Larry also asked the task force to look at the audit process as though it were a factory operation.

> My view of administrative processes is that they are all really factories. Whether you are in a banking institution clearing checks or whether you are a secretary worrying about your own in-box and out-box, you can view your operation as a factory. The secretary gets things from a supplier, does something with it, and then ships the goods out to a customer. What she is doing is running her own little factory. I urged them to think horizontally not vertically.

Task Force Results

In two weeks the task force had met all of its mission goals. It defined the audit department's customers and the products they "buy;" defined the audit process; defined what a defective product was, where defects were likely to occur, and critical success factors in avoiding defects; developed a way to measure defects in the process as though auditors were running their own factory; developed two questionnaires to measure the quality of the audit process; and produced a series of recommendations for things to work on in the future.

Customers: The task force identified five major customers: the audit committee of Motorola's Board of Directors, senior Motorola management, the divisions or departments which are audited, the company's external auditor, and the internal auditors themselves.

The audit committee of the board looks to the internal auditors as an extension of itself, the independent eyes and ears of the audit committee throughout the corporation.

Senior Motorola management depends on the audit staff to play an important role in monitoring and improving the quality of systems throughout the company.

Each division or department that is audited obtains the internal auditors' help as well as top-level exposure as the auditors communicate about the internal control environment to senior management and to the Board.

The external auditor (KPMG Peat Marwick) gets two benefits from the audit department. First, the work of the internal auditors lays the groundwork for the external audit—KPMG relies on Motorola's internal audit findings to determine the scope of their work. Second, the quality of Motorola's internal audit staff is so highly regarded by KPMG that Motorola staffers on loan to KPMG now do roughly one-half of KPMG's audit research.

The department's own audit staff is the fifth customer. Audit is a developmental area: identifying and hiring promising individuals, training them, exposing them to many parts of the organization, and then placing them in new positions throughout the company. Should the audit department fail to develop its personnel properly, not only would audit performance suffer, but staff members would be more likely to fail in their subsequent job assignments. Such failures would, in turn, make it more difficult to send future audit staffers on to their next jobs.

Products: The task force initially struggled with the definition of the department's product. Their first approach, modeled after the operational areas of the company, was to look at the tangible output of the department: the product they were "shipping" to their customers. As a result, they defined their product as audit reports, a definition accepted by the rest of the audit department. However, over the course of the next several years, they realized they were really evaluating and promoting an internal control environment. As a result, they redefined the finished product to be the individual audit condition or audit finding. The audit report is "simply the box they ship it in." Larry Grow identifies this insight as one of the most important learnings of rethinking the internal audit process.

In addition to the audit report, eventually modified to be the company's internal control environment, the task force identified three other products: control of external audit costs, development of future managers, and the running of the department itself.

By the quality of their internal audits, their professionalism, and their ability to work with Motorola's external auditor, audit department members impact the amount of the company's external audit costs.

By training audit department staffers and giving them wide exposure to the organization, the audit department contributes to the development of future managers for Motorola.

By their actions and their choice of management practices, audit staffers contribute to the administration of their own department.

That can be done in an efficient or inefficient way. We found that we were not very efficient. We suspected that if finance functions in other companies went through some of the things we went through, they would find it rather shocking how poorly they actually administer their own areas.

The task force matched the products with customers and concluded that each of the five customers "purchased" at least two products. One customer, Motorola's senior management, purchased all four.

Defining the audit process: Each of the four audit department products was decomposed into its component parts and documented. As Larry Grow said:

We took each one of the finished products and broke it down using an organizational chart format. [The chart the team developed in 1987 for performing an audit is shown in Figure C.1.] We didn't do it in the traditional quality management way. If we were doing the charts today we would use mapping processes, fish-bone charts, and all the quality tools that are now in the academic world, but we did not use those tools at that time.

The process of performing an audit was broken into five steps: scheduling, planning, fieldwork, reporting, and post-audit.

We really did not know how to measure performing an audit, so we took each one of the steps and asked what kinds of things go into building a good audit? We looked at it as a bill of materials, working backwards—exploding things a little bit. First you schedule an audit. Second you plan the work you are going to do. Third, you execute the field work. Fourth, you publish the report. Fifth, you do some post-audit work or wrap-up work at the end, where you try to figure out what you can do better the next time.

Defining a defective product: The task force also identified what each of the five customers might define as a defect in each of the four products. One obvious defect is an audit report that contains something factually incorrect. A more serious error—the ultimate auditor's nightmare—is missing something material to the audit, leaving the auditor asking "what was not done that should have been done?" The audit department does not claim to have the answer to that question, but Larry Grow believes the processes put in place to evaluate audits and the feedback the department gets from its clients have mitigated that risk substantially.

In the audit world, timely news is the right news; late news does not help anyone. The timeliness of reports is a potential defect area. Audit costs can be excessive either internally or externally, so how costs are managed and the perception of how they are managed could give rise to defects.

FIGURE C.1 **Detailing the Audit Process**

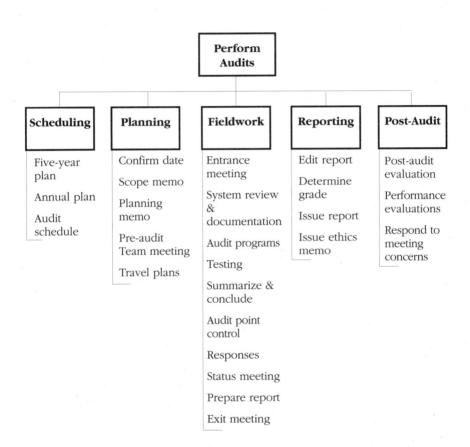

If an auditor resigns from the company, something probably was not done correctly in the hiring or training processes. The department might have to let somebody go, which implies a hiring mistake. Or somebody could spend 24 to 36 months with them, move on to one of the operational units, and then fail in the next job. "That is a 2 year problem we didn't detect." All those things would be considered defects.

The team quickly realized that there was too much to measure, so Larry suggested they focus on key areas. They decided to concentrate on performing audits—the department's major business and potentially the area with the biggest opportunity for improvement. The team concluded that the planning process, field work, and reporting were the three areas where they could make the greatest quality and cycle time improvements.

Next, the task force brainstormed places where there were opportunities for error. As they analyzed their flowcharts, Larry reported,

> A phenomenon happened that we did not anticipate. All of a sudden, I had six quality experts saying: "holy smoke, 56 things could go wrong and we have only looked at three processes. We know those things are broken today and it is absolutely amazing we get anything out the door on time and correct." So we had 6 people running around the department with this weird look on their faces, and I had a bunch of other people saying "what happened to those folks?" Instead of the small learning curve lead we thought we were going to have with the task force team, we had this giant leap in understanding—a big gap we had to narrow very quickly. That is where the subsequent training became so important.

The team also recognized there was no way they could measure effectively 56 kinds of opportunities for errors, so they divided those 56 items into four areas: administrative error opportunities, technical error opportunities, work paper documentation error opportunities, and personnel related error opportunities.

The attempt to interpret the audit process in six sigma terms was a particular challenge.

> We were producing only about 150 audit reports a year, while our factories produce thousands of pagers and radios, and millions of semiconductors. If we defined the audit report as the unit of measure, errors in only one report would put us at four sigma. We would never get to six sigma if we measured that way. The question became: 'How do we reframe our processes to make them look like a large factory? What is it that we produce a lot of that we can measure?'

The team decided to count the individual work papers generated by auditors as the unit of output rather than the final audit reports.

> By counting paper, we can identify millions of "products," so we have an opportunity to match up with the volumes of output that our factories typically produce.

Measuring the quality of the audit process: The task force developed two questionnaires to be filled out at the end of every audit to evaluate the quality of the audit process and all the work papers. One questionnaire is filled out by an audit department peer who was not a participant on that audit—so the person can make an independent professional evaluation. It contains 39 questions (originally 36) and is designed so the respondent can complete it in roughly one hour. Each question is answered simply "yes" or "no" with a no answer indicating a defect somewhere on that item. The second questionnaire is filled out by the customer to get feedback. It contains 19 questions answered on a one–to–five scale plus room for written comments. The survey form is given to the customer with the final audit report and is to be returned directly to the senior manager in charge of the audit department.

The Improved Audit Process

A scoring system was developed allowing the audit evaluation question-naires to be scored in six sigma terms. Using that measurement system, errors in performing audits fell from almost 10,000 parts per million defective in 1988 to the realm of 20 parts per million defective in 1991. In sigma terms this was an improvement from 3.8 sigma to 5.6 sigma.

When the task force began its work, 20 percent of audit work papers and reports were issued without error. By mid-1990, 80 percent were error free. And cycle time for issuing the final report fell from 51 days to five days after completion of field work. These and other improvements arose from changes in each stage of the audit process.

Scheduling: The staffing schedule is arranged to make the two year assignment as unique a learning opportunity as possible. The depart-ment does not want anyone to visit the same location twice, to spe-cialize in any aspect of the business. At the end of each month the staffing schedule for the next 90 days is published and the first 60 days of that is "locked in concrete."

> We go out of our way to avoid changes at all costs, even at the expense of trying to delay special projects that may come along. We try to push those out and get them in the staffing schedule at a later date.

With the Bechtel Corporation, the department has developed a pilot version of an automated scheduling system, a form of artificial intelli-gence that matches auditor profiles with audit profiles. They consider the current version to be "marginally successfully."

> The philosophy is to run the schedule like most people run their factories in a just-in-time manufacturing environment. We look at the auditors as suppliers, supplying resources to the audit department. You have to make a firm schedule commitment to your just-in-time supplier to make the sys-tem work efficiently. If you cannot give them good access to your schedul-ing window, they cannot keep the production line flowing for you.

Planning: Because of the advance and predictable scheduling, audit teams have time to plan each audit so every member has a clear under-standing about where they are going, who they are going to work with, and what their responsibilities will be.

To plan the audit, the department prepares a scope announcement telling the client who will be on the audit team, when the team will be coming, and what they will look at. In a pre-audit meeting, a detailed planning memo is prepared for the auditors on the team. The memo identifies the time to be spent on each item by each person, what is to be audited, the work programs to be used, and the appropriate tools and techniques.

The improvements in scheduling and planning led to significant savings in travel.

> We are very efficient on how we manage our travel costs. Because we're on the road 50% of the time, we spend $1 million a year on travel in our department. It is one of the largest travel budgets in the building. Our ability to schedule so well really allows us to maximize our purchasing power. We buy a lot of nonrefundable tickets, and we don't waste very many of them.

The planning step is also being completed faster. Audit questionnaire responses indicate that the cycle time for planning has been cut in half. Audit staffers now know twice as early what they will be doing and where they will be going.

Fieldwork:

> We manufacture the audit report as we go along, building it in a just-in-time environment. We have entrance meetings with customers to describe what we will be doing and status meetings once a week to discuss the issues. We hand them all findings the day we find them, and customers are required to give us responses to findings in three working days. As a result, the status meetings are not a debate about the findings. We say, 'Here is the issue we gave you on Tuesday; what is your response?' As soon as we get an issue resolved and the response agreed to, it goes into our computers, our finished goods warehouse.

Reporting: When the task force began to rethink the audit process, reporting was a separate step, distinct from fieldwork. Auditors would return to their offices to draft the audit report, have it reviewed, assign the grade, and write the ethics memo, before the report was forwarded to the customer. Now all that work, including the ethics memo when possible, is done as part of the fieldwork.

The final audit report is issued the last day of fieldwork when the auditor meets with the client at an exit meeting.

> By the time we get to the last day of field work, we have already compiled the report in our laptops. We are able to hand the client the final

report on the spot. All that's left when we come back to the office on Monday is to hand the secretary the diskette: she runs it through the PC, prints the report on the laser printer, checks the style sheet to make sure the report is in the right format, puts the yellow cover on, stamps the grade that is assigned, and the report goes out the door.

Post-Audit: In 1986 the department developed a 19 question customer feedback survey. Two years after the completion of the task force's work, the department reported a 94 times improvement in their scores on the post-audit questionnaire.

Performance evaluations for auditors are faster and more effective. As Larry Grow said,

> The auditors now know what they have to do well on those 39 areas to succeed. Everyone knows what the performance standard is. We have achieved a three times improvement in the feedback on performance evaluations. It used to take us 30 days to tell somebody how they did. We operate on a four-week cycle: our audit teams are typically out in the field for a month. If we wait 30 days to tell them how they did on that audit, they've already messed up the next one. If we tell them three days after the audit is over how they did, they now can fix any problems on the next audit.

Additional Payoffs in the External Audit Process

Improvements in the internal audit process have also paid off in the external audit process. In 1983, when Motorola's revenues were about $4.8 billion, some 24,000 hours were devoted to domestic audit. Those working hours were about evenly split between KPMG Peat Marwick and Motorola's internal audit department. In 1991, the company's revenues had grown to $11.3 billion, but domestic audit took only 12,000 hours. Motorola feels they reduced the scope of that audit by 35 percent by asking such fundamental questions as "What are we doing today that we did yesterday? Why can't we change it? What do we need to do to improve cycle times?" They calculate they achieved a two times improvement in the cycle time of the external audit, resulting in a $1.8 million cost avoidance in additional audit fees.

Larry believes KPMG Peat Marwick is a major beneficiary of the improved processes.

> The Peat Marwick people in Chicago kill to get on this account. They don't work any overtime. I think the Peat Marwick senior auditor at the corporate office worked two days of overtime last year. Yet, although they bill us fewer hours, I am sure their profits on our relationship are higher than they were before.

Ongoing Quality Initiatives in Finance

The quest for higher quality is never ending at Motorola. In October 1989, the company engaged the consulting firm of A.T. Kearney to benchmark Motorola finance against world class practices. The study found Motorola's finance group to be "near world class" in functional capability and cross-functional partnering, but only average in productivity and efficiency. In response, Motorola finance began a series of "key initiatives" to increase productivity, implement superior financial systems, improve the relevance of the data provided to operating management, and make finance more of a change agent within the business, all with the goal of becoming best in class in each area.

Motorola finance has created a series of "Finance Councils," cross-functional task forces to deal with new technologies and changing environmental conditions. Several pursue quality-related initiatives, investigating financial management systems that improve quality and further reduce rework and cycle time:

1. *The Finance Metrics Council* evaluates new and evolving concepts in management measurements and implements those that promise better management information. Among the measures considered by this task force are those which capture the quality characteristics of the company, especially as they relate to Motorola's financial performance.

2. *The Internal Controls Council* evaluates existing control systems and participates in the design of new control systems to ensure they are efficient and add value to the company.

3. *The Accounting Policy Council* ensures corporate-wide consistency in accounting policy. It also evaluates new technologies for collecting and reporting financial data to improve accuracy and reduce cycle time.

Payoffs from Motorola's Investments in Quality

Motorola's financial executives believe the payoffs from investments in quality, both in finance and throughout the company, have been very high. These payoffs are most obvious on the income statement: increased revenues and decreased costs. Less obvious benefits may be hidden on the balance sheet. Beyond the financial statements, other benefits are found in the responsiveness, adaptability, and flexibility of the organization, and in what W. Edwards Deming calls "joy in work."

Motorola has not estimated the benefits of its quality investments on the revenue side, but its global competitiveness, and in many cases leadership, in industries frequently dominated by the Japanese is based upon its quality, technology, and cycle time successes. In telecommunications, integrated circuits, space exploration, and its other product markets, high quality and low cycle time in developing, improving, and delivering new products are the price of admission. Without its progress in quality, Motorola would probably no longer be a player, let alone a leader, in these markets.

On the cost side, Motorola has calculated the cost of poor quality for each of its divisions since 1987. From 1987 to 1992, the manufacturing savings on a cost of poor quality basis has been calculated at $2.2 billion, and the company estimates the cost of poor quality has fallen from about 14.5 percent of sales to about 7.5 percent over that time. These estimates do not include savings in support activities such as finance, accounting, legal, and human resources. Although the finance department does not attempt to calculate its own cost of poor quality, it does keep track of improvements on individual projects.

David Hickie has suggested there are other quality benefits the company does not yet know how to quantify.

> The measurement of cost of poor quality is a P-and-L measurement. I submit that there are incredible balance sheet savings that we are not recognizing. When you go through our factories you do not find huge areas to store inventories. We are in the process of converting factory space to office space because our factory space as a percent of total space has decreased. So we do not have to put up a new building because of our improvements in quality and cycle time. Our receivables are interesting. For years we always said as our international business goes up, our total receivables should keep increasing in terms of weeks of receivables. But they have not because the quality improvements in the order entry system and the billing system make it easier for the customers to pay us—so they pay us. When we quote 30 days and they pay us in 6 weeks it is because of their saying things like "We don't know who to call," and "I don't agree with the bill." The whole quality thing has helped us tremendously with assets and receivables, even though we have not been able to get the finance profession to step up and figure out what the savings are.

Motorola estimates that $65 million was spent in training and educating employees in 1991, not including the salaries of the people being trained. As Bob Galvin had argued in 1978, these costs are not seen as expenses, but as investments in current and future organizational responsiveness, adaptability, and flexibility. Every employee is still required to have at least 40 hours of formal training each year. The audit department proudly reports that it averages twice that number.

"Joy in work" comes from many things, not the least of which is the satisfaction of a job well done at the leading edge of customer service and technology—the ability to ship a uniquely configured and freshly manufactured pager from the Boynton Beach, Florida, plant less than an hour after a sales person takes the order anywhere in the world, or the ability to brag about providing communications and other electronics for over 1,000 space launches without a single failure. However, it also comes from the removal of petty annoyances in the day-to-day workplace. For example, Motorola employees no longer need to arrange advances for travel expenses, nor wait weeks for their expense reports to be processed. A new computerized system allows a clerk to enter data from an employee's expense report, checks for errors, converts foreign currency into the local currency, submits the completed form for payment, and cuts a reimbursement check in four hours, long before the employee's credit card statement arrives.

Motorola's 1992 to 1997 Challenge

Perhaps the greatest payoffs from Motorola's investments in quality are the challenges it is now able to lay before itself. In a speech to the company in May 1992, George Fisher, CEO and Chairman of the Board, reported that the company had come close to, but not reached, its target of achieving six sigma performance in all activities by 1992, estimating the company was at a 5.4 sigma level—40 defects per million opportunities. Then he updated the five-year challenge his predecessor, Bob Galvin, laid down in 1987. The 1992–1997 challenge has three priorities: first, continuing and increasing Motorola's commitment to total customer satisfaction—higher levels of success in making the customer the focus of everything the company does; second, recognizing that the company's quality goal of parts per million performance needs to be replaced by a parts per billion mentality—going way beyond six sigma; and third, increasing the company's emphasis on time-based management—seeking the goal of a ten times cycle time improvement in everything Motorola does by 1997! By accepting these challenges, George Fisher told the Motorola community, they would be "daring to dream of becoming the finest company in the world."

People Interviewed

Larry Grow, Senior Manager of Internal Audit
Dave Hickie, Executive Vice President and Chief Corporate Staff Officer
Ken Johnson, Vice President and Corporate Controller

Fordham Student Research Team

Ralph Terracciano, case assistant
Karen Byrne
Greg DeRosa
Don Quigley
Marie Sabia

Solectron

At Solectron, quality is a moment-by-moment way of life in every part of the organization. A contract manufacturer of electronic components and systems, Solectron lives in an environment of continual change and has to be nimble to survive. Solectron has succeeded by becoming extraordinarily responsive to its changing environment: by listening to and working closely with its customers, by monitoring and improving its own operational effectiveness every day and in regular weekly meetings, and by creating extreme flexibility in its processes. Underlying Solectron's success is a commitment to total quality management throughout the company.

Solectron's finance organization plays an important role in the company's tqm activities. Within the finance organization, the quality philosophy is fully embraced by the top leadership, and quality management tools are used to improve the department's own processes, such as reducing receivables, handling payables, improving cash flow, and limiting asset exposure. Perhaps more important, there is a remarkable degree of integration between the finance group and the rest of the company. Finance professionals work with each functional group to provide relevant information and sound financial analysis. A particular achievement at Solectron is the way the finance organization is involved with customers: from their identification and qualification, to bidding and pricing, to account cost and profitability analysis, and ultimately to account performance improvement.

Measurement plays an important role in Solectron's tqm activities. The company's quality database contains information for measuring and meeting the needs of customers, employees, suppliers, shareholders, and the community, and for improving the performance of employees, organizational processes, and suppliers. The data are reviewed daily for trends, process variation, and problem analysis.

A 1991 winner of the Malcolm Baldrige National Quality Award, Solectron has successfully integrated the Baldrige application process into its management systems, using it as an opportunity for ongoing self-study—to compare itself to other quality companies and to monitor its quality progress.

D
Solectron

We would like to win the [Malcolm Baldridge National Quality] award, but more importantly we want to use the application as a process for critical self-examination, goal setting, and continuous improvement. We see the application as a journey: a journey to excel, to improve, and to become the best in the world. Through this rigorous process, American companies can beat the best foreign competitors and revitalize their competitiveness.

—Winston Chen, Chairman and Co-CEO
Solectron won the Baldridge Award in 1991

Few companies are better at systematic self-improvement than Solectron. Every procedure and process at the company is under constant review, and change is a way of life. If the ability to adapt rapidly has become a key to survival, Solectron is well poised for the coming years. Len Wood, former manager, Internal Audit, at Solectron, puts it another way: "When you operate with a gross margin in the range of 13–14 percent, you have to be pretty good to be profitable. We're profitable!"

As a contract manufacturer of electronic components and systems, Solectron lives in an environment of continual change. Customer requirements vary from day to day, and occasionally from hour to hour. Material prices, especially for electronic components, adjust so quickly that any purchase may be made at a price different from the preceding one. Advances in technology occur with such rapidity that it is difficult to know what products the company will be manufacturing from month to month. As a result, Solectron has to be nimble to survive. Solectron has succeeded by becoming extraordinarily responsive to its changing environment: by listening to and working closely with its customers, by monitoring and improving its own operational effectiveness every day and in regular weekly meetings, and by creating extreme flexibility in its processes.

Underlying Solectron's success is a commitment to total quality management throughout the company. Solectron competes for business with companies that operate plants in third world countries—where labor and facilities cost a fraction of what Solectron pays—and with the in-house manufacturing operations of its own customers. This places immense pressure on Solectron's profit margins, leaving little room for waste or error. Winston Chen, along with other Solectron managers, is convinced that the company's tqm approach has been a critical component of its success.

Solectron's finance organization plays an important role in the company's tqm activities. Within the finance organization, the quality philosophy is fully embraced by the top leadership and quality management tools are used to improve the department's own processes, such as reducing receivables, handling payables, improving cash flow, and limiting asset exposure. Perhaps more important, there is a remarkable degree of integration between the finance group and the rest of the company. Finance professionals work with each functional group to provide relevant information and sound financial analysis. A particular achievement at Solectron is the way in which the finance organization is involved with customers: from their identification and qualification, to bidding and pricing, to account cost and profitability analysis, and ultimately to account performance improvement.

How Solectron has so tightly fused its finance activities with the remainder of the organization forms the heart of our case profile.

Solectron's Entry into Quality Management

In a sense, Solectron has been involved in quality management since 1978, when Dr. Winston Chen invested $100,000 to purchase 50 percent of the struggling, one year old, 15-employee company. From the beginning, Winston brought to the business his deep-seated belief in the worth of people and their ability to contribute to the organization and a desire to provide the highest degree of product excellence and service quality to customers. Winston had spent eight years with IBM, and in 1988 he invited his friend and former boss at IBM, Dr. Ko Nishimura, to join him at Solectron. Both fully embraced IBM's three guiding principles: customer service, respect for the individual, and pursuit of excellence in every activity.

An "Emergent" Quality Management System

The process of adopting and adapting tqm approaches at Solectron began as an "emergent" rather than a "planned" process. In providing direction to the company, Winston and others applied their values in a step-by-step fashion. As the results of each step became apparent, they would build upon them by taking what looked like the logical next step.

In the first few years, the company's responsiveness to its customers led its members to work long and hard hours attempting "to inspect quality into the product." In 1981, the company embraced quality circles, as did many other American companies at the time.

The first major quality breakthrough for the company occurred in 1984, when it discovered the power of statistical quality control and applied it to its manufacturing operations. Kaizen (continuous improvement) concepts were applied systematically beginning in 1986. In 1987, Solectron started making good progress on shifting its quality efforts toward the prevention mode and in making QPI (Quality and Productivity Improvement) teams widespread and effective. In 1989, a second breakthrough occurred with the adoption of the Malcolm Baldrige National Quality Award criteria as an integrating framework for the company's various quality efforts and with the adoption of Motorola's six sigma approach and metrics.

Intense Competition and the Need for Tqm

Even if Solectron's founders had not been predisposed toward quality, the industry they elected to enter left them little choice. Contract manufacturing is a highly competitive business. It is characterized by ease of entry and by significant competition from companies that choose to manufacture in low cost, often third world venues, and also from its customers, which can simply keep their manufacturing in-house. Success in contract manufacturing depends on delivering high quality assemblies at a competitive cost, and frequently on being able to deliver them faster than the customers' own production facilities. Success in contract manufacturing of electronic devices depends also on achieving a high degree of flexibility and responsiveness since customer requirements change often and without warning.

In part, Solectron became a tqm company simply to be competitive. Because management understood the intensity of its competition, it relied on tqm-like practices since its founding. As a result, there was no need for a massive shift in practices to implement tqm. Quality management principles were always there and created much of the company's vital early competitive advantage.

Advantages of a Diverse Workforce

The diversity of its workers further reinforced Solectron's use of quality principles. Reflecting the company's philosophy of providing opportunity to those in need, many Solectron employees are recent immigrants who suffered hardships and dislocations on their way to the U.S. Solectron offers a "family" environment where differences among employees are valued and their personal growth encouraged. To walk through Solectron's facilities is to meet people from virtually every part of the world. Dozens of cultures are represented; dozens of languages spoken.

The need to communicate across language and cultural lines sensitized employees to become better listeners and to discard prejudices that might inhibit working with "different" people. It also gave Solectron skills in communication that were adaptable to dialogue with customers and suppliers.

Learning from the Baldrige Award Process

As Winston Chen's remarks in the opening paragraph of this case study reveal, Solectron used the Baldrige application as an opportunity for self study. Winning the award was not the driving force in applying; in fact, most of the people involved in preparing the Baldrige application, including senior management, did not expect to win for many years if at all. Rather, the Baldrige Award provided Solectron the chance to compare itself to other quality companies and to monitor its quality progress. Susan Wang, Senior VP and CFO, says the company was "pleasantly surprised by the results of our first application" when it scored above the median of the companies that applied for the Baldrige Award in 1989.

For Ko Nishimura, now Solectron's President and CEO, the Baldrige application process was the opportunity to bring together and formalize the disparate quality initiatives taking place throughout the company. True to its entrepreneurial style, Solectron had encouraged each part of the organization to pursue tqm in its own way. Ko saw the Baldrige criteria as one possible set of unifying guidelines for a tqm organization. As he remarked,

> We looked at it as a key business process that we should use in the company to integrate the pieces. Why should we go out and invent one of these when there were a lot of people who thought this out pretty well? I looked at this and said "Gee, this is great. It doesn't do everything, but it does a lot of things and it's going to move the company forward if we use it every year."

By writing the application, company members were required to share their quality approaches and take a serious look at the consistency of their processes.

Solectron first applied for the award in 1989, and received useful feedback about its strengths and weaknesses. In response, Solectron set about improving areas identified as below par, including employee communications, corporate standards, training, and recognition. An employee opinion survey was initiated. Corporate guidelines for manufacturing and testability were written, and the company adopted Motorola's six sigma system to measure defect rates. Solectron University was founded, offering a varied set of courses taught on-site, on company time, and free to all employees. The company created a President's Award for quality improvement team contributions and a Chairman's Trophy to recognize outstanding divisional performance. Responding to the 1990 feedback, Solectron strengthened its use of structured process analysis and improvement tools, increased its community involvement, and extended its benchmarking activities.

In 1991 when they won, Solectron received a site visit from a team of Baldrige examiners who followed up with written reports containing still more useful guidance. Commenting on the worth of applying for the award, Ko remarked,

> By asking serious questions about how we stacked up against the Baldrige criteria, we involved everyone throughout the organization in quality and learned a lot about where we had the opportunity to improve as well. Where else could we get such low cost, high quality consulting?

Mixed in with the elation of winning the Award in 1991 was the realization that winners were proscribed from applying again for a five-year period, five years during which the Baldrige Award feedback would no longer be available to Solectron. There was also concern that some employees might think the company "had made it" and be tempted to relax. Instead, Solectron found new ways to challenge itself. In 1992, partly prompted by its international expansion, it began to pursue ISO 9000 certification. The company sees ISO 9000's focus on standardization and documentation as a good way to address gaps in documenting processes, gaps recognized by the company and identified by the Baldrige examiners. Solectron is extending standardization and documentation "compliance" beyond a product focus to include more business processes than formally required, while working to prevent standardization from creating bureaucracy as the company continues to grow.

Beyond ISO 9000, Solectron is continuing to use the Baldrige criteria to focus its improvement processes and to measure its progress. It is acting on the priority improvement areas identified by the 1991 Baldrige examiners, has set five-year goals for those areas, and may reapply for the

Baldrige Award in 1996 when the competition will have evolved to a much higher standard of excellence. Solectron is also thinking of applying for the Japanese Deming Prize. As Ko says,

> We have compared ourselves to the best in the United States so what's next? To compare ourselves to the best in the world and strive to reach that level.

Finance as a Quality Partner

Finance was encouraged to be involved in tqm from the start of Solectron's systematic quality management efforts and to move forward in implementing tqm at its own pace. At first, finance reached a common, if erroneous, conclusion: tqm was merely a way to speed up production, to produce more at a faster pace. However, they soon realized that quality management did not simply mean speed, and that faster production without improved processes would only result in producing a lot of "junk."

To learn more about tqm, finance started using the same types of QPI teams to examine its own operations that finance members were joining to improve processes in manufacturing and other parts of the company. The first team examined the order entry process and succeeded in creating process flowcharts, making some process improvements, and achieving some reduction in cycle time. However it soon became apparent that the team did not possess the skills to do a root-cause analysis of the problems in the process, and was unable to eliminate them. This insight led to the creation of an eight-week training program in problem solving and statistical process control designed specifically for finance, and attended by all finance members.

Over time QPI team members continued to identify lack of training in tqm improvement processes and knowledge of the tqm tools as barriers to full implementation of tqm in the finance area. What appeared at first as resistance to the quality approach turned out instead to be people trying to grasp and use the new techniques without sufficient understanding to be able to use them effectively. When the finance staff began to receive formal training in behavioral and statistical process control techniques, the teams became more effective and enthusiasm for the new approaches became more evident. Task forces were assigned to identify problems and discover their root causes—not to lay blame, but to look systematically at each process and where it might be going awry.

Cross Training

As finance progressed in its work with its own QPI teams and those initiated by other areas, problems in communicating with other departments about financial issues and financial analysis techniques started to surface. Concluding once again that the communication problems arose not from resistance to the new approaches or from attempts to protect turf, but from lack of knowledge and skills, finance recommended that every other area of the company be given some training in working with costing and other financial information. Susan Wang observes,

> It seems logical now that if we in finance wish to have another area communicate with us then we should be speaking the same language. Providing financial training serves to bridge the gap.

Finance's experience with training was shared by other areas within Solectron. Each group needed to learn quality management tools, and each found it important for other areas of the company to learn about their work. As a result, Solectron has developed a belief that all areas of the company should have cross-functional training. No area is off limits. For example, when he was manager of internal audit, Len Wood completed a week of training in the latest soldering techniques used on the factory floor in order to improve his understanding of that part of the business.

Solectron University supports both the tqm training and the cross-training needs of the company with its courses in tqm, business, English as a second language, and many more subjects. The company's employee training goals and accomplishments are impressive: each employee was slated to receive 85 hours of training in FY 1991 and 95 hours in FY 1992. Virtually everyone reached those targets. The targets for the next three years are 110, 125, and 150 hours.

Measuring Quality

Solectron constantly collects quality data in all its operating areas. The information is compiled in a computer database accessible from more than five hundred personal computers throughout the company. The quality database contains information for measuring and meeting the needs of customers, employees, suppliers, shareholders, and the community, and for improving the performance of employees, organizational processes, and suppliers. The data are reviewed daily for trends, process variation, and problem analysis. Analyses and actions are communicated within the company and to many customers through E-mail. Among Solectron's more important quality measurements, and the starting places for many of its quality improvement efforts, are those related to customer service, particularly its internal and external Customer Satisfaction Indices (CSIs).

Customer Satisfaction Indices

Solectron's first customer satisfaction index was based on surveys developed by the marketing area and filled in by external customers. Each week, marketing distributes the CSI survey form to all customers, asking how Solectron is doing on five dimensions: product quality, delivery, communication, service responsiveness, and overall company performance. Customers score the company on a letter grade scale with a matching point score for each letter: A(100 points), A-(90), B+(85), B(80), B-(75), C(0), and D(-100). The scale is a severe one. "A" is the only acceptable score; even an A- is well below the corporate goal of 97.

Space is provided on the form for comments, which are encouraged. Customers are asked to FAX the form to Solectron by Monday afternoon each week. The results are distributed to the operating divisions over E-mail each Tuesday and presented at the Thursday morning executive management meeting. Division managers responsible for action plans responding to customer feedback also present their progress. The meeting is attended by most senior people, and open to all employees, a fair number of whom attend as well.

By collecting feedback every week, Solectron creates an open dialog with its customers so it can quickly sense any change in customer expectations and how well they are being met. By sharing the results with the entire company, vital feedback—both good and bad—is provided, and all employees can participate in remedying any problems that arise. By sharing the results with its customers, Solectron communicates that it is aware of problems and is working quickly to correct them.

CSIs for Finance

In 1990, finance began to survey its own customers' satisfaction. Surveys using the same scale and the same or very similar dimensions as the external customer forms are distributed to finance's various internal customers. CSIs are computed and reported on a monthly basis. The philosophy is the same as that of the external customer CSIs: finance understands it can best learn what its customers want by asking them.

All finance units collect CSIs. While those who respond indicate a high degree of satisfaction with their finance suppliers, the response rate is lower than desired. Finance is currently looking for ways to create a higher level of interest so more of its internal customers will regularly return the CSIs.

Breaking Down the Barriers with External Customers

The idea of approaching a potential customer armed with statistical data outlining not only how the customer will benefit but also clearly detailing what one's company will gain certainly sounds like an innovative business practice, yet how many companies are successful in doing so? The idea of using the first set of data to sell the prospect is certainly logical but the idea of sharing both sets of data may seem far less logical—unless the goal is to build a long-term relationship based upon mutual benefit and trust. But even then, how many companies seeking long-term relationships are willing to take the risks in such an approach? Yet, this is just the type of thing Solectron does, and it goes a step further—communicating that its goal is to achieve a 6 percent pre-tax margin on the work it does and providing customers data to verify its successes and failures in doing so.

Many companies have been accused of thinking only short-term and going for the fast buck. And the finance function is frequently fingered as a particularly guilty party in this respect. These accusations may be true about some other American companies, but short-term thinking and financial short-sightedness are not charges that can be leveled at Solectron—or at its finance department.

Integrating Finance into the Process
of Developing and Satisfying Customers

The heart of Solectron's business—the process of obtaining and retaining satisfied customers—demonstrates the progress Solectron's finance function has made in making sure that it adds value to the company's day-to-day business operations.

The following discussion focuses on Finance's role in four aspects of the process of obtaining and retaining satisfied customers: identifying promising prospects, approaching potential customers, establishing successful partnerships with them, and working to make those partnerships increasingly effective. Although this discussion emphasizes

Finance's role in these processes and the success of the Finance Department in working as a team member with the other functions—just as all the other cases in this study provide the same focus and emphasis—it is important to remember that the other functions at Solectron, as in the other companies discussed, make similar contributions and have achieved very similar levels of integration and sense of teamwork and partnership.

Identifying Promising Prospects

Solectron seeks the same thing from customers that many companies committed to quality want—solid, long-term relationships. In identifying promising prospects, finance plays an important role in supporting sales, marketing, and other personnel in evaluating each prospect's potential. In Solectron's industry, there are four major reasons why a company might use a contract manufacturer for some or all of its production: to conserve capital and/or cash, to gain access to production technology it lacks, to save time if a contract manufacturer can "ramp up" production faster, and to achieve quality levels greater than possible with the company's existing facilities and management system. Solectron summarizes these reasons as giving its customers the lowest total cost solution to their manufacturing needs, where total cost includes not only the direct cost of manufacture, but also the costs saved due to high quality, on-time production, capital expenditures avoided, and the like.

Over the years, Solectron has developed an effective team-based process for identifying promising customer prospects, evaluating them, and making decisions on their suitability. However, recent attempts to improve a step that used to come relatively late in the prospect identification process have considerably improved finance's contribution to the entire process. That step involves the decision on the credit worthiness of the prospect and the amount of credit the prospect would be eligible to receive.

Integrating credit analysis with strategic customer acquisition: In Solectron's early days, there was no formal procedure for checking a customer's credit worthiness. The company was small and did not have appreciable financial resources to extend to customers. In addition, the early customers tended to be well established companies or were identified as prospects through personal contacts and were well known to management. By the mid-1980s, however, Solectron had grown to the point where extension of credit was becoming increasingly important and appropriate.

In 1985–86, finance developed an internal credit matrix, a fairly elaborate and traditional credit analysis process similar to commercial bank systems. Unfortunately, the process proved quite cumbersome. Since few members of the sales force had finance skills or desired to take time away from selling, credit analysis was done within the finance organization. Sales people lost considerable time as they contended for the attention of the company's sole analyst, lobbied for credit approval, and were forced to wait for the credit decision. It was difficult to be responsive to prospects. A negative decision meant the time invested with a potential customer was wasted, leaving the sales staff, and very likely the rejected prospect, angry and frustrated.

Simplifying the credit decision and distributing it to the field: In early 1992, Myron Lee, Financial Manager with credit responsibility, introduced a simplified process. Finance divides potential customers into three groups: "A customers," which are large and financially healthy and require no credit check, "B customers," the middle-sized prospects for which it is important to check credit, and "C customers," those that are financially weak and are not to be pursued unless a special strategic rationale exists. Sales people are free to pursue A customers without further financial review. For B customers, the sales person now fills out a credit scoring sheet developed by Myron and his colleagues. The form uses easily obtainable data and is simple to fill out. A potential customer's score translates directly into the credit line Solectron is willing to extend.

The new process has empowered the sales staff to make preliminary credit decisions and has eliminated the frustration of the prior system. Sales people now know how finance will react before approaching a customer, and no longer waste time selling to unacceptable credit risks. Because it is so easy to understand, the form itself teaches the sales staff how and why finance makes the credit decision. Finance staffers are now seen as a support system and are no longer the "bad guys" who interfere with sales. By distributing some of his skills to the sales force, Myron Lee eliminated much of his routine work and can now devote more time to supporting strategic marketing decisions.

Bringing strategic dimensions to the field: In the process of simplifying and distributing the credit analysis process to the sales force, Solectron has also assisted the sales force in keeping strategic factors in mind at the very first step in the prospect identification process. The credit scoring sheet provided to the sales force summarizes key dimensions of customer attractiveness, each of which is scored on a one to three scale. Sales uses the rating scheme to decide which prospects are likely to be attractive to the company in both the short and long term and to communicate this evaluation if the prospect actually is recommended as a customer. The form enables the salesperson to include strategic marketing, technological, production, and financial perspectives into the very earliest stages of account prospecting and enables Solectron to "distribute" these traditional functional and upper management perspectives to the company members closest to potential customers. It also enables the salesperson to predict not only the amount of credit the prospect would be eligible for but also the likelihood the prospect will be approved as a customer.

Moving from inspection to prevention: In addition to empowering the sales force to make early decisions with a strategic perspective and to make preliminary credit decisions, the new system can also be looked at as shifting the process of credit analysis and granting from an "inspection mode" to a "prevention mode." Instead of the credit decision coming at the end of the sales process after a salesperson has invested much time and effort to cultivate a potential customer, it is now done up front, before the customer is approached.

Approaching the Potential Customer

Once a potential customer has met Solectron's selection criteria, a team of marketing, finance, procurement, and production staff approaches the prospect. Since Solectron is interested in developing long-term relationships and desires support throughout its customers' organizations, the team attempts to meet with a wide variety of people from the prospect company. The goal is to present Solectron as offering a total manufacturing solution to the prospect's needs. Together the prospect and Solectron discuss opportunities to outsource production.

The finance team member is active throughout the customer approach. A presentation of the financial benefits of contract manufacturing is frequently made to the prospect company's CFO. The finance team member participates in a technical and cost analysis of the relevant business; often, as Solectron learns of the prospect's design and production technology, it discovers a higher quality or lower cost way to manufacture that it passes on to the potential customer.

In response to Solectron's presentation and analysis, the prospect can do one of three things. Should the prospect reject Solectron's approach, the Solectron team attempts to determine why, and if given the opportunity, goes over its proposal with the prospect step by step to determine if there were any incorrect assumptions on either side. Solectron may modify its proposal as it learns more about the prospect's products and needs. Alternatively, the prospect may reconsider Solectron's proposal, especially as the customer more fully understands the total cost of using Solectron—direct manufacturing cost adjusted for savings due to high production quality, quick response time, and not supporting the production in house. A second response could be a request for more information, which normally also leads to a detailed review of the proposal with the potential customer. Third, the prospect could agree to engage Solectron, in which case the relationship continues and develops.

Building Customer and Supplier Partnerships

Solectron's finance staff works closely with its customers and suppliers to create and support a relationship that encourages honesty and openness, creates trust, and promotes continuation and expansion of their business. In many cases, Solectron's finance people meet regularly with their counterparts in the customer's or supplier's organization to facilitate rapid communication and sharing of problems and successes. Working together is also facilitated by connecting Solectron's E-mail directly with the E-mail of its large customers.

Division controllers participate in an ongoing problem-solving process as members of QPI teams composed of personnel from both the customer and Solectron. Examples of recent teams are:

- overtime premiums—a team to reduce overtime premiums stemming from customer rescheduling,

- price quotations—a team to reduce complexity in quantifying variances from quote where the customer and Solectron have different accounting systems, and

- price changes—a team to improve price list maintenance due to rapid changes of specifications and cost of materials.

Often the work of the QPI teams not only solves the immediate problem, but leads directly to other improvements in the way Solectron does business. For example, the team working on price list maintenance designed a centralized pricing database and a better change order procedure to deal with the immediate issue. These improvements led to the creation of an automated price list system that is now shared across the company and available to all customers.

Russ Kilidjian, one of the division controllers, has become a leader in a user group for the financial software package used by Solectron. He established a cost accounting task force that has attracted membership from throughout the West. By sharing their experiences, members of the task force solved many common problems, for example, reconciling the inventory sub-ledger with the general ledger. The task force has been so productive that the software company that wrote the package now sends representatives to meetings to learn how to improve its product and provide better service to customers like Solectron.

Reducing the cycle time for responding to orders: In August 1990, a cross-functional QPI team began to work on customer complaints that Solectron took too long to process and distribute purchase orders (POs). The team discovered that customers' needs regularly changed during the time contracts were being negotiated. This would lead to modifications of a product's specifications or the quantity to be manufactured which would, in turn, require the PO to be rewritten. Delays were preventing Solectron from beginning work in a timely manner.

In response, the QPI team devised a preliminary purchase order that would contain the product's original specifications and would be sent to the customer for approval the same day. The team also redesigned the computer screen used to input PO data. This reduced input time and made it easier to enter changes after the preliminary PO was cut. In total, the average time to get a PO into the system was reduced from eight to ten days to same day entry, drastically reducing customer complaints.

Seeking moment-by-moment awareness of progress and problems in operations: Because of the volatile nature of its business, Solectron calculates, analyzes, and responds to its profitability on a weekly basis. Through the device of the "weekly P+L," the company carefully monitors its business with each customer, identifies any changes in revenues or costs, and tracks the overall profitability of each division. Changes in revenues or expenses surface quickly, permitting prompt response, and the data are used to improve the accuracy of the company's financial forecasting.

Solectron began weekly profitability reporting in its early days when it had few turnkey contracts. Most business was on a consignment basis, was subject to volatile market conditions, and could change significantly from week to week. In many ways, the company was living "from hand to mouth, making it critical to know where we stood" recalls Gerry Bain, Solectron's Consolidations Manager.

Each week, Finance produces an income statement for each division of the company. Revenues are then further split out by customer to identify deviations from the forecast of that customer's business. Also generated by division on a weekly basis are month-to-date income statements, which are the accumulation of the weekly P+Ls and an updated forecast for the current month, which is the beginning of month forecast adjusted by the weekly actuals.

The weekly P+L results are presented formally at Solectron's Tuesday morning meeting, at which the profitability of each division and the trend of each major customer's business are discussed. Until 1992, the report was presented by Gerry Bain for all six major divisions, but this often led to challenges from division controllers and others about the report's accuracy or interpretation. Now each division controller presents the report for that division; the divisions now "own" the weekly P+Ls and take responsibility for their accuracy, interpretation, and for addressing any problems that surface. A full accounting close, in which all expenses are fully allocated by division, is done at month end. Each division receives a P+L for each of its customers, and the divisional customer P+Ls are aggregated for Solectron's 10 largest customers (who typically do business with more than one division and represent a large part of Solectron's revenues) to produce company-wide customer P+Ls.

For its weekly P+Ls, Solectron uses ratios reflecting prior expense levels to allocate costs by division. For its monthly reporting, however, Solectron makes creative use of Activity Based Costing (ABC) to attach costs to each customer. Some accounts—such as revenues, wages, commissions, and materials—are hard data and do not require allocation. Others are connected to cost drivers such as labor dollars (certain fringe benefits), materials dollars (purchasing, warehousing), employee head count (supplies, human resource department), fixed assets (facilities costs, interest expense), and number of invoices (purchasing). Corporate administration is seen as protector of the company's two primary assets: employees, and shareholders' investment in capital resources. Accordingly, one half of administration is allocated based on head count and the other half on the sum of receivables, inventories, and fixed assets.

Tom Clawson, who as director of finance is responsible for managerial accounting, is challenging his staff to continue reducing the cycle time for producing internal reports. Solectron now closes its books at month end in three days, has a goal of one day, and looks ahead to the possibility of closing after every transaction so statements are available in real time. Along the way, finance is improving its use of ABC to permit weekly, or perhaps daily, P+Ls by customer.

Improving Customer Account Performance

If a customer's way of doing business is inconsistent with Solectron's continuous improvement process, or if the relationship is simply not profitable, Solectron will try to improve the account. To address problems in the quality of the relationship, Solectron will offer to educate the customer in tqm, inviting customer personnel to attend sessions at Solectron University. If the problem is financial, the divisional controller will work with the customer to review Solectron's cost and profit structure and to renegotiate the economics of the relationship. Often these efforts succeed in rescuing the account.

As a last resort, Solectron will terminate a nonperforming customer. Disengagement is done slowly to avoid disrupting the customer's business. Solectron will do its best to locate a competitor that will take over the business and will cooperate with the competitor to make the transfer as easy as possible for the departing customer. With the opening of its Penang, Malaysia plant in 1991, Solectron has created the opportunity to transition maturing production for some customers that might otherwise have been lost to lower-priced third world competitors.

Breaking Down the Barriers with Internal Customers

Solectron distributes members of its finance staff to the operating divisions in the form of divisional controllers. Each controller, who is physically located in the operating division (some work with more than one division), is responsible for bringing finance skills to the company's day-to-day activities. Controllers are also a major link for coordination between support functions and operating divisions as they meet weekly to share their experiences and ideas.

On a daily basis, divisional controllers provide support to the decision making and business processes within the division. As discussed above, they participate with divisional personnel in direct customer related activities. Internally, they provide financial analysis of production activity, of materials purchases, and of inventory and capital expenditure proposals. They manage data collection and reporting within their division. Ultimately, the controllers' work with their internal customers helps the division provide external customers the best mix of product quality and service at low cost.

Division controllers are active participants on QPI teams, both within and across divisions, working with production, sales, division managers, etc. to solve specific problems and to improve processes. Examples of recent teams are:

- Pricing consistency—a team to create consistency in the pricing and quotations presented to customers (who often deal with several Solectron divisions).

- Unscheduled issues of inventory to production—a team to improve the physical and accounting handling of raw material issues beyond a product's bill of materials due to shortages or damaged work in process.

- Physical inventory—a team to improve the accuracy and reliability of the ongoing inventory cycle count to the point where it is no longer necessary to take a regular physical inventory (avoiding shutting down the plant for one day to complete the physical inventory would save about $250,000).

- Accounting standardization—a team to improve and standardize the recording and reporting of areas such as subcontracting costs, manufacturing variances, and scrap.

Reducing Inventory Exposure

In its role as protector of the firm's assets, Solectron's financial management is charged with minimizing unusable inventory occurring because of changes in customer requirements. Its efforts have resulted in high inventory turnover and very little waste.

As a first step, the company elected not to speculate in inventory. All raw materials are purchased against a specific customer's turnkey contract with the exception of a few generic parts where volume discounts are significant. (There is no exposure with consignment business in which inventory is provided and owned by the customer.)

On a quarterly basis, divisional controllers review a summary of the weekly analyses prepared by the materials planning organization comparing inventory levels and turnover to each customer's business volume. The analyses include raw materials on hand (a small amount, since many of Solectron's operations are on a just-in-time basis) plus material on order. Excess inventory, defined as anything greater than the forecasted amount required to service a customer for the next six months, is identified and worked through the system.

To prevent surplus inventory from accumulating, Solectron works with its suppliers to build volume and delivery flexibility into each materials purchase contract. The company also works with its customers to ensure that changes in business volume do not cause inventory excesses. By establishing a close relationship with each customer, Solectron attempts to learn of possible volume changes as the customer considers them, providing the longest possible lead time to adjust material purchase orders. Should a customer change its level of business after Solectron has committed to purchase materials, Solectron makes every attempt to dispose of the unusable inventory at no cost. In addition, contracts with customers are generally written so that if a customer changes its volume inside specific order delivery windows, it bears the liability for excess inventories on hand or on order, a remedy used only as a last resort.

Self Audit

When he was manager of internal audit, Len Wood began changing the role of the internal auditor at Solectron. While internal audit retains its responsibility for promoting solid internal controls, it no longer serves as the primary enforcer of that environment. In a shift of approach similar to what Myron Lee has accomplished with credit analysis, internal audit is moving from performing inspections after the fact to eliminating problems through prevention.

Len points out that traditional audit procedure is based on assumptions that may never have been true, and are contrary to Solectron's tqm culture. The traditional audit model assumes that people are weak and possibly bad, are uninterested or afraid of accurate record keeping and reporting, and are prone to hide their errors. They will take advantage of the company and have to be closely watched. The role of the audit system is to act as a police force, looking over people's shoulders expecting to find deficiencies. Auditors identify problems after they have occurred, find fault with the people involved, and put them on notice that they will be watched even more closely. As Len colorfully puts it, "In the traditional audit system, we went around bayoneting the wounded after the battle." He continues,

> The problem isn't the people, it's the system. But in the traditional system, we rarely get to the root causes that lead to the problems we discover. We end up blaming the people and treating the symptoms, and the problem is still likely to be there when we go back next year.

In a tqm perspective, people are seen very differently. People are presumed to be strong and good, are honest and therefore comfortable with record keeping and reporting, and wish to learn of their errors so they may improve what they do. They are loyal to the company and will protect its resources. With its policy of constant respect for people and its high degree of support for employees, Solectron's culture reinforces this behavior. Consistent with these assumptions, Len began a self audit program in which each area of the company performs much of the audit job itself. Len's role became that of a teacher, training the operating units in the need for controls, in the design of control systems, and in the statistical methods that can test for reporting accuracy. Much of what Len taught helped operating staffers understand their processes better so they could be proactive in finding and eliminating potential problem areas. Operations now "owns" its controls and is much more interested in making them work. Once again, Solectron has distributed the skills of finance to its operating personnel, empowering them to act better, smarter and faster—and at lower cost.

KPMG Peat Marwick, Solectron's external auditor, reports that its job has been simplified since the self audit process began. Much of the work Peat Marwick would otherwise do is now done directly by the operating units. Solectron is particularly open, reporting problems to Peat Marwick as they arise throughout the year. As a result, the external auditors discover little with their formal annual audit they don't already know. They complete the audit in much less time than before, and at a lower cost to Solectron. Peat Marwick auditors find the Solectron account such a fascinating learning experience, they compete to be assigned to it.

Integrated Planning and Budgeting

Planning is difficult in Solectron's volatile environment. The consignment portion of its business is highly unpredictable, changing from day to day. Turnkey contracts rarely extend for more than several months. In the past, the company's forecasting horizon was limited to a six-month period, with accurate forecasts possible for only the next 90 days.

Recently, however, Solectron elected to extend its forecasting horizon to a full year. In part this was driven by the company's strategic effort to increase its business stability by expanding the proportion of turnkey contracts in its job mix. With less consignment work, Solectron's business would become more predictable. But the change was also due to the work of a QPI team that applied statistical process analysis to forecasting accuracy. The team found that one large customer accounted for much of the deviations from forecast. It is now working with that customer to identify how much variability is beyond its control and how the customer's forecasts can be improved.

Each month, finance receives information from all manufacturing and sales departments. Detailed forecasting is done for the coming four months. The primary input is from the manufacturing divisions, is based on contracts in hand, and is broken down by customer and by assembly. Marketing estimates any business coming on line but not yet available to manufacturing. A more general forecast is made for months five through 12. Based primarily on marketing's estimates of future business, the forecast is sliced by customer, but not detailed more finely. Customers have been very responsive to Solectron's request for forecasting information as they understand that this helps Solectron plan for their needs and keep manufacturing costs down. Once the forecast is produced, Solectron's cross-functional capacity management committee looks at the implications for capacity allocation and needs, and updates its plan for steering work to the various divisions and for capital expansion.

Given the volatility of its business environment, the results of Solectron's forecasting efforts are impressive. Over the first three months, actuals run within 5 percent of forecast. Actuals are within 10 percent in months six through 12.

Results for the Finance Function and the Company

Solectron's commitment to tqm has paid off in many ways, including the dedication and satisfaction of its employees, improved financial processes, and significant returns for external stakeholders. Winning the Baldrige Award confirmed many of these benefits and set Solectron on the path to its next higher level of performance.

Benefits for Company Members

Tqm at Solectron reinforced and extended a culture that plays a big role in the company's success story. By insisting all company members act out of respect for each other, by providing a high level of education and training, and by promoting cultural diversity, Solectron makes important statements to its people. For many employees Solectron is like a family, a home in which they feel valued and comfortable. While this is particularly true of Solectron's immigrant population whose former homes were left far behind, it is also true for those with domestic roots. Many employees cannot conceive of working anywhere else. There is a palpable feeling of joy in being part of the company that translates into many hours of dedicated work. Staff often work well beyond an eight-hour day due to their loyalty and concern for the company. Solectron's commitment to its employees' personal growth is well understood within the firm. Company members share a feeling that the company places no limits on their success, no ceiling on their professional progress.

Within the constraints of production requirements, hourly employees have flexibility in their work hours and can choose to work a four-day week. And, although customer requirements often dictate the use of overtime, Solectron is very aware of the disrupting effect this can have on employees' personal lives and income stream, and has been successful in offering its hourly employees a balanced schedule to avoid high time and salary "volatility."

Solectron's finance people report a particularly high degree of satisfaction in their work. They are seen throughout the company as cooperative partners with important skills that can help the operating divisions increase profits leading to more job opportunities and higher compensation. As Steve Ng, Vice President of Corporate Materials, commented, he couldn't live without his division controller any more. CFO Susan Wang's personal style echoes that of the company, providing education and opportunity, and encouraging innovation. There is a shared feeling among the finance staff that they are pushing back the envelope in finance and quality, a source of considerable pride for many.

Improvements in Financial Processes

Tqm has provided the technology used by Solectron to bring systematic improvement to its business processes. Credit analysis, marketing support, profitability analysis, inventory control, internal audit, and budgeting are among the finance activities that have been and are still being significantly strengthened through the application of tqm. Running through the stories of each of these improvements are the tqm threads of process focus, team-based problem solving, continuous improvement, distributed financial expertise, and a focus on prevention rather than inspection.

Benefits for the Company and Its External Stakeholders

Tqm has helped Solectron offer its customers high quality manufacturing at low cost. The types of quality improvements and cost savings found in any effective tqm implementation have, of course, been realized by

Solectron. For example, Solectron's 1991 Baldrige application reported the reduction of one major component of rework costs, the cost of rework labor, as follows:

> Rework labor cost has been declining over the last three plus years. When we started tracking this indicator in 1987, average rework cost was over $22,000 per week ($1.1 million annually). This amounted to about 1.9 percent of our annualized revenue. At our average revenue growth rate of over 50 percent for the last four years, rework cost would normally grow to $4.5 million per year in 1991, but improvements in processes and process controls have reduced it to around $4000 per week ($200,000 annually). This amounts to a saving of 22 times our 1987 rework cost.

By creating partnerships with its customers, Solectron has made itself easy to do business with and very responsive to its customers' changing needs. From 1989 to 1991 the number of quality awards it had received from its customers grew from 14 to 41. Its overall customer satisfaction index rose from 91 percent to 93 percent. Its reputation in the electronics industry continues to increase, and the company continues to experience a high rate of sales growth. From 1989 to 1991 sales grew from $129 million to $265 million. In 1992 the growth continued, with sales reaching $406 million. Its success has permitted overseas expansion to provide additional services for its customers. New opportunities have opened up as industry leaders look to new relationships with Solectron. For example, toward the end of 1992, Solectron successfully completed the acquisition of IBM manufacturing plants in North Carolina and France.

Solectron's sales growth has been accompanied by a corresponding growth in earnings, rising from $4.3 million in 1989 to $9.2 million in 1991 and to $14.5 million in 1992. Share price has risen even more dramatically, from $6 when the company went public in November 1989 to about $40 in early 1993 after a two for one split. Solectron is highly regarded by financial analysts. Its stock was recently listed on the New York Stock Exchange and it has very good access to banks and the capital markets.

Benefits (and Costs) of Winning the Baldrige Award

The Baldrige Award is this country's highest confirmation of success in using tqm. It has identified Solectron to the world as one of America's best managed companies. While it is the result and not the cause of Solectron's excellence, the Award has raised the company's profile, attracting new customers, suppliers, and investors.

There are some costs to winning the Award, but they are small. Solectron is obligated to share its story with other interested companies, something it was doing already and something very consistent with the company's belief in returning its successes to the community. And Solectron will have to look elsewhere for the advice that came from Baldrige examiners since it cannot apply again until 1996—but this has only spurred the company on to scale other heights.

Perhaps the greatest benefit of winning the Baldrige Award is the satisfaction that comes from being widely recognized as one of the best, a satisfaction that is shared throughout the company. There is a pride in being leaders in tqm, and in contributing to U.S. competitiveness in an industry dominated by foreign concerns. Winning seems to have drawn the company family even closer and elevated the already high commitment to outstanding performance.

Reviving U.S. Competitiveness

Solectron is a company comfortable with change. In learning to be nimble to deal with its volatile business environment, the company developed the comfort with change that helped it adopt and deploy the tqm management technology rapidly. Solectron recognizes that, as good as it is, it is far from perfect. To build upon its successes, all company processes must be improved continuously or competitors will surpass it in product quality and customer service.

The deep involvement of finance has been an important part of the company's achievements in using tqm. As Susan Wang advises the finance staff, "Change is our friend. We want to embrace it. But we want to direct the change, not just pass through it." Russ Kilidjian, one of Solectron's division controllers, points out that in an ever more rapidly changing environment, it is critical that basic systems and controls be in place. And he emphasizes the importance of accepting change when he points out how many innovations have been unintended but serendipitous by-products of QPI teams working on process improvements.

Solectron's long-term goals are clear. The company will continue to set the highest standards for itself, seeking to be among the best in the world. Winston Chen recently used the story of Wal-Mart Stores to demonstrate what is possible for Solectron and to challenge the company's members to build upon its successes. Solectron hopes to continue to grow rapidly in contract manufacturing. It hopes to compete globally, a task made easier, and perhaps possible in the first place, by the quality systems and processes already in place. It will continue to use every available device to examine and test its progress, including the Baldrige criteria, and pursuit of ISO 9000 certification and the Deming Prize.

Solectron's management harbors strong feelings that the company has an obligation to contribute to the community. Reflecting on the company's success, Ko Nishimura pointed out that many of the company's resources and skills—its people and their education, technology, quality management, quality of life, the freedom to be entrepreneurial—came from others. "We have learned and prospered from all of this. We have an obligation to give back what we can." Already active in contributing to its community, Solectron recently began a program to award 15 scholarships to local high school seniors who excel in the arts and sciences and as all-around contributors. But Solectron's feelings of responsibility run much deeper. Reflecting its strong commitment to the country that the majority of its people feel blessed to call home, Winston has said that, "Solectron's ultimate goal is to show how U.S. manufacturing competitiveness can be revived."

People Interviewed

Gerry Bain, Consolidations Manager

Ling Chan, Division Controller

Li–Hua Chang, General Accounting Supervisor

Winston Chen, Chairman and Co-CEO

Tom Clawson, Director of Finance

Ann Dy, Assistant Corporate Controller

Russ Kilidjian, Division Controller

Myron Lee, Financial Manager

Stedman Lowe, Accounts Payable Supervisor

Stephen Ng, Vice President, Corporate Materials

Ko Nishimura, President and Co-CEO

Dave Podsadecki, Division Controller

Robert Sorakubo, Operations Controller

Gailon Turner, Senior Financial Analyst

Susan Wang, Senior Vice President and CFO

Walt Wilson, President, West Coast Operations

Len Wood, Manager of Internal Audit

Len Zanoni, Treasurer

From KPMG Peat Marwick

Mary Pat McCarthy, Partner

Fordham Student Research Team

Candi Childers, case assistant

Kim Allen

Javier Basuri

Cathy Borzon

Julie Brennan

Marianne Craig

Raphael Porras

Southern Pacific

The Southern Pacific experience shows that a company does not have to spend many years to get into and start reaping the benefits from a quality management system. Although relatively new to tqm and not yet nationally recognized for its quality efforts, Southern Pacific may be the best example of a large company adopting tqm at an accelerated rate, attempting to use the lessons of the past to move faster than other companies have.

To install its new quality management system, senior management used the vehicle of a fully integrated planning process, uniting the company's strategic, operational, financial, and quality goals. The budgeting portion of the process is driven out of the CFO's office, and has significantly improved how the finance group functions internally, as well as how it works with and is perceived by the rest of the organization.

Because of strong top-down direction, all parts of the company began to implement tqm at the same time, so the finance group had few role models within the company. But while much of the theory and language of quality was new to the finance staff, many of the concepts were not, as aspects of a tqm culture were already present.

Today multiple initiatives are occurring in finance as it and the rest of the company commit to quality. Finance is extending the concept of benchmarking by doing "financial benchmarking," the systematic collection and analysis of publicly available data to identify what is possible and to prioritize opportunities for improvement. The financial planning process now incorporates increased inputs from the operating departments and is integrated with the company's long-term strategic plan—including the major strategic dimension of adopting tqm management technology. The quality components of the financial plan have enhanced the company's credibility with its bankers and its ability to access the financial markets by supporting cash flow forecasts and profitability improvement. Finance staff are active members of quality improvement teams. One such team is rapidly improving billing accuracy after a customer survey identified invoicing as one of the processes that created the most frustration for Southern Pacific's customers.

E

Southern Pacific

Quality made all the difference in our credibility with the banks—in our being able to convince the bankers to proceed with the financing we needed.

—Larry Yarberry, CFO

In February 1992, senior executives of the Southern Pacific Transportation Company made a presentation to the company's lead bank, Bank of America, and its syndicate group of 20 other banks. Present at the meeting were the president of Southern Pacific and every senior vice president. The meeting was an important one for the railroad: unless management could convince the bankers to move forward with a $125 million, four-year revolving credit facility, Southern Pacific would find itself without backup liquidity.

During the previous decade, Southern Pacific had lost the leadership it once held. It was slow to respond to deregulation, and a planned merger with the Atchison Topeka and Santa Fe went awry. The merger was first negotiated, then held in suspense for five years, and then finally restricted by regulatory considerations to non-railroad property. The Southern Pacific Transportation Company, the line that had opened the West and was once the largest and most profitable railroad in the U.S., was stripped of many of its assets and sold off to join the Denver and Rio Grande Western.

A year and a half before the February 1992 meeting, Philip Anschutz, the new owner and chairman of Southern Pacific, had made a decision to "bet the railroad's turnaround on quality." Quality experts had been hired, and a broad-based quality effort had made remarkable progress in a short time. The bank presentation included a lot about quality: how the company had adopted the tqm management technology, how it was starting to be managed through a fully integrated strategic/operational/financial/quality plan, and how specific quality initiatives had already produced dramatic improvements and promised more. Even though Bank of America had originally advised Southern Pacific to delay the loan syndication, the inclusion of quality in the company's plans convinced the bankers to proceed with the financing.

In some ways, Southern Pacific Transportation Company's case is different from the preceding four. Unlike the other companies, Southern Pacific is relatively new to tqm and has not been nationally recognized for its quality efforts. However, Southern Pacific may be the best example of a large company adopting tqm at an accelerated rate, attempting to use lessons of the past to move more rapidly than other companies. Southern Pacific is demonstrating that a company can move rapidly to adopt tqm and need not wait years for quality to pay off.

Prior to Phil Anschutz's decision to install quality management, tqm approaches were known and starting to be practiced in only a few parts of the company. Systematic quality management came to Southern Pacific in the form of a mandate to change, and with the hiring of industry and quality experts to facilitate the transformation as quickly as possible. As a result, all parts of the company, including the finance function, began to embrace quality at roughly the same time. In this respect, finance was neither a leader nor a follower, but an integral part of a company-wide program to change the way the business was managed.

To install its new quality management system, senior management chose to use the vehicle of a fully integrated planning process, uniting the company's strategic, operational, financial, and quality goals. The budgeting portion of the process is driven out of the CFO's office and has significantly improved the way the finance group functions internally, as well as how it works with and is perceived by the rest of the organization. This case emphasizes the broad scale and rapid implementation of tqm at Southern Pacific and the important role of the integrated strategic, operational, financial, and quality plan. It also reports other financial successes related to the use of publicly available information, improved financial market access, and improved internal financial processes.

From near-zero familiarity with tqm less than two years ago, Southern Pacific has progressed to a point where it has become focused on the needs of its customers, where there are hundreds of Quality Improvement Teams (QITs) working on opportunities to save millions of dollars, and where more and more of the company's employees and financial advisors are fully convinced that tqm will enable the company first to survive, then to become significantly more competitive, and ultimately to prosper.

Southern Pacific's Entry into Quality Management

In a speech at the Impro 1991 Conference sponsored by the Juran Institute, a research and consulting organization internationally recognized for its leadership in tqm, Phil Anschutz described briefly the romance, importance, and potential of the railroad industry in general and of Southern Pacific in particular, and then contrasted them with the condition of the railroad when he acquired it in 1988:

> But regardless of the romance and regardless of the potential, what I found when I got to Southern Pacific was . . . an industry with declining market share . . . and steeply rising costs. [A] company that had been in trust for almost five years. [Being] in trust for those many years is a difficult situation for a company, for its leadership, and for its employees, much less for its customers. We found a company with low morale and high costs. And we found low customer satisfaction with the performance of our company. So the company, obviously, had a problem and we needed to fix it—and quickly.

An Old, Proud Company Loses Its Way

Some aspects of quality management existed at Southern Pacific long before Phil Anschutz's arrival. There was a philosophy, promoted by Senior VP Ed Ahern, recently retired after 56 years with the company and known fondly as "Mr. Railroad," that the most important part of the business was its employees. Ed Grady, Southern Pacific's Treasurer, relates that when he joined the company in the early 1960s, Southern Pacific was ranked number one among Class I (large, interstate) railroads on many dimensions, including revenues and profitability, and the finance department was recognized throughout the railroad and financial service industries for its excellent work.

However, after many years of industry leadership, Southern Pacific lost its focus on the railroad business in the mid-1970s. Following the fashion of the day, management began a diversification program, purchasing companies in a variety of businesses including telecommunications, title insurance, pipelines, vineyards, and real estate development. Distracted by its new units, Southern Pacific was unable to make the rapid changes required when the Staggers Act deregulated the rail industry in 1980. The company continued to operate as if still regulated, and it began to fall behind its more nimble competitors. To insure the railroad's survival, management began merger talks in 1980 with the Atchison Topeka and Santa Fe railroad, culminating in a decision to merge in December 1983. However, the Interstate Commerce Commission held that the adverse effect on competition from the merger of these two major western railroads would exceed the advantages from efficiencies or economies of scale. It directed the new entity to divest one of the railroads, either the Santa Fe or the Southern Pacific. For five years, until Phil Anschutz purchased it in October 1988, the Southern Pacific railroad was held in trust. (Southern Pacific's telecommunications venture evolved into SPRINT which was ultimately sold to GTE in May 1983 for $750 million. The title insurance company was sold for $270 million in September 1983. All but $150 million of this was lost to the Santa Fe in the merger.)

Southern Pacific continued to make some major investments during the five-year trust period, most notably $1 billion in track and roadbed improvements and the building of the Intermodal Container Transfer Facility (ICTF) serving the ports of Long Beach and Los Angeles. The investments in its right of way gave Southern Pacific perhaps the highest standard mainline in the country, and the ICTF put the company in a commanding position in the rapidly growing market for transferring cargo containers between sea and rail carriers. However, in many ways the trust period was a difficult one for Southern Pacific, its employees, and its customers. Anticipating the merger would be approved, Santa Fe's management discouraged upgrading, replacing, or expanding Southern Pacific assets, which might be redundant in the combined railroad. Employees faced considerable uncertainty about their future. Southern Pacific lost a significant amount of business: some customers transferred to Santa Fe anticipating it to be the survivor of the merger, while others deserted out of fear that the merger might not go through and leave Southern Pacific in a weakened condition.

From 1988 to the initiation of its quality program in the fall of 1990, Southern Pacific's condition did not improve greatly. The Interstate Commerce Commission's R1 reports, annual submissions from all railroads that detailed operating and cost data, showed Southern Pacific's costs to be higher than its competitors in most categories. An employee survey in July 1991 identified high levels of dissatisfaction with training, communications, accountability, and recognition. And the company's first customer satisfaction survey in May 1991 identified that, compared to its competitors, Southern Pacific ranked dead last in every category save one.

Early Quality Steps

One of the earliest formal applications of tqm practices at Southern Pacific took place in Houston in late 1987. Southern Pacific had several important customers in the chemical industry that were early tqm adopters. They were beginning to demand quality performance from all their suppliers. To retain this business, Southern Pacific had to get involved in tqm. Ed Kammerer, then vice president, Chemicals in the Distribution Services Department, and now a quality consultant with the Juran Institute, responded by appointing Art Kielty to a newly created position in the same department: Director of Quality and Hazardous Material Safety. In November and December of 1987, a joint Southern Pacific/customer quality improvement team including Ed and Art studied rail car switching problems at customer facilities and made recommendations for improvement. The study and resulting recommendations were successful and led to a very positive reaction from the chemical industry customers, as well as Southern Pacific's Houston employees.

Ed Kammerer and his team presented their successes to the board of directors in 1988 and again to Phil Anschutz and other top managers at the company's annual management meeting in January 1989. They identified some $70 million in potential savings from extending their switching project throughout the company and recommended that other quality improvement teams be formed to pursue these and other opportunities. However, the board and management groups were not quick to grasp the nature and possibilities of tqm, doubted that such large savings would actually result, and gave the team a lukewarm reaction. Quality was not yet the way at Southern Pacific.

Phil Anschutz's Leadership

When he purchased the railroad in October 1988, Phil Anschutz did not do so with a plan to install total quality management. But by mid-1990, he was convinced that a major change in the way Southern Pacific did business was required and that tqm was the way to engineer the change. Perhaps he remembered the pilot study on switching Ed Kammerer had presented at the January 1989 management meeting. Perhaps he recognized that Southern Pacific was one of only two Class I railroads without a formal quality improvement process. Perhaps his decision came from hearing that Union Pacific had already saved $300 million through its tqm efforts and there was the potential for similar savings at Southern Pacific. Regardless of its origins, the extent of his conviction about the importance of systematic quality processes has since become clear from his actions and from an answer he has given a number of times to the question why he chose to invest in quality. His reply: "Because it's my money!"

Once Phil Anschutz made the decision to move to tqm, the transformation took off rapidly. An accomplished deal maker, Phil understood the financial implications of a rapid $300 million savings and pressed for quick action. But other forces also worked in the company's favor. There was a widely shared understanding within the company that the railroad was in need of a prompt turnaround, that it could not continue to sustain an annual $100 million operating loss. And the company's culture supported the change. Most employees had a fond feeling for the company and its history—many had worked for the railroad for a long time or had come from families in which working for the railroad was a tradition. They were very loyal and wanted the company to succeed.

Phil began to search for proven quality talent, people who had been part of and had led quality successes at other companies in the transportation industry. From American President lines, he hired Don Orris to become executive vice president of Distribution Services and Pete Routsi as vice president—sales for Distribution Services. And, at Union Pacific, he found his new quality director in Kent Sterett. Kent had previously been the quality chief at Florida Power and Light Company. In 1989 FP&L became the first non-Japanese company to win Japan's Deming Prize, Japan's highest award for quality management.

At the October 1991 Impro Conference, Phil described his initial guidelines to the quality team:

> My needs and my requests to this group were fairly simple, I thought. There were four things:
>
> 1. Develop a fast-track program for us; kick-start this program for Southern Pacific and let's get it underway.
>
> 2. Go outside for the best people, but combine these with the best people in our own organization so that we form a team of outside and inside people.
>
> 3. Don't reinvent the wheel—you can beg, you can borrow, you can steal, you can do anything you like, but let's get started and we'll improvise on the way.
>
> 4. And, last of all, you've got to do this on a somewhat limited budget. I would just as soon arrive at my destination in a Ford as in a Mercedes.

Rolling Out the Quality Process: "Short-Cycle Deployment on All Fronts"

Within six months of the November 1st arrival of Kent Sterett as Executive VP for Quality, Southern Pacific had:

- achieved a high level of top management commitment combined with considerable knowledge of tqm,

- articulated a quality-driven strategy and supporting mission statement,

- developed approximately 120 Key Performance Indicators (KPIs) driven from that strategy and mission statement with prime movers, measurements, and tracking systems for each one,

- staffed a 14 person quality improvement department to catalyze the implementation and lead specific initiatives,

- designed and initiated a series of quality training programs,

- inaugurated 275 QITs (Quality Improvement Teams), working on projects throughout the organization, and

- started building suppliers into the quality process.

Although there was clear sequencing of the various steps, there was little or no delay in initiating them, and there was no apparent waiting for an early step to be fully "digested" before a step building upon it was initiated. For example, processes and events for celebrating and rewarding the successes of the QITs were designed and ready for implementation before many of the teams had gotten deeply into their quality improvement projects, let alone completed them.

In another paper presented at the October 1991 Impro Conference, Bob Scanlon, director of Quality & Reliability Engineering, described the first nine months of design and installation of the company's quality management system. What Southern Pacific needed was:

> . . . a process to unify the company, dramatically improve customer satisfaction by improving service reliability, make SP an easier company to do business with, grow revenue by taking back traffic that had been lost to trucks, and most importantly, return SP to operating profitability. The Quality Process was the only vehicle known that could accomplish this.

Bob went on to divide the initial period into three three-month phases: design, introduction, and implementation. The following builds upon that description with some modifications. While several pages are devoted to the specifics of Southern Pacific's quality transformation, the most striking aspect of the process should be kept in mind: the great rapidity with which various elements of an entire tqm system were initiated—the near-simultaneous initiation of many elements of a tqm system in many parts of the company.

Phase I—Building leadership and direction (November 1990 through January 1991): During the first three months, Southern Pacific designed and planned the tqm implementation, recruited a quality team, built top management commitment, established a quality strategy and corporate mission statement, started benchmarking the competition, and started integrating quality and other plans by cascading quality objectives throughout the organization.

- *Designing and planning the quality implementation:* Kent Sterett led the design of Southern Pacific's quality effort, drawing upon his background with Florida Power and Light and Union Pacific, quality leaders he had worked with and learned about as a senior Baldrige judge, and his other experiences.

- *Recruiting a quality team:* As the planning proceeded, Kent was also recruiting a team for a newly established quality department. He recruited from outside the company, drawing upon contacts from his previous work, and from inside the company where earlier quality efforts had made key inside people visible. The job of the quality improvement department was to get a new, quality-based management system installed. It was designed as a transitional organization, facilitating and coordinating the quality efforts of the operating and staff departments—not executing them itself. The new staff started as a team in mid-February.

- *Building top management commitment:* Phil Anschutz underlined his commitment to quality to his senior managers in several ways. He was successful in luring his number one choice for leader of the quality effort away from Union Pacific, a key competitor. He gave Kent the title executive vice president—quality, reporting directly to the President. He supported the development of a very substantial quality department. He also mandated that the top management group visit a series of recognized quality leaders (Milliken, Xerox, Ford, and Florida Power and Light) and begin formal training in quality management.

- *Establishing a quality strategy and corporate mission:* Phil's decision to adopt tqm as the company's new management system was the core of the new corporate strategy. This major strategic choice was supported by a short set of strategic initiatives and a new corporate mission statement:

> Southern Pacific Lines' mission is to anticipate and satisfy the requirements of its customers for highly responsive and cost effective transportation and distribution services.

The corporate mission statement was supported by mission statements by each of the major staff groups. Finance's mission statement is:

> To provide the financial direction, accounting controls, planning and analysis, management information, and financial resources which will enable the company to fulfill its corporate mission.

- *Starting to benchmark the competition:* In addition to the informal benchmarking of quality leaders that formed the basis of its quality management system, Southern Pacific also started using the Interstate Commerce Commission's R1 reports to identify where costs might be out of line with other major western railroads and to signal high priority areas for cost reduction. The finance department issued reports that compared detailed operating and financial information supplied by major competitors with Southern Pacific's own R1 data. The reports included two calculations of the potential savings for each line item—first, the savings if Southern Pacific matched the average performance of its competitors and second, if it reached a "world class" status—matching the performance of its best competitor at each activity. These comparisons led Southern Pacific to conclude that at least $400 million dollars could be saved by bringing current operations in each activity up to the standards of the most comparable competitor.

- *Integrating quality planning by cascading quality objectives:* In this early period, Southern Pacific also began to integrate its quality plans and initiatives with its other plans by establishing approximately 120 Key Performance Indicators (KPIs) based upon the quality strategy, R1 benchmarking, and other information. One or two managers took responsibility for each KPI, and processes for measuring and reporting progress on a monthly basis were implemented in the next phase.

Phase II—Building capabilities and starting organizational movement (February 1991 through April 1991): During the second three months, Southern Pacific put the new quality team to work, started building organization-wide commitment, started quality management training programs, developed company structures and processes for reviewing progress, started to build suppliers into the quality management system, and continued and extended the activities from the preceding phase.

- *Putting the quality team to work:* The newly recruited quality team began work on February 17, 1991. It divided up the initiatives and started pushing each one forward.

- *Building organization-wide commitment:* Phil Anschutz kicked off the company's quality campaign at Southern Pacific's January 1991 management meeting. For the first time in the company's history, union leaders were included in the meeting, beginning the process of breaking down the railroad's often rigid labor-management, departmental, and hierarchical barriers. A panel of important customers related tales of good and bad experiences with Southern Pacific, and pointed out that their continued business depended on the railroad's willingness to provide high quality service. To help employees move in the same direction, the new company mission statement was presented. An eight-year financial plan was introduced, taking the focus away from any thoughts of a quick fix, and the goals of the plan's first phase, dubbed "The Road to '92," were presented.

  Over the next few months, this initial management meeting was extended to "town hall meetings" throughout the company. As Phil said at Impro: "We insisted that all the senior managers go and be represented at one or more of the meetings, starting with me." Eventually, approximately 125 of these meetings were held every six months.

  Communication about the quality effort also occurred in other meetings and activities. These included regular meetings with the 54 general chairpersons of the company's unions, workshops, new and existing company publications, "management workdays" in which senior managers "walked the talk" by rolling up their sleeves and working at the individual contributor level, and the new quality training programs.

- *Establishing quality management training programs and QITs:* Building upon quality training programs developed by recognized quality consultants and modified for Southern Pacific's unique situation and industry, a major quality training effort began. With the aid of programs to train quality team leaders and facilitators, the few demonstration QITs that had started with Ed Kammerer's Houston switching project increased to 571 by the end of 1991 and 882 by mid-1992.

- *Developing company structures and processes for reviewing progress:* The finance, quality, and other departments began to develop reports to record and share the progress of the QITs, on the KPIs, and on other quality activities. Monthly "cross functional management committee" meetings were initiated to review progress, and a monthly "Red Book" containing the prior month's KPI data was designed and issued. Individual KPIs were modified in definition and some responsibilities changed as Southern Pacific gained experience. Progress in reaching KPI goals entered the compensation system of individual managers.

- *Starting to build suppliers into the quality management system:* In February 1991, QITs were initiated with suppliers as full team members. During the next month, design work for a "supplier certification program" was initiated.

- *Continuing and extending earlier activities:* Each initiative from the first phase was continued and extended, with particular emphasis placed on integrating the strategic, quality, operating, and financial plans into a single annual plan within an eight year financial budget.

Phase III—Continuing and deepening the process (May 1991 onward): By the end of the first six months, a great many of the elements of a tqm system were designed and initiated. In the next few months, processes and programs for recognizing and celebrating successes were begun, customer and employee satisfaction data were collected with surveys of each, customers were invited to join QITs, and quality training reached increasing numbers of managers and nonmanagers. Data from customers and employees were used in an ongoing process of fine-tuning the KPIs and other quality initiatives.

Because the quality team had at its disposal the "lessons learned" by many quality pioneers that preceded Southern Pacific, the team began with the knowledge of what a fully integrated tqm system might look like once it was in place. They were able to design and start implementing all the pieces without waiting for early steps to signal and create the need for subsequent steps. A month-by-month Gantt chart based upon the Baldrige application categories was used to plan, track, and communicate progress on implementing the various components of the new quality management system.

Southern Pacific was able to avoid many of the delays and problems experienced by quality pioneers, since, by 1990, tqm was becoming increasingly understood as a management technology. Among these pitfalls are starting without clear top management leadership and support, waiting patiently for a few key resisters to become persuaded of the importance of tqm, insisting on inventing one's own unique approach to quality rather than borrowing aggressively from quality leaders, asking managers to produce quality improvements while rewarding only traditional operating results, and setting up a quality plan separate from and not integrated with the existing strategic and financial plans.

But, of course, not all missteps were avoided. When Phil was asked at the Impro Conference what one change he would make if he could go back and do things differently, he replied that he would spend more time working with middle management to help them embrace the changes that were occurring.

Finance as Part of the Quality Transformation

Because of the strong top-down direction from Phil Anschutz, all parts of the company began to consider tqm at the same time, and the finance group had few role models within the company. But while much of the theory and language of quality was new to the finance staff, many of the concepts were not, as aspects of a tqm culture were already present at the beginning of the transformation.

The finance group had a history of excellence in their work. They had a good reputation in the financial markets for their forthrightness and trustworthiness and had always been successful in prior financings. They had earned the confidence of the banking industry for a high degree of accuracy in check processing and account reconciliations. They had been active in industry and professional organizations and had contributed advice and financial systems to the industry.

Southern Pacific's finance staff had long recognized the value of a highly trained workforce. Staff members had attended a wide variety of training programs, courses, and degree programs. Often finance pushed against and exceeded its training budget.

The finance group also had conducted "benchmarking-like" activities well before the concept came to Southern Pacific as part of tqm. They had systematically searched out best practices throughout the industry, had attempted to adapt their findings to Southern Pacific, and had measured their performance against best in class.

However, much like the rest of the company, the finance staff had been affected negatively by the company's drift during the 1980s. For example, cutbacks in headcount had reduced the accounts receivable staff so much that the value of delinquent accounts had risen to a point where their cost more than exceeded the personnel savings.

New Initiatives

By early 1991, top management's demand for rapid change and the expert guidance of the quality improvement department had moved the finance staff to begin exploring tqm. Today multiple initiatives are occurring in finance as it and the rest of the company commit to quality:

- Using the ICC R1s, finance is extending the concept of benchmarking by doing "financial benchmarking," the systematic collection and analysis of publicly available data to identify what is possible and to prioritize opportunities for improvement.

- Financial planning is being redefined to connect to the company's long-term strategic plan, in particular incorporating the major strategic dimension of adopting the tqm management technology.

- The budgeting process has been reworked to increase input from the operating departments. One important addition is budgeting for planned, quality-driven benefits. Involvement in planning for quality improvements has created ownership of the improvements and budget numbers by operating managers.

- The quality components of the financial plan are being used to enhance the company's credibility with its bankers by supporting cash flow forecasts, and hence borrowing requests.

- Finance staff are active members of many QITs. One of the more visible ones is rapidly improving billing accuracy after a customer survey identified invoicing as one of the processes that created the most frustration for Southern Pacific's customers.

The Integrated Plan

One of the more important, quality-driven innovations at Southern Pacific is the development of a management system focused on change using a variety of elements all coordinated with only one document—an improvement-focused plan integrating strategy, quality, operations, and finance. Early in its tqm efforts, Southern Pacific made such a plan a primary objective, to ensure that all parts of the company were marching in step toward a common goal.

The Prior System

In past years, Southern Pacific used a traditional top-down planning methodology. Sometime in the third quarter of the year, the marketing departments would be surveyed to obtain a projection of the upcoming year's operating volume (measured, for example, in gross ton miles: the product of tons of freight carried and distance traveled). The finance department would then convert these estimates into monetary terms, applying pricing schedules to derive a forecast of operating revenues and unit costing data to predict railway operating expenses. Other revenues from planned real estate sales would be factored in. A second survey would be made of the operating departments for their projections of capital needs. When all the details were in, the finance department would forecast corporate profit by combining revenue and expense projections and then run the figures through a cash flow model to identify any cash excess or shortfall.

Since the mid-1980s, it was more common for the forecast to show an operating loss than a profit. However, even when the model forecasted a profit, there was usually a gap between projected operating profit and cash flow and the profit and cash flow desired by senior management. Management would respond by mandating operating expense and capital investment budgets for each operating unit for the coming year, budgets that were nearly always lower than the units had requested. For the most part, these budgets were based upon accepting marketing's revenue projections while reducing expense and capital projections, effectively demanding that the projected volume level be reached at lower cost than in prior years. (Occasionally, higher revenue targets were requested although the focus was nearly always on cost reduction in the belief that operating units have more control over costs than over revenues.) Expense cuts were made largely across the board (for example, a flat 10 percent applied to all departments) and were made with little if any operating department input. The budgets tended to be made available too late in the year (about October or November) for the operating departments to have much input to the process or to change their plans before the new year had started.

The operating departments responded to this process with a mixture of gaming, commitment, and fatalism. To some extent, they tried to "trick the process" by inflating their capital requests in anticipation of cutbacks. To some extent, they tried to meet their budgets but with relatively low buy-in. Some divisions made their budget targets, others did not. When the targets were missed, the consequences were not severe or predictable (if there were any at all) because of the recognized arbitrariness of the process and the late time frame of the budget.

The New Planning Process

Unlike the old system, the new planning process is set into the context of Southern Pacific's long-term plan, integrating the company's strategic, financial, operating, and quality objectives. Each year is seen not as a separate, stand-alone phenomenon, but rather a step on the way to a series of goals with a seven- to eight-year time horizon. The plan is driven from Southern Pacific's corporate strategy, which is framed in terms of short-term survival, medium-term competitiveness, and long-term strength. As an important element, it contains financial objectives of satisfactory and regular profitability that will permit the restructuring of the company's long-term debt to remove existing restrictive covenants. It is tied closely to operating performance and results. Quality is the facilitator, the mechanism for identifying opportunities to improve and make the required transition to being a world-class organization.

Also factored into the process are Southern Pacific's new Key Performance Indicators that identify prime opportunities for operating expense and service quality improvements. As discussed earlier, KPIs are developed from a variety of data sources, especially customer surveys, employee surveys, and the Interstate Commerce Commission's R1 report of comparative operating costs. A senior management committee selects, prioritizes, and designates responsibility for KPIs, thus setting a series of intermediate-term targets for the entire company to follow.

Compared to the old system, each year's planning cycle begins much earlier—for the 1993 plan the cycle started in mid-June 1992—and the planning period is longer, lasting through November. This provides time for negotiation. Currently, negotiations occur between the operating departments and finance. The goal is to move toward direct negotiation among departments to allocate any needed cost reductions, removing finance from the process. The longer planning cycle also gives operating departments the ability to locate detailed opportunities for reductions, making them more real and achievable. Assistant VP—Finance Joe Doherty who leads the budgeting process points out,

> In effect, the new planning process asks each department to create its own business plan so the budget won't lose integrity out in the field.

The planning process still begins with a survey of the marketing departments to develop a projection of operating volume and revenue. However, the budgeting of expenses is significantly changed. For one, it is far less arbitrary than before. It now begins with the seven- to eight-year targets from the long-term plan, further broken down by the finance organization into targets for the coming year. For another, it makes far better use of data pointing toward opportunities for cost reduction. In particular, it makes creative use of financial benchmarking, using the ICC's R1 report to compare Southern Pacific's costs to those of its competitors on nearly a line item by line item basis. Areas in which other railroads operate at a lower cost are identified and prioritized for quality improvement. KPI data are also used to help plan expense reductions so that across the board cuts are no longer demanded.

As a by-product of the new process, the capital budget is better understood by both finance and the operating departments. Some 75 percent of capital expenses are for roadway repair, necessary for operations and similar to maintenance expenses in other industries. Another 15 percent is spent on government-mandated projects, including those that are safety related, for which there is no choice. Only the remaining 10 percent is truly competitive among departments, a fact often overlooked under the prior system. At present, decisions on how to allocate this 10 percent are made by senior management to conform to the company's strategic thrusts.

The new planning process has already changed the operating managers' receptiveness to the budget and created a perceived need to operate according to the plan. Managers are now responsible for their budget line items. They have the opportunity to share in the planning and must buy-in when the plan is completed. They are expected to achieve their budget targets. And their compensation package includes a factor for their performance against budget.

Improved Financial Market Access

Adopting tqm has allowed Southern Pacific to change the way it approaches the financial markets. The company is now able to justify its income and cash flow projections with specific cost saving plans grounded in quality improvement. As a result, Southern Pacific has enhanced its ability to access the money and capital markets.

The February 13, 1992 Presentation

On February 13, 1992, Southern Pacific's top management team made a presentation to a syndicate of 21 banks at the offices of its lead bank, Bank of America. The loan request was important to Southern Pacific as the company was without any backup lines of credit at the time and needed the increased liquidity. Mike Mohan, Southern Pacific's president, led the presentation at which every senior vice president spoke. What made this presentation different from those of the past was the prominent role played by total quality management.

Southern Pacific had always enjoyed a good relationship with Bank of America. Yet, at the time of the presentation, Southern Pacific's credibility with its bankers had reached a low point. The railroad was consistently unable to make a profit during the late 1980s, and its bankers were looking for evidence that a turnaround was possible. In addition, the initial income and cash forecasts prepared to justify Phil Anschutz's $1 billion acquisition financing request had proved overly optimistic. Later, these projections were updated but with minimum input from Southern Pacific's finance and operations departments and again proved unrealistic. Southern Pacific's bankers became progressively more cautious in interpreting the company's income and cash flow projections.

Concerned about Southern Pacific's credibility and a weak market, Bank of America loan officers asked the company to consider delaying its request until more evidence of the claimed turnaround was visible and until the credit markets were more suitable for financing. But Southern Pacific was convinced it had a good story to tell—the story of how the company's tqm efforts would make the turnaround happen, and happen sooner than anyone would have predicted just a short time ago.

At the same time, many of the syndicate members, including Bank of America, were acquiring their own experience with tqm through in-house quality management efforts and exposure to other customers pursuing quality management. Within the transportation industry these loan officers followed, several companies had already demonstrated quality successes, most notably Union Pacific. The hiring of Don Orris, Pete Routsi, and especially Kent Sterett who came from Union Pacific, gave considerable credibility to Southern Pacific's claims of moving toward quality.

In preparing for the meeting, Southern Pacific identified some 75 quality improvement opportunities and quantified the anticipated benefit from each. However, Bank of America loan officers were afraid the 75 opportunities would overwhelm the other syndicate members and asked Southern Pacific to limit its presentation to no more than ten. Yet, even with fewer than ten quality improvement savings in the projections, Southern Pacific's numbers looked good. The remaining quality projects gave the bank a sense there was a real cushion in Southern Pacific's chances of meeting its cost reduction targets.

Ultimately, the ability to identify such good cost reduction opportunities, and to justify them through quality initiatives, convinced Bank of America officials to proceed with the presentation and convinced the syndicate members to proceed with the loan syndication, even in a less-than-perfect market.

Capital Market Reaction

The long-term debt markets reacted to Southern Pacific financial difficulties in much the same way as its banks. Whereas the company's senior debt was once considered rock solid, always drawing an investment grade rating, by the late 1980s it had declined to a below investment grade rating of Ba_1,B+, even though the railroad's equipment debt, with its specific collateral, continued to be rated A.

Ed Grady, Southern Pacific's Treasurer, is convinced that quality improvements will be an important force in restoring the company's long-term debt rating through its improvement of income and cash flow. As he points out,

> Restoration of the debt rating is not only important in that it will lower our interest costs, it is crucial for our refinancing plans which are an essential part of the new corporate strategy. Right now we can't realize the full benefits from the combination of the Southern Pacific and the Denver and Rio Grande Western railroads because of restrictive covenants which prevent us from fully integrating the two lines. Quality-driven savings should lead to significant profit improvements, then to refinancing the debt, and then to even more savings as we fully combine the two railroads.

Ed Lincoln of Kidder, Peabody, who recently led a successful $70 million private placement for new locomotives agrees:

> Southern Pacific is clearly taking the right steps to identify and implement ways to generate the improved operating results that will enable the company to regain its investment grade debt ratings across the board. We have been for some time impressed by the candor of the treasury and finance

staff and their commitment to doing things right the first time. This is where improvement starts and reflects the attitude of senior operating management. More recently, we have noted management's intensified daily focus on customer service and cost control. In the recent locomotive transaction we had several new investors as well as historical lenders who, after due diligence, bought into management's dedication to quality improvement. In our business few things are more important for capital access and, ultimately, lower cost of capital, than broadening a client's investor base.

Billing Accuracy

Soon after he arrived at Southern Pacific, Kent Sterett designed and sent out the company's first customer survey. Among other things, the survey found that of all the company's finance processes, customers were most dissatisfied with billing accuracy. Fully 13 percent of all bills were objected to as wrong, most identified as too high. In response, Brian Kane, Southern Pacific's Controller, began a quality project to improve billing accuracy.

Within the controller's office are 97 rate clerks, all members of the Transportation and Communications Union, who price customer invoices. To a large extent, they work with a paper-driven system in which pricing, or "rating," involves matching the service provided to a customer with unit pricing information from multiple databases kept in several locations. Some invoices are only for services provided by Southern Pacific and can be rated using the company's own tariff schedule, which is maintained within the accounting department. Other invoices, while only for Southern Pacific services, involve special volume or discount pricing specified in contracts kept in a marketing database. Still other invoices might include charges for interline services, such as storing another railroad's cars or switching a car from another railroad to Southern Pacific's track, and must be rated using the tariffs of other carriers or with interline tariffs maintained by industry service bureaus. While some invoices are rated automatically by computer, others require some minor manual intervention, and some are so complex that they have to be done entirely manually. At present there are 85 to 90 possible steps in tracking down the proper price to put on an invoice, although most invoices can be rated in three or four steps. The majority of extra steps is due to pricing exceptions. An invoice is normally handled multiple times before being sent out. Each person working on an invoice is expected to inspect it for accuracy, raising the possibility that with so many inspectors, no one takes real responsibility.

Tracking Contentions

After seeing the survey results, accounting started to track "contentions," complaints by customers that their invoice was not correct. Brian Kane's office began to graph the number of contentions per week hoping to get a sense of what fraction of each week's invoices were bad, but a problem quickly surfaced. Contentions could be about an invoice sent at any time in the past. Thus the graphs showed a mix of old and new problems, rather than measuring the problems created each week. Because old contentions could arrive in a bunch, the graph was a wildly fluctuating line. To smooth the data and get a clearer picture of the number and trend of misrated invoices, the graphs were changed to show a 12-week moving average.

In December 1990, soon after the graphs were first begun, there were some 1850 contentions out of roughly 17,950 freight bills rated per week, a contention rate of 10.3 percent. Most contentions reflected overbilling, primarily from basing the rate on the standard tariff rather than a more favorable negotiated rate. Some contentions arose because the customer used its own computer to rate the bill and came up with a number different from Southern Pacific's; these invoices could be overbilled or underbilled. (There is some amount of underbilling that will be paid and not show up as contentions, although internal samples of paid bills suggest this is a small problem.)

By early 1991, accounting had enough data to begin analysis. A sample of 500–600 contentions was taken and the various problems that showed up were classified by nature (such as, type of commodity being shipped, customer, geographic location, and so on), and by cause (clerical error, rating information not received, poor input from field regarding car movement or content, and the like). In particular, significant numbers of contentions were found within the grain group, and an early quality improvement team was formed to study these problems in more detail.

After classifying the contentions, 10 to 12 categories of problems were brainstormed in an attempt to discover their root causes. Twenty-six processes were identified as critical but not functioning at acceptable levels of reliability and became the first phase of the improvement efforts.

Putting Quality Improvement Teams to Work

Much of the rating problem was traced to lack of communication between marketing and accounting. Joint accounting/marketing QITs were formed to share concerns and improve cooperation. A program was organized to educate marketing personnel about the rating system. To heighten marketing's awareness of the rating problem, Brian Kane organized sessions where marketing people would spend a day in accounting, rating invoices and experiencing frustrations along with the accounting staff.

One QIT studied contentions on shipments of various commodities and concluded there was a need for faster sharing of pricing data, especially when specific to a customer or commodity. Another looked at the structure of the rating department leading to a reorganization of the department by commodity group to align with the marketing organization. QITs were formed to improve and simplify the communication from marketing to accounting about price escalations built into customer contracts.

Other QITs were set up to improve paper flow and to ensure that accounting receives correct and complete data the first time. Brian points out that

> Not only did this quickly cut down on errors and processing time, it forced reliability on the data. Now there is one consistent set of prices coming from marketing, rather than the bits and pieces we used to get which were often not believed by accounting.

Information technology provides a significant opportunity for improving rating accuracy. Together, accounting and marketing are moving toward a single, computerized rating database, based on published rates, which would be authoritative for both price quotes to customers and for rating the subsequent invoices. This step has led marketing to consider the potential benefits of simplifying what is now a complex pricing structure, in much the same way as the passenger airlines are struggling with the issue. The hope is that simplification of prices will permit a substantial increase in the automatic computerized rating of invoices. (Today, the pricing structure is so complex that on forwarded traffic, traffic beginning on Southern Pacific tracks, only 14 percent of invoices are automatically rated by computer; on received traffic—traffic coming to Southern Pacific from other railroads—no invoices are now fully rated by computer.) Southern Pacific is also moving toward electronic data interchange (EDI) with other carriers to simplify the rating of interline shipments and is participating in the development of the "Rate EDI Network (REN)," an industry-wide electronic system for the interchange of rates.

Still another opportunity for quality-driven improvement came directly from customers. Because some customers were pursuing their own quality programs, they were demanding quality service from Southern Pacific. Customers were discovering the cost arising from billing errors and the resulting contentions and wished to eliminate their rework in processing Southern Pacific's invoices. Many customers were open and sometimes eager to participate with Southern Pacific in process improvement projects, and this led to a half dozen joint Southern Pacific/customer QITs working on rating and other invoice problems.

Improvements in Billing Accuracy

The results of the initial billing accuracy efforts have been excellent and have come quickly. Underbillings have been reduced to about 0.5 percent of all invoices. Accounting performs a quarterly sample to locate underbilled invoices, re-rate them, and re-bill those customers. In only 1 1/2 years, from December 1990 to June 1992, contentions have been reduced from an estimated 13 percent in mid-1990 to 5 percent of all invoices, a rate of improvement far ahead of initial expectations. Rework has been slashed, reducing the cost of servicing an account. And, since the 8 percent reduction in contested invoices represents millions of dollars of receivables per day, the company's cash flow has improved dramatically.

Payoffs from Quality

In moving massively and rapidly in implementing tqm across the company, Southern Pacific is getting the payoffs from quality very quickly. Many of the benefits are monetary: improvement can be seen in the trend of KPIs, and Southern Pacific is able to identify significant savings from the company's early investment in quality. Both Larry Yarberry and Kent Sterett suggest that the payback period for the company's quality efforts is well less than one year and in some cases may be as little as one month. But other gains from tqm are less immediately measurable in dollar terms, even though they are expected to produce monetary benefits in the near future.

Benefits for the Company

Perhaps the biggest company-wide, non-monetary benefit is a palpable shift in the competitive health of the organization. After many years of distractions from its rail operations, personnel cut-backs, and reduced ability to acknowledge and reward people's contributions, there is an increasing sense of optimism throughout the company. Southern Pacific's quality management system and the managers who are using it are gaining growing support among union leaders and members.

There is an increasing willingness and ability of all organizational members to "manage by fact." This comes from the quality culture that emphasizes the need to collect and use data in decision making rather than relying on opinions and guesswork. It also comes from the greater availability of meaningful data, including the ICC R1 analysis and the existence of KPIs. In addition, the improved quality of budget numbers and the greater believability of pricing data have promoted the notion of a common set of agreed-upon facts.

Southern Pacific is starting to create a culture that supports rapid change. The business environment of the coming decades is likely to be volatile for the transportation industry as new technologies, demographic shifts, and regulatory philosophies change the way business must be done. As Southern Pacific discovered in the negative when the industry was deregulated in 1980, the ability to react quickly to environmental changes is vital for survival.

Quality has permitted Southern Pacific to move forward on the key financial strategic task of refinancing its debt. The recent bank syndication would not have been accepted without at least three quality items in place: the quality component of the company's strategy on which the seven- to eight-year financial projection was based, the specific quality cost savings initiatives identified, and management's clear commitment to quality evident in the presentation itself.

Benefits for the Finance Function

Finance officers at Southern Pacific report that since tqm became their way of life, they are able to do their jobs significantly better. Their relationship to the rest of the organization has changed away from contention and toward cooperation. They have more time available to work on ways to improve the company, rather than fight fires. They are better managers because of their quality training and experiences.

Brian Kane reports that he has become much more proactive in his role as controller and is moving away from simply being a bookkeeper reporting on events after the fact. He sees his staff getting much more involved in supporting economic decision making.

Some Important Learnings

Southern Pacific exemplifies the emerging second generation of tqm companies. A latecomer to quality, Southern Pacific is demonstrating how it is possible to learn from the successes and mistakes of its predecessors. While tqm must still be adapted to fit the culture and characteristics of each company, there is no need to wait years for quality to take hold, nor for the benefits to accrue.

Larry Yarberry and the finance organization provide another important lesson. Quality is just as easily absorbed and implemented within finance as in any other part of a company. There is no need for finance to wait until quality has been proven elsewhere. In fact, there can be significant benefit if finance is an early participant in a company's quality efforts.

Just as it takes many people to run a railroad, it takes many contributors for a company's quality efforts to have such a big impact. Phil Anschutz provided the rolling stock by creating a mandate and the sense of urgency. Kent Sterett and his staff brought the quality expertise that put the train on the right track. Operating units of the company fired up the locomotive and got it moving. Larry Yarberry's organization climbed on board to help the train go in the right direction. Together they are giving a new sense of spirit and competitiveness to a historic, 135-year-old company.

People Interviewed

Brendan Collins, Vice President—Quality Management Systems
Joe Doherty, Assistant Vice President—Finance
Justin Fox, Director—Quality
Celestine Gebrier, Director—Quality, Information & Replication
Ed Grady, Treasurer
Roy Gelder, Director Quality Economics
Ed Kammerer, Vice President—Quality Systems
Brian Kane, Controller
Art Keilty, Director, Quality–Team Development
John Kerins, Assistant to the Vice President of Operations
Bob Scanlon, Director of Quality & Reliability Engineering
Kent Sterett, Executive Vice President, Quality
Larry Yarberry, CFO

From Bank of America

Jeff Bonzon, Vice President, Corporate Banking
Mark Lies, Assistant Vice President, Capital Markets Division
Patricia Ward, Vice President

From Kidder Peabody

Ed Lincoln, Senior Vice President

From the Transportation Communication Union

Bob Brackbill, General Chairman

Fordham Student Research Team

Ann Hardy, case assistant

Research Methodology

The goal of this research was to find finance functions which are adding exceptional value to their companies and to capture their stories in writing. To seek that goal we identified and qualified target companies, invited company finance members to make presentations at a seminar at the Fordham University Graduate School of Business Administration, visited the selected companies to conduct interviews and collect other data, and worked with members of the companies and research teams from the seminar to describe and interpret the company activities.

Research Characteristics

The research approach we adopted was marked by three primary characteristics: a focus on leaders in total quality management, an appreciation for successes and best practices, and a sharing of the inquiry process. By examining leaders in finance and total quality, we identified ways financial executives are participating in and profiting from the emerging "global quality revolution." By seeking successes in the application of new tools and techniques, we uncovered examples which, we believe, are of particular interest and utility to financial executives. By partnering with members of the subject companies and with our students, we built a strong support system, increasing the breadth of our work and the accuracy of our reporting.

Focus on Quality Management

We began the study with the observation that a new way of managing organizations, often called total quality management or "tqm," is revolutionizing the way many successful companies are operating. Considerable evidence exists that the operating units of companies adopting this new management technology are discovering exceptional opportunities to add value to their firms. We hypothesized that the finance functions of companies which are leaders in tqm were also likely to find exciting new ways to add value as they adopt and adapt the quality management approaches that the rest of the company is using. Beginning with this premise, we sought companies for the study that met three criteria: the company was a recognized leader in quality; the finance function was a recognized leader in applying quality approaches to the corporate finance function; and the top management, quality professionals in the company, and the finance function all believed the company had a good story to tell about the integration of total quality management and financial management.

Appreciation

A second characteristic of the research is "appreciation," an approach that focuses on successes and best practices: things that work. This approach is similar to the methods of "appreciative inquiry" used by a growing number of researchers, including David Cooperrider, Suresh Srivastva, and their colleagues, and is described in their book *Appreciative Management and Leadership*. It is also similar to the work of Tom Peters, Robert Waterman, and their colleagues, and to the tqm management tool of competitive benchmarking used by the companies and finance functions we studied.

We feel there is much to learn from the study of best practices in finance. Innovations in financial management are often made in the field, not in the research laboratory, and can be shared by being reported via field research such as this work. Excellence in another company can demonstrate clearly that a higher level of performance is real and achievable and can often serve as a blueprint for improvement. Few finance functions cannot learn from their peers, and, in fact, each of the finance leaders who participated in this study was keenly interested in what it could learn from the others.

Co-inquiry

The third characteristic of this research approach is "co-inquiry" the partnership of researchers and "researchees" in attempting to discover and describe the phenomenon being explored. In this study, co-inquiry, occurred in two ways: one with the participating companies, and one with the student research teams that worked with us in conducting the project.

In the companies, co-inquiry took the form of sharing the basic research objectives with the company participants from the beginning, working with them to find illustrations of the new financial management practice and perspectives we were seeking, and working with them to capture examples, experiences, and perspectives accurately in our writing. Our steering committee members played a major role in this process and provided indispensable guidance, assistance, and support.

With our students and co-researchers, co-inquiry took the form of participating in a seminar on corporate finance and total quality management held at Fordham, joining in field visits to three of the companies, developing first drafts of four chapter cases, writing essays on a variety of issues in finance and tqm, and collecting a set of readings relevant to the topic. Officers of four of the participating companies visited Fordham and made presentations in the seminar. Five of the seminar members also continued their work on the project in tutorials or informal collaboration on the research after the seminar was over.

Company Identification and Qualification

To find companies and finance functions which met our criteria of quality management leadership we drew upon a network of quality professionals, many of whom had assisted us in the same way in our earlier research with similar theme and focus, *Remaking Corporate Finance*. We relied very heavily on their recommendations and list their names with much gratitude in the acknowledgments which accompany this book. When a finance function became a candidate for participation in the study, we then relied on members of the company's finance and quality functions to judge whether there was a good story to tell and, also, whether work loads would allow key members to participate fully.

Field Research and Data Collection

We spent from four to six days at each company, interviewing senior corporate executives, finance members, and members of the corporate quality department. At three of the companies, we attended the formal quality briefing given to suppliers and other interested parties. In addition, we were given many company documents relating to tqm efforts and progress in both the company as a whole and within the finance function.

In each interview, as in the seminar presentations, we asked:

- how the finance function and company became involved in tqm,

- for their best examples of using tqm within corporate finance,

- how the finance function was changing as the company continued to adopt tqm and adapt it to its needs, and

- for evidence of payoffs from tqm.

Integrating, Report Drafting, and Follow-up Interviews

Early drafts of each case were reviewed with members of the participating companies and were used to guide subsequent research interviews. In most of the companies, follow-up field interviews were conducted using drafts of sections of each company case as inputs for further interviews. In this manner, we encouraged company members to play an active role guiding our writing and interpretations. To ensure that the cases capture the "voice of corporate finance" in the companies accurately, the final drafts were reviewed with and approved by each company, and each interviewee who was quoted approved the accuracy of each quotation.

Suggested Readings

The following readings are divided into four parts: readings on the five case study companies (emphasizing their quality efforts), readings on quality in corporate finance and financial services, readings on the quality revolution in general, and readings on the tools of tqm and on adopting quality management. We have indicated where the material can be obtained if it is not available from a book publisher or in a journal or magazine.

For the second set of readings, dealing with quality in corporate finance and financial services, we have included all the readings in finance and quality management we can find. While the literature in corporate finance and quality management is sparse, there is considerable literature in accounting and quality management and several references on quality in financial services. We have included a few of the available references in these last two categories because of the scarcity of references that relate directly to quality and corporate finance.

Selected References on the Case Study Companies

Corning Incorporated

Corning Total Quality Digest . . . to be World Class. (catalog number 2-90-5111). (Corning, N.Y.: Corning, Inc., 1990.) Available from Director of Quality, Corning Incorporated, HP-CB-06-4, Corning, NY 14831.

Hammonds, Keith H. "Corning's Class Act: How Jamie Houghton reinvented the company." *Business Week*, May 13, 1991: 68-73. Available from Corporate Communications, Corning Incorporated, HP–AB–01–13, Corning, NY 14831.

To Be World Class—Quality Milestone VII. Corning, NY, Corning, Inc., June 5-6, 1991. Available from Director of Quality, Corning Incorporated, HP-CB-06-4, Corning, NY 14831.

Federal Express

American Management Association. *Blueprint for Service Quality: The Federal Express Approach.* New York: American Management Association, 1991.

Federal Express Corporation Quality Profile. A summary of quality related processes and systems at Federal Express. Available from Federal Express Corporate Relations Department, 2005 Corporate Avenue, Memphis, TN 38132.

The Finance Division Quality Improvement Process Charter. Available from Chauncey Burton, Federal Express Corporation, 2007 Corporate Avenue, Memphis, TN 38132.

Motorola

Bhote, Keki R. "Motorola's Long March to the Malcolm Baldrige National Quality Award," *National Productivity Review*, VIII, 4 (Autumn, 1989):365-375.

"The Company that Saved Itself," chapter 6, in Lloyd Dobyns and Clare Crawford-Mason, *Quality or Else: The Revolution in World Business.* Boston: Houghton Mifflin, 1991, 127-150.

Thompson, Kenneth R. "A Conversation with Robert W. Galvin," *Organizational Dynamics*, XX, 4 (Spring, 1992): 56-69.

Solectron

Haavind, Robert. *The Road to the Baldrige Award: Quest for Total Quality.* Stoneham, Mass.: Butterworth-Heinemann, 1992, 91–96.

Solectron: Malcolm Baldrige National Quality Award Application Summary. (undated). Solectron Corporation, Marketing Department, 777 Gibraltar Drive, Milpitas, CA 95035

"What Drives Quality?," *Internal Auditor Magazine* (April 1992): 39–45.

Southern Pacific

Lhermitte, Patrick R., and Robert J. Scanlon. "Applying TQM to Purchasing." Presented at the National Association of Purchasing Managers (NAPM) Conference, San Antonio, TX, May 3, 1993.

Scanlon, Robert J. "Installing a Quality Process in Record Time," 1991 Juran Impro Conference. Wilton, Conn.: The Juran Institute, 1991: 8A-1-13.

Welty, Gus. "Southern Pacific's Quality Comeback," *Railway Age* (November 1992): 30–34.

Quality in Corporate Finance and Financial Services

Aubrey, Charles A. II. *Quality Management in Financial Services.* Wheaton, Ill.: Hitchcock Publishing Company, 1988.

Gabor, Andrea. "The Quandary in Total Quality," *Treasury and Risk Management,* XII, 3 (Fall 1992): 28-31.

Johnson, H. Thomas. *Relevance Regained: From Top-Down Control to Bottom-Up Empowerment.* New York: Free Press, 1992.

Johnson, H. Thomas, and Robert S. Kaplan. *Relevance Lost: The Rise and Fall of Management Accounting.* Boston: Harvard Business School Press, 1987.

Keating, Patrick J. and Stephen F. Jablonsky. *Changing Roles of Financial Management: Getting Close to the Business.* Morristown, N.J.: Financial Executives Research Foundation, 1990.

Latzko, William. *Quality and Productivity for Bankers and Financial Managers.* New York: Marcel Dekker, 1986.

Stoner, James A. F., and Frank M. Werner. *Remaking Corporate Finance—The New Corporate Finance Emerging in High-Quality Companies,* New York: McGraw–Hill Primis, 1992.

The Quality Revolution

Deming, W. Edwards. *Out of the Crisis.* Cambridge, Mass.: MIT Center for Advanced Engineering Study, 1991.

———. *The New Economics for Industry, Government, and Education.* Cambridge, Mass.: MIT Center for Advanced Engineering Study, 1993.

Dobyns, Lloyd, and Clare Crawford-Mason. *Quality or Else: The Revolution in World Business.* Boston: Houghton Mifflin, 1991.

Gabor, Andrea. *The Man Who Discovered Quality.* New York: Times Books, 1990.

Garvin, David A. *Managing Quality: The Strategic and Competitive Edge.* New York: Free Press, 1988.

Goldratt, Eliyahu M., and Jeff Cox. *The Goal,* 2nd rev. ed. Croton-on-Hudson, N.Y.: North River, 1992.

Ishikawa, Kaoru. *What Is Total Quality Control? The Japanese Way.* Translated by David J. Lu. Englewood Cliffs, N.J.: Prentice-Hall, 1985.

Juran, J. M. *Managerial Breakthrough: A New Concept of the Manager's Job.* New York: McGraw-Hill, 1964.

Peters, Tom. *Thriving on Chaos: Handbook for a Management Revolution.* New York: Knopf, 1987.

Stoner, James A. F., and Charles B. Wankel. *World Class Managing: Two Pages at a Time.* New York: Fordham University, 1990.

Womack, James P., Daniel T. Jones, and Daniel Roos. *The Machine that Changed the World.* NewYork: Rawson Associates, 1990.

The Tools of Tqm and Adopting Quality Management

Aubrey, Charles A. II, and Patricia K. Felkins. *Teamwork: Involving People in Quality and Productivity Improvement.* Milwaukee, Wis.: Quality Press, 1988.

Berry, Thomas H. *Managing the Total Quality Transformation.* New York: McGraw-Hill, 1991.

Camp, Robert C. *Benchmarking: The Search for Industry Best Practices That Lead to Superior Performance.* White Plains, N.Y.: Quality Resources, 1989.

Juran, J. M. *Juran on Quality by Design.* New York: Free Press, 1992.

————. *Juran on Leadership for Quality.* New York: Free Press, 1989.

————. *Juran on Planning for Quality.* New York: Free Press, 1988.

Mizuno, Shigeru, ed. *Managing for Quality Improvement: The 7 New QC Tools.* Cambridge, Mass.: Productivity Press, 1988.

Scholtes, Peter R. *The Team Handbook.* Madison, Wis.: Joiner Associates, 1988.

Spendolini, Michael J. *The Benchmarking Book.* New York: AMACOM, 1992.

Stalk, George, Jr., and Thomas M. Hout. *Competing Against Time: How Time-Based Competition Is Reshaping Global Markets.* New York: Free Press, 1990.

The Malcolm Baldrige National Quality Award

Brown, Mark Graham. *Baldrige Award Winning Quality: How to Interpret the Malcolm Baldrige Award Criteria,* 2nd edition. White Plains, N.Y.: Quality Resources, 1992.

Steeples, Marion Mills. *The Corporate Guide to the Malcolm Baldrige National Quality Award,* Revised edition. Homewood, Ill.: Business One Irwin, 1993.

Individual copies of two U.S. Government documents—*The Malcolm Baldrige National Quality Award Criteria,* and *The Malcolm Baldrige National Quality Award Application Forms and Instructions*—may be obtained at no charge from

Malcolm Baldrige National Quality Award
National Institute of Standards and Technology
Route 270 and Quince Orchard Road
Administration Building, Room A537
Gaithersburg, MD 20899
Telephone: (301) 975–2036
Fax: (301) 948–3716

Fordham Student Research Team

Jeff Deiss
Margaret Edwards
Jeffrey Goddard
William Halford, Jr.
Melissa Horan
Rick Pederson

Index

Graf, Alan, 3, 6, 63, 126, 141–42, 143
Gray, Debra, 65, 119, 127, 128, 132, 134, 135, 137, 139, 146
Grow, Larry, 160, 161, 163, 164, 166, 169

Halford, William, Jr., 240
Hardy, Ann, 146, 229
Helton, Sandy, 45, 56, 93, 99, 100, 101, 102, 103, 104, 105, 115
Hickie, David, 154, 171
Horan, Melissa, 240
Houghton, Jamie, 94, 95, 96, 99

Imagineering, 52
Information
  emergence of new, 8–9
  in financial theory, 86
Integrative techniques, finance's use of, 12
Internal audit process at Motorola, 158–69
Interrelationship diagram, 51
Investment management at Corning, 111–12
Investor relations at Corning, 109–11
Ishikawa, Kaoru, 18
ISO 9000's focus on standardization, 181

Jablonsky, Stephen F., 60, 62
Japanese management system, 29
Johnson, Ken, 74, 155, 160
Juran, Joseph M., 18, 99

Kammerer, Ed, 209
Kane, Brian, 223, 224, 225, 227
Keating, Patrick J., 60, 62
Key Results Indicators (KRIs) at Corning, 93, 97, 103–5
Kielty, Art, 209
Kilidjian, Russ, 190, 199
King, Phil, 133, 136–37, 139, 140
K.J. diagram, 51

Lee, Myron, 187, 194
Lincoln, Ed, 222

Maier, Peter, 108–9
Management, focus of, 37

Management methods, 50, 54–57
  behavioral methods, 51, 53
  competitive benchmarking, 53–54
  numerical and analytical methods (tools), 50–51
  transitions in, 24–25
Management system, attitude toward the, 38–39
Matrix data analysis, 51
Matrix diagram, 51
McKinsey and Company, 25
Measurement and reward systems, 14
Measurement horizon, 38
Measurements, emergence of new, 8
Mohan, Mike, 221
Moment-by-moment management, 56–57
Motorola, xviii, 5, 6, 147, 149–73
  audit department at, 45, 159–69
  challenges for, 172
  commitment to learning at, 151
  corporate purpose of, 63
  Corporate Quality Council at, 150
  cycle time reduction at, 154–56, 167–69
  defining defective product at, 164–66
  defining audit process at, 164
  entry into quality management at, 150–51
  Finance Councils at, 170
  finance function at, 54
  Fordham student research team for, 173
  improved audit process at, 167–69
  internal audit process at, 158–69
  investment in quality at, 170–72
  involvement of finance in quality movement at, 153–56
  leadership at, 78
  measuring quality of audit process at, 166–67
  ongoing quality initiatives in finance at, 170
  payoffs from, 169, 170–72
  payroll accuracy at, 156
  people as critical resource at, 151–52
  people interviewed at, 173
  quality in corporate finance in, 4
  quality vision at, 152–53

About the Authors

James A. F. Stoner is Professor of Management Systems at the Schools of Business Administration of Fordham University. He received his Ph.D. from the MIT School of Industrial Management (now the Sloan School) in 1967. He also earned an S.M. in Management from MIT in 1961 and a B.S. in Engineering Science from Antioch College in 1959. Dr. Stoner is author and co-author of a number of books and journal articles. These include *Management,* 5th edition, Prentice Hall; *Introduction to Business,* Scott Foresman; and *World-class Managing—Two Pages at a Time,* Fordham University. He is a member of the Academy of Management, the American Finance Association, the American Society for Quality Control, the Financial Executives Institute, the Financial Management Association, and the Organizational Behavior Teaching Society, of which he is a former board member. In addition to his responsibilities at Fordham, Dr. Stoner advises several major companies on the movement toward total quality management and teaches in executive seminars on quality and management. He has taught in executive programs in North and South America, Europe, Africa, and Asia. In 1992, Fordham University established the James A. F. Stoner Chair in Quality Leadership.

Frank M. Werner is Associate Professor of Finance at the Schools of Business Administration and Associate Dean of the Graduate School of Business Administration of Fordham University. He received his Ph.D. in Finance from Columbia University in 1978. He also received an M.Phil. in Finance from Columbia in 1975 and an M.B.A. from Harvard in 1968. His undergraduate degree was in Engineering and Applied Physics, also from Harvard, in 1966. Dr. Werner is the author of a variety of journal articles, a computer-based simulation of corporate finance decision making, and numerous monographs and cases for instructional use. He is a member of the American Accounting Association, the American Economics Association, the American Finance Association, the American Society for Quality Control, the Financial Executives Institute, the Financial Management Association, and the Institute of Management Sciences.

In addition to his responsibilities at Fordham, Dr. Werner advises companies in the areas of corporate finance and total quality management. He has given seminars on various quality and finance topics, in both English and Spanish, throughout the U.S. as well as in Europe, South America, and the Caribbean.

In collaboration with student research teams at Fordham, Drs. Stoner and Werner have produced *Remaking Corporate Finance—The New Corporate Finance Emerging in High-quality Companies,* McGraw-Hill Primis, 1992. The monograph examines changes in the corporate finance function and the job of the Chief Financial Officer in companies which are leaders in the movement toward total quality management. They are currently working on two additional books. The first, scheduled for completion in 1994, is a study of how progress toward tqm is changing the internal audit process. The second, *Modern Financial Management—Continuity and Change* (HarperCollins), is a new-generation textbook in corporate finance consistent with the principles of tqm which will be available in October 1994.